FIGURATIVE LANGUAGE AND THOUGHT

COUNTERPOINTS: *Cognition, Memory, and Language*
SERIES EDITOR: Marc Marschark

Rochester Institute of Technology
National Technical Institute for the Deaf

STRETCHING THE IMAGINATION
Representation and Transformation in Mental Imagery
C. Cornoldi, R. Logie, M. Brandimonte, G. Kaufmann, D. Reisberg

MODELS OF VISUOSPATIAL COGNITION
M. de Vega, M. J. Intons-Peterson, P. N. Johnson-Laird,
M. Denis, M. Marschark

WORKING MEMORY AND HUMAN COGNITION
J. T. E. Richardson, R. W. Engle, L. Hasher,
R. H. Logie, E. R. Stoltzfus, R. T. Zacks

RELATIONS OF LANGUAGE AND THOUGHT
The View from Sign Language and Deaf Children
M. Marschark, P. Siple, D. Lillo-Martin,
R. Campbell, V. Everhart

GENDER DIFFERENCES IN HUMAN COGNITION
P. J. Caplan, M. Crawford, J. S. Hyde,
J. T. E. Richardson

FIGURATIVE LANGUAGE AND THOUGHT
A. Katz, C. Cacciari, R. W. Gibbs, M. Turner

FIGURATIVE LANGUAGE AND THOUGHT

ALBERT N. KATZ
CRISTINA CACCIARI
RAYMOND W. GIBBS, JR.
MARK TURNER

New York   Oxford
OXFORD UNIVERSITY PRESS
1998

Oxford University Press

Oxford   New York
Athens   Auckland   Bangkok   Bogotá   Buenos Aires   Calcutta
Cape Town   Chennai   Dar es Salaam   Delhi   Florence   Hong Kong   Istanbul
Karachi   Kuala Lumpur   Madrid   Melbourne   Mexico City   Mumbai
Nairobi   Paris   São Paulo   Singapore   Taipei   Tokyo   Toronto   Warsaw

and associated companies in

Berlin   Ibadan

Published by Oxford University Press, Inc.
198 Madison Avenue, New York, New York 10016

Oxford is a registered trademark of Oxford University Press

Library of Congress Cataloging-in-Publication Data
Figurative language and thought / Albert N. Katz . . . [et al.],
p.   cm.—(Counterpoints : cognition, memory, and language)
Includes bibliographical references and index.
ISBN 0-19-510962-7; ISBN 0-19-510963-5 (pbk.)
1. Psycholinguistics.   2. Figures of speech.   3. Metaphor.
4. Thought and thinking.   I. Katz, Albert N.   II. Series:
Counterpoints (Oxford University Press)
P37.F54   1998
401'.9—dc21   98–19101

1 3 5 7 9 8 6 4 2

Printed in the United States of America
on acid-free paper

Contents

Contributors

Albert N. Katz, Department of Psychology, University of Western Ontario, London, Ontario, Canada

Mark Turner, Department of English Language and Literature and Doctoral Program in Neuroscience and Cognitive Science, University of Maryland, College Park, Maryland

Raymond W. Gibbs, Jr., Department of Psychology, University of California, Santa Cruz, Santa Cruz, California

Cristina Cacciari, Department of Psychology, University of Bologna, Bologna, Italy

FIGURATIVE LANGUAGE AND THOUGHT

CHAPTER 1

Figurative Language and Figurative Thought

A Review

Albert N. Katz

Imagine a race of creatures with the head of a human and the body of a lighthouse. As far as I am aware no such creature exits, and there is no noun, in any language, to label that race. And yet we know that people can, with little effort, create such concepts. Analogous (albeit equally fictional) creatures have been conceptualized—and labeled—in the past: the sphinx (head of man/body of lion), the centaur (head of man/body of horse), or, in more recent years, transformers (toys that turned into half-person, half-killing machine).

The creative interplay of language and thought is particularly evident in figurative language. The use of such language is not rare or limited to poetic situations but rather is a ubiquitous characteristic of speech (see, for instance, Lakoff and Johnson, 1980; Pollio, Smith, and Pollio, 1990). Although hundreds of possible figures of speech have been described (see Lanham, 1991), most interest and research has focused on just a few of these. Roberts and Kreuz (1994) list eight such commonly used forms, though one can easily add to their list (they do not mention metonymic or proverbial language, for instance). Among the prominent (and studied) forms are *metaphor* (an explicit or implicit comparison, which is literally false: "my car is a lemon," "Juliet is the sun," "chair leg"); *irony* (a statement contrary to intended meaning: "what a fine friend" intending to convey that the friend is not good); *idioms* (conventionalized expression in which the intended meaning often is difficult or impossible to recover from the words making up the expression: "He kicked the bucket"); *indirect requests* (a request phrased as a nonrequest: e.g., one can be asking

3

whether one possesses some material when one intends to ask someone to actually perform some action with the material, such as stating, "Do you have a dollar?").

Traditionally metaphor and the other tropes described above have been taken as a property of, and a problem for, language, not surprising because figures of speech are, naturally, expressed in language and not in some other medium. There are, for instance, no obvious idiomatic facial expressions or gestural indirect requests or tactile proverbs.

However, another aspect of nonliteral language must be recognized. Novel metaphors are often only novel as a linguistic expression but not as a deeper conceptual relation. For instance, Lehrer (1978) studied the point at which specific metaphors enter a language. She found that a basic conceptual relationship or root metaphor (e.g., PERSONALITIES are like TEXTURES) is first instantiated, then followed rapidly by a host of novel instantiations (e.g., "he is a smooth talker," "he is rough around the edges"). A similar analysis has been demonstrated for poetic metaphor (Kittay and Lehrer, 1981). More recently, Lakoff and Johnson (1980) and Gibbs (1994) have argued that root or conceptual metaphors motivate our understanding and use of language in general. This last point should be emphasized: as Lakoff (1993) describes it, metaphor should be understood as a property of our conceptual systems, not as a property of language per se. If Lakoff is correct, metaphor is not a property of (and problem for) language but rather is a property of (and problem for understanding) our conceptual system.

This volume, as the title proclaims, is about the relation of language and thought, especially figurative language and thought. This review consists of three sections. First, I review some of the traditionally posited relations between language and thought; this literature consists almost totally of the relation of *literal* language and thought. Second, I review some of the major themes in figurative language theory and research; most of this will involve metaphor. Finally, I consider how literature on figurative language has implications for the more general issue of language-thought relations.

LANGUAGE AND THOUGHT: OVERVIEW

The naive psychology of Western thinkers makes a distinction between language and thought as quite separate entities. In a general sense, thought has been considered as a form of mental experience that mediates intellectual activities (see, for instance, Johnson, 1972). Thought has both structural and processing components. Folk descriptions of the structures include entities such as ideas, concepts, images, and propositions. The actual format in which these entities are represented is somewhat controversial, with some arguing for symbolic representation and others for a connectionist architecture. These entities can be marshaled as "trains" of thought, usually conceptualized as directed at solving a problem (via reasoning) but also involving nondirected arousal (such as the "thoughts" that come to mind while one reads a poem or the unconscious inferences one draws in understanding discourse).

Language has been conceptualized also in terms of structures (e.g., phonemes, lexical units, phrases) and processes (e.g., rules that govern syntax). In a more basic way, many have distinguished between language-as-used and language-as-an-ideal, in a way that has not occurred for thought (but see Jackendoff, 1992, chap. 2). An early distinction (Varro, circa 100 BCE; see Dinneen, 1967) was made between the actual speech produced by an individual speaker and the more abstract language knowledge shared by members of a linguistic community, a distinction elaborated at the turn of this century by Ferdinand de Saussure (1857–1913). Saussure drew a useful analogy of a symphony to contrast the abstract score written by the composer from any specific performance or interpretation of the score. As applied to language, the actual speech act, or, in Saussure's terms, "la parole," is an idiosyncratic reflection of an abstract structure (Saussure's "la langue"), namely a semantic-grammatical system that makes speech possible. Chomsky (1965) made an analogous distinction, between performance (the actual production or comprehension of speech that is influenced by secondary factors, such as memory load or attention) and competence (the ideal, abstract knowledge that underlies performance). Chomsky argues that describing competence should be the aim of linguistic theorists.

Unlike thought, language has traditionally been assigned a social communicative role. Although the communicative functions of language undoubtably are, like thought, based on cognitive structures and processes—that is, la langue of Saussure, or the competence-based grammars described by Chomsky—language has an interpsychic component missing in our conceptions of thought. A generated thought has no social impact unless put into some medium of behavior; spoken language has social impact whenever someone else is present.

An enduring problem in Western culture has been conceptualizing the relation between thought and language. Given the communication function of language, one would expect that generated language serves to make social and public the private and privileged thought of a person, and communication involves decoding the public act so that it can be understood by the cognitive systems of individuals. As one prominent linguist has put it: "Meaning, of course, is presumably the reason for there being such a thing as language at all, since the language faculty is at bottom a device for externalizing and communicating meaning" (Jackendoff, 1992, p. 7). The seeming "obvious" relation described by Jackendoff has not proven so obvious to others, and one can discern several different relations in the literature, some of which I describe below.

First, one can envision that language and thought are functionally independent. Taken to the extreme, the functional independence position would suggest that what we say can be unrelated to what we think; in fact, this position has been proposed for young children. Some current modular models of mind argue for a less extreme variant of this position, even for adults. In this variant, functional independence occurs at some levels of language (such as those involved in processing syntax) but not in others (such as understanding the intent of a speech act). Consider, for instance, someone asking: "Can you close the window?" Presumably, syntactic analysis and word recognition might proceed independent of general knowledge; however, acknowledgment of the indirect request (i.e., please close the window) would involve general knowledge structures.

One can also envision the other extreme relation between thought and language, namely that the former might be reducible to the latter. Thus, in an evolutionary sense, human thought developed with the emergence of human language. But what aspect of language? The most commonly proposed variant of this position in the twentieth century has been the argument that thought is dependent upon *speech,* that is, on the specific language used in a linguistic community. In some variants of this position, two modes of thought are envisioned, one language(speech)-based and one nonlinguistic (see, for instance, Paivio and Begg, 1981). An implication of this position would be that nonhuman animals, or pre-linguistic children, either do not think or think in a manner fundamentally different from the thought of mature humans. If only *some* thought is language-based, a second implication would be that, even with adults, humans may have thoughts that cannot be adequately or completely translated into language.

One of the most famous versions of this position has elaborated upon another implication of the thought-as-speech position: if thought depends upon speech, then linguistically different communities would think differently—people with different speech would conceptualize and understand the world in fundamentally different ways. This hypothesis, variously labeled linguistic relativity or, after its two most prominent proponents, the Sapir-Whorfian hypothesis, has had a seductive impact on modern conceptions of language and thought. If this hypothesis had been examined just a few years ago, most theorists would have argued that its emphasis on speech per se is misguided and the whole enterprise flawed. In recent years there has been, in the words of one psycholinguist, "a remarkable revival of the Whorfian hypothesis" (Denny, in press).

I argue that an alternative version deserves serious consideration. In this variant the suggestion is that language, rather than merely serving a communication role, is a form of representation of the world (Bickerton, 1990). The emphasis here is on language principles shared by all and not on the specific languages used by different communities.

LANGUAGE AND THOUGHT: REVIEW OF POSITIONS: LANGUAGE AND THOUGHT ARE FUNCTIONALLY INDEPENDENT

A version of the independence hypothesis can be found in the work of Vygotsky (1962), who proposed that language and thought are separate independent activities in the very young child. According to Vygotsky, a child's earliest attempts at problem solving reflect thinking without language, and the earliest speech (babbling) reflects language without thought. The two activities join and change when the child reaches about two years of age, when as Vygotsky puts it, thought becomes verbal and speech rational.

Unlike Vygotsky, who conceptualizes the independence of language and thought only for the very young, Chomsky (1965) and Fodor (1983) describe independence in adult language use. From his earliest work onward, Chomsky has stressed the independence of specific language functions (such as between syntax and semantics) and language as an autonomous function separate from other cognitive processes. The independence proposal was explicitly Fodor's focus. Fodor (1983) proposed that the mind contains a central cognitive system, as well as a set of specialized, autonomous modules. Within a module, when processing commences, it proceeds uninfluenced by information that arises elsewhere in the cognitive system, a property of modules called informational encapsulation. Encapsulation presumably allows the system to operate rapidly, somewhat like a reflex, without having to consider (and hence be hindered by) potentially relevant information arising from elsewhere in the cognitive system.

Fodor's argument that language input acts as one such module has attracted many supporters in recent years (see for reviews Damasio and Damasio, 1992; Pinker, 1994). As applied to the relation between language and thought, the modularity hypothesis implies that the processing of language proceeds somewhat independently of thought, and that, only after some preliminary analysis of language is completed (in the language module), are the *results* of the analysis made available to the central system. Accordingly, some aspects of language are not influenced by knowledge of the world or by pragmatic considerations. The modular approach would hold for both nonliteral and literal language, and, if applied to the issue of figurative language, any processing or conceptual differences with literal language would have to reside in the general cognitive system.

The modularity hypothesis has been very influential. I present only selected aspects here.

Language is functionally dissociated from thought. One testable implication of the modularity hypothesis is that, in principle, one should be able to demonstrate a double dissociation between language and thought. Some (see Pinker, 1994) argue that such a dissociation is evident in the contrast of various clinical syndromes. For example, one can contrast Down's and Williams syndromes, both of which lead to severe cognitive impairments. In Down's syndrome, language performance lags behind cognitive development. If language depended on overall cognition, one would expect that the language of people with Down's syndrome would parallel their cognitive abilities: they should (but do not) produce and understand speech appropriate for a person of the same mental age. Thus, some have taken this as an example of the single dissociation: thinking abilities without comparable language abilities. In contrast, those with Williams syndrome have been described as having the opposite single dissociation: linguistic abilities in the absence of comparable cognitive abilities. For instance, Williams Syndrome children develop extensive vocabularies, expressive and comprehension proficiency with some grammatical constructions (e.g., passives and conditionals), and very good narrative skills. Yet, at the same time, they tend to fail Piagetian tasks traditionally taken to reflect transitive reasoning, class relational thinking, and other basic cognitive tasks solved by the normal nine-year-old child.

The dissociation between language and thought described in these two syndromes has been controversial, not surprisingly, especially because Williams syndrome, in contrast to Down's syndrome, is a relatively unstudied pathology. Maratsos and Matheny (1994) point out some problems with assuming that Williams syndrome children indicate language independent of cognition. First, they note that the major evidence in favor of a language-thought dissociation employs Piagetian tasks as the measure of cognitive abilities and that failure to perform these tasks does not necessarily indicate a failure to develop basic cognitive skills but can reflect attention or memory problems. Second, they argue that the children in question do not really exhibit a dissociation between language and thought inasmuch as their speech is not only syntactically but always semantically correct (i.e., they do not produce syntax-correct word salad). Finally, they argue that some of the other grammatical features of these children's speech that has been posited as evidence of language independent of cognition (e.g., competence with passives and with conditionals) is not unique, for young children of the same mental age as the syndrome children also show competence with these features. Clearly more work is required before the hypothesized double dissociation can be accepted unconditionally.

Language is hardwired. A second source of support has been the claim that modules might be biologically hardwired. Language-specific functions might be evident in the brain, whereas no such specialization might be present for thinking processes in general. For instance, numerous books include chapters on language and the brain but few on a topic such as deductive reasoning and the brain, presumably reflecting the belief that language, but not reasoning, is somewhat independent of general intellectual abilities.

A long history in psychology has demonstrated "areas" of the brain dedicated to language. The evidence gathered from both clinical populations (e.g., people with localized brain damage) and the performance of nonclinical participants on tasks that tap cerebral asymmetries all indicate a left-hemisphere (LH) dominance in language, at least for right-handers (see Hellige, 1990). This specialization can be shown for those who communicate via sign language (Poizner, Klima, and Bellugi, 1987), suggesting to some that the LH is specialized for language per se, not just for sound-based speech.

Two areas in the LH have been specifically implicated, namely Broca's and Wernicke's areas. Damage to the latter (a central, more posterior) area produces an aphasia, which, on surface, seems to indicate a disruption of semantic processing but sparing syntactic processing. Wernicke aphasics speak fluently but often meaninglessly, substituting, for example, one word for another or using pronouns without clear reference. Broca aphasics, on the other hand, use semantically appropriate speech connected to context but have difficulty in producing output and, some claim, they are deficient in using syntax (see Hellige, 1990). Because one can find evidence for Broca's area from the early hominid fossil record, a common assumption by paleontologists until recently was that language was present well before the emergence of our species, *H. sapiens sapien*. Some at least now believe that true language emerged only with our species (e.g., Bickerton, 1990; Walker and Shipman, 1996).

This evidence is all consistent with a modular concept of language hardwired in the LH of humans. However, in recent years the picture has become more complicated and less obviously indicative of the type of specializations I described.

First, there is ever-growing evidence that the right hemisphere (RH) also plays an important role in the processing of language: for instance, priming studies indicate that one can get semantic priming in the RH (Chiarello, Burgess, Richards, and Pollock, 1990). Moreover, there is also ever-growing evidence that the RH is especially important to the processing of nonliteral language: damage to RH is related to impairments in understanding various forms of nonliteral language, such as indirect requests, idioms, and metaphor (see Burgess and Chiarello, 1996). One could argue that nonliteral language depends more on context and knowledge of the world than more "standard" literal language and that damage to the RH is affecting the contribution of these functions to comprehension. Gardner (1983) makes a similar point, claiming that evidence for (LH-based) modularity is strongest "when one focuses on phonological, syntactic, and certain semantic properties" but that "once one encompasses broader aspects, such as pragmatic functions, the picture of linguistic autonomy becomes less convincing" (p. 89).

A second problem is that a finer analysis of aphasic patients have shown that the syntactic (Broca) and semantic (Wernicke) distinction between types of aphasic patients is somewhat problematic. Wernicke aphasics are not as asemantic (see Heeschen, 1985) and have more syntactic (Kolk, Van Grunsven, and Keyser, 1985) problems than originally thought. Moreover, Linbarger, Schwartz, and Saffran (1983) find that so-called agrammatic aphasics are quite good at making sophisticated judgments about the syntax of sentences. That is, Broca aphasia might be better characterized as a disruption of performance and not of language competence.

A third problem, related to the second, follows from Kimura (1993). She argues that the LH is specialized for motor selection of both oral and manual musculature. Kimura, as had others before her, noted that aphasia is often associated with difficulties in performing motor movements (apraxia). Moreover, she claims that differences in apraxia underlie the deficits seen in language. Unlike previous studies, Kimura's classified patients by the locus of the brain damage, and not a priori, on the basis of disrupted functioning. When given a set of tasks, patients with damage to Broca's and Wernicke's areas performed similarly on tasks of production and comprehension but differently on tasks of oral and other motor movements. Thus, as in the conclusion above, evidence for so-called modular effects may reflect differences in performance, not in linguistic competence.

Modules are informationally encapsulated: experimental tests. Recall that, according to Fodor, a defining characteristic of a module is that it is informationally encapsulated; that is, processing within the modular proceeds independent of information outside the module. This aspect of the modularity hypothesis has been extensively tested in two language domains: lexical access and syntactic analysis.

Lexical modularity.   Research has examined the access of meaning for lexically ambiguous items, such as homographs in which a given word (e.g., bat) has multiple meanings (e.g., flying rodent vs. baseball equipment). If lexical access is modular, then access of meaning would proceed independent of other information available to the cognitive system. One implication from the modular perspective is that both meanings of a homograph would be accessed, regardless of sentential context. Early data favored a modular explanation (e.g., Swinney, 1979), but more recent work indicates that the strength and type of context, as well as the relative frequencies of each meaning, play an important role in determining whether one or multiple meanings are accessed (see Tabossi and Zardon, 1993). Moreover, recent constraint-satisfaction computational models can produce results that appear to support encapsulation, even though they are interactive, taking into account context, strength of major meaning, and the like

(Kawamoto, 1993). Thus, in general, there is little support for a strong modular explanation of lexical access based on the access of multiple meanings, either empirically or logically.

Syntactic modularity.   The issue here is analogous to that observed with access to a lexicon. Namely, is the original syntactic analysis of a sentence dependent on a set of rules that work independent of semantic and contextual information? Naturally any empirical test of this proposition depends on the nature of any proposed syntactic parser. As an example consider an early and influential model by Frazier (1987). She argued that two basic strategies underlie syntactic analysis: late closure and minimal attachment. Late closure refers to the tendency to attach on-line each term to the clause or phrase being processed, and minimal attachment refers to the tendency to add that term in a way that will build the simplest syntactic structure. Note that these rules act independent of pragmatic or semantic influences.

One testable implication of this model is that when one processes a sentence on-line, the parser might at some juncture prefer a syntactic structure that later information proves to be incorrect: so-called garden pathing. Parsing might be led down the garden path by application of either principle.

For instance, consider a sentence such as "Since Jay always jogs a mile and a half seems like a short distance"(1). According to the late closure principle, initially one treats as a unit the phrase "a mile and a half." On encountering "seems" this interpretation is no longer possible and a new syntactic structure is required. Some early studies in which eye movements were tracked during reading indicated that garden pathing occurs. For instance, Frazier and Rayner (1982) found that fixation durations increased in the part of the sentence where the inconsistency occurs (i.e., on encountering the word "seems") and regressive eye fixations returned to where the ambiguity originates (e.g., the verb, "jogs").

From a modular perspective, one would also predict that garden pathing should *not* be influenced by semantic or by contextual information. The evidence here is more controversial. Rayner, Carlson, and Frazier (1983) studied sentences in which garden pathing is induced by the minimal attachment principle. For instance, in the sentence "The lady sent the flowers was very pleased"(2), minimal attachment would have "sent the flowers" as the verb phrase attached to the noun phrase, "the lady." A nonminimal attachment construction would have "The lady sent the flowers" as a noun phrase for an upcoming verb phrase. Rayner et al. recorded eye movements for sentences such as 2, or its pair, "The florist sent the flowers was very pleased"(3). Their argument was that if pragmatic factors were important, then it is more likely that ladies would be sent flowers than would florists, and, as such, a minimal attachment strategy would be less likely for sentence 3 than sentence 2 (or, to put it another way, garden pathing would be more likely to occur for sentence 2). However, they found that garden pathing was equally strong for both types of sentences, suggesting that parsing occurs without regard to pragmatic plausibility.

A similar conclusion can be found in Ferreira and Clifton (1986). They studied sentences that are ambiguous because the verb form is used for both the past tense and past participle. Based on minimal attachment logic, on encountering ''The defendant examined'' one would expect that defendant is the subject of the verb playing the thematic role of the agent described by the verb, and thus should be followed by a noun phrase. When completed as the reduced relative clause such as follows, ''(The defendant examined) by the lawyer was found to be unreliable,'' garden pathing should occur because now the original noun phrase (the defendant) is the grammatical object of the verb and plays the role of patient. Such sentences do produce garden path effects, as expected. Of more relevance here was the manipulation introduced by Ferreira and Clifton. They manipulated the animacy of the head noun for reduced relative clause sentences (e.g., ''The defendant examined by the lawyer turned out to be unreliable'' versus ''The evidence examined by the lawyer turned out to be unreliable''). The inanimate status of ''evidence'' rules out the possibility that the head noun is acting as the agent and, if that semantic information is being taken into account during initial syntactic analysis, then one should find garden pathing for the animate (''defendant'') but no (or, at least relatively less) garden pathing for the inanimate version. Ferreira and Clifton found no difference in garden pathing as a function of animacy, suggesting that such semantic information is not being used.

The data presented earlier are consistent with a strong modular view of syntactic processing. Other data are less supportive. For instance, Rayner et al. (1983) found effects of pragmatic plausibility for sentences of the type: ''The spy saw the cop with the revolver (the binoculars).'' The minimal attachment principle would lead to the prepositional phrases ''with binoculars'' and ''with the revolver'' being attached to the verb phrase in both cases; however, the former but not the latter is more pragmatically plausible. And it was with the latter sentences that participants lingered at the prepositional phrase, suggesting that pragmatics was having an early effect on syntactic processing.

More dramatic effects are found when sentences are put into an elaborated context. Consider sentences such as ''He told the woman that he was having trouble with to leave.'' Readers prefer to interpret ''the woman'' as a simple noun phrase, not as the more complex noun phrase containing a relative clause (''the woman that he was having trouble with''). However, this preference can be changed by context, such as by presenting a preceding sentence that introduces information suggesting that a relative clause interpretation is plausible, such as ''The therapist saw two women'' (cf., Altmann and Steedman, 1988).

Thus, resolution of a syntactic ambiguity is informed by contextual information and not just by rules in an autonomous syntax-module.

Other research has shown also that pragmatic and semantic factors inform syntactic analysis. For instance, the initial syntactic preference has been shown to depend on how one expects the sentence to be completed, as well as on principles such as minimal attachment. Thus, pragmatic content, not syntax, can be shown to affect the speed at which reading occurs (e.g., Tarban and Mc-Clelland, 1988). Moreover, there is an ever-growing list of studies showing that frequency information is used to resolve local ambiguities. For example, although the verbs "claim" and "remember" can both be followed by a noun phrase ("John remembered my book") or a sentence complement ("John remembered my book is due at the library"), the verb "remember" is more frequently completed with a noun phrase, whereas the verb "claim" is more frequently completed with a sentence complement. Trueswell, Tanenhaus, and Kello (1993) demonstrated that such frequency information is used on-line to resolve syntactic ambiguity.

In summary, the history of studies on syntax is one in which the early, but not the more recent, studies supported a strong modular position. More recent model building has shifted the emphasis away from a strong dichotomy between modular (autonomous) and nonautonomous processes to one in which syntax-based information is used interactively with nonsyntactic information. Some of the shifts have been relatively minor, with some arguing only for weak interactions (e.g., Altmann and Steedman, 1988). Most recently the emphasis has been on a strong interactional approach in which even the most basic of syntactic resolution involves using multiple constraints (syntactic, semantic, pragmatic) in a continuous manner.

The history of research on syntactic resolution thus parallels the history for the other sources of support of the modularity position: early promise has given way to approaches that do not demarcate between language and more generally based thought processes.

LANGUAGE DETERMINES THOUGHT

In contrast to the position that language and thought are, at least at some levels, functionally independent, linguistic determinist positions argue for the primacy of language in shaping thought. Schaff (1973) traces the history of this position to the eighteenth-century writings of Herder, who argued that the language spoken by a people shapes the weltanschauung of that people. This general proposition was forcefully elaborated on a hundred years later by von Humboldt, and, as Schaff demonstrates, his ideas influenced later generations of European thinkers.

The North American tradition has been associated mainly with Benjamin Lee Whorf and Edward Sapir. There are two elements to the discussion, namely linguistic determinism, or the argument that language is primary and determines thought, and linguistic relativity, or the argument that members of different linguistic communities have differing views of reality. Hill (1988) argues against any version of linguistic determinism, pointing out that even speakers of the same language can appear to have different worldviews and that, in any event, linguistic patterns are often very flexible and have been shown to change when one culture comes into contact with another. Moreover, Whorf's claims about the structure of the languages that he did study (see Whorf, 1956) have been questioned, as well as his reliance on surface level representation. For instance, consider the following two sentences: "John is easy to please" versus "John is eager to please." If one were to employ the methodology used by Whorf, one would be oblivious to the fact that in the latter case John is the subject and in the former the object of the sentence. Hill (1988) provides an excellent critique of various methodological problems with the enterprise, though some (e.g., Denny, in press) have demonstrated some support for the hypothesis, even when Whorf's original data are re-analyzed with better methodology.

Despite the shortcomings of Whorf's original work, the underlying hypotheses have proven seductive. An extensive literature has attempted to test them, even though the specific aspect of linguistic determinism and relativity has itself been controversial (see Fishman, 1960; Miller and McNeil, 1969). In general, the experimental paradigm is to identify two or more languages that differ in some specified way and then to see if this difference is reflected in a corresponding difference in worldview that cannot be traced to cultural differences per se. Fishman (1960) contrasts differences that occur in lexical, semantic, syntactic, and pragmatic levels of language.

Differences in the lexical/semantic domain. The commonly used example is that of the Inuit who, apparently, have a number of words for snow, whereas the standard English speaker will have only a few. Does this mean that English and Inuit speakers have different understanding of a physical phenomenon (snow)? We do not have, for instance, a lexical item to describe the type of snow that, as a child, you awaken to on a cold clear Sunday morning, bright and clean, glistening and pure. But does that mean we do not have the concept for it? I would fear that an answer in the affirmative would indicate the impossibility of poetry or the impossibility for lexical creativity. And yet, as I argue in the first paragraph of this chapter, humans have a remarkable capacity to create words for concepts, presumably indicating that such concepts do not depend for their existence on the preexistence of a word.

The experimental evidence has for the most part employed color terms. Cultures differ in the number of colors that they label, and color perception itself is related to a wavelength of light, so all cultures should be dealing with same basic physical input. Until recently the mapping of a lexical term to light wavelength was assumed to be relatively arbitrary; presumably a culture is not constrained in how it partitions the physical input. The initial experiments appeared to support the Whorfian hypothesis: linguistic "codability" (the agreement on the name, speed with which it is given, and length of name) predicted one's memory of the color—a "cognitive" measure (Brown and Lennenberg, 1954)— as did another linguistic measure, communication accuracy (Lantz and Stefflre, 1964). More directly relevant, Lennenberg and Roberts (1956) reported that Zuni speakers made more recognition errors for yellows and oranges than did English speakers. Zuni speakers have only one term for those two colors, and, presumably, the errors reflect a failure to make the real-world distinction that English speakers (who have separate terms) do make.

However, more recent work has not been as positive. First, as Brown (1976) noted, the similarities across cultures in memory for color, despite widespread differences in language, are much more impressive than are the few differences. Second, the basic assumption that color labeling is arbitrary does not appear to be correct. Berlin and Kay (1969) found that the speakers of 20 different languages, while disagreeing on the boundaries of color (i.e., when a lexical term is no longer appropriate) show remarkable agreement on the best examples of colors corresponding to basic color names, what they label focal points or focal colors. Third, and most relevant, Heider and Olivier (1972), found that the Dani, a culture with only two color terms, remembered focal colors better than nonfocal colors, and, even though they had no preexisting names, learned "names" for focal colors easier than for nonfocal colors. More impressive, both Dani and English speakers were given the same color recognition tests. The errors made on this test can be used as an index of conceptual similarity (colors that are psychologically similar are more likely to be confused with one another). When the errors were analysed, the resulting conceptual structure of color was remarkably similar for the Dani and English speakers. That is, the Dani, with only two terms (mili, for dark cold colors, and mola, for light warm colors) had a conceptual structure involving the same three factors found in English (with six basic color terms): hue, saturation, and brightness. Clearly, the color domain cannot be taken as support for the Whorfian hypothesis, though several theorists have argued that perhaps evidence for the hypothesis might still be found in other cognitive domains (e.g. Brown, 1977).

Differences in the grammatical domain. Languages differ in the information they obligate one to give (such as the basic distinction between singular and plural) versus information that is optional. For instance, in French one is obligated to distinguish between a formal (e.g., "vous") and informal (e.g., "tu") form of personal address, whereas in English the distinction has long disappeared and we are left with only the formal form (e.g., "you"; the informal forms of "thee" and "thou" now being obsolete). The Whorfian position would be that these differences should reflect differences in how the speakers of different languages understand their world.

Carroll and Casagrande (1958) note that in Navaho there is obligatory shape marking so that the form of a verb used depends upon the shape of an object being discussed. They report an early study which demonstrated that Navaho-speaking children tended to group objects by shape more than do English-speaking children from the same reservation, a finding consistent with the hypothesis. However, they also report that age-comparable English speakers from Boston performed more like the Navaho-speakers than the English speakers from the reservation. As such, language per se is at best only weakly implicated.

More recently, Bloom (1981) noted that Chinese speakers do not mark counterfactuals in their language, whereas in English we do so with ease. For instance, we use special verb forms, such as the use of "might have" in the following: "If Hitler won the war, then we might have had a 1000-year Reich." Does this mean that Chinese speakers cannot efficiently think in counterfactual terms? To test this possibility, Bloom presented analogous English and Chinese text to Chinese and English speakers. Counterfactual situations were discussed in the text, marked as above in the English version but in the standard non-marked manner in the Chinese version. Later the participants had to choose the correct counterfactual actions of the characters on a multiple choice test. The English speakers performed nearly perfectly, whereas the Chinese speakers almost to a person missed the counterfactual implication. Bloom concluded that the form of language was accompanied by differences in thought, a position, of course, consistent with Whorfian logic. However, the bloom was soon off Bloom's study: Au (1983) argued that the Chinese translation used by Bloom was poor. When better materials were employed, the so-called differences in thought disappeared. Other research has also failed to find differences between language structure and other aspects of thinking, such as syllogistic reasoning (see Scribner, 1977). However, in recent years, some support has been found in some domains (e.g., plural marking of a noun [Lucy, 1992]; transitive reasoning on spatial location [Pederson, 1994]), suggesting that the Whorfian hypothesis may still be viable.

Differences in pragmatic aspects of language.   It is a given that our ability to comprehend speech is closely tied to cultural and real-world knowledge (see Hill, 1988). In fact, because so much is left "unsaid," full communication has to go from what is actually expressed linguistically to what is unsaid. Grice (1975) has described conversational implicatures that are required for communication to proceed, and it is likely that these, or a very similar list of, implicatures are necessary in all human languages. As such, any test of the Whorfian hypothesis would not only have to address lexical or grammatical differences, but differences in the knowledge held by members of different linguistic communities. And, if these differences in knowledge are, as Whorfians would claim, themselves dependent on the structure of the language, then we are left with a nontestable hypothesis. In any event, I am not aware of any study in the Whorfian domain in which pragmatic aspects of language have been controlled for, let alone tested.

Does language facilitate or inhibit thought?   If, as the previous review indicates, there is no convincing evidence that language determines thought, is there evidence for a weaker version, namely, that language can facilitate or inhibit thought? The evidence here is somewhat more positive. Over 60 years ago, it was demonstrated that the verbal label given ambiguous figures influences how that figure is later remembered (Carmichael, Hogan, and Walter, 1932), and the labels given to objects in a problem-solving task can either aid or hinder problem solution, depending on whether the label emphasizes or disguises an element of an object that is required for correct problem representation (e.g., Glucksberg and Danks, 1968).

An example of one place in which language has been shown to influence thought is analogical reasoning, a thinking task especially relevant to the discussion of metaphor, given the long-standing tradition that associates metaphor with analogical thought (see Katz, 1992, for a review). Holyoak and colleagues (e.g., Gick and Holyoak, 1980, 1983) have shown that the spontaneous transfer of a solution from one problem to an analogical isomorph becomes increasingly more unlikely as the verbal descriptions of the isomorphic problems become increasingly more distinct. In an ingenious study, Gilovich (1981) presented one of two analogical isomorphic problems involving a foreign conflict; the task was for the participants to choose the best alternative for U.S. action. The manipulation was very subtle: description of the isomorphic passages so that, in one case, events were described in terms reminiscent of events that led to either World War II (in which most participants agreed with U.S. intervention) or the Vietnamese conflict (in which most believed intervention was not in the United States' best interest). Although the events were formally the same, in the former case participants choose as the best alternative an interventionist alternative, whereas in the latter, the choice was of nonintervention.

So, at least for some aspects of thinking, language plays a role. The Whorfian extension of these findings would be that languages that label "ambiguous" real-life events (such as, as originally thought, color) should have a cognitive advantage over those that do not and also that verbally framing the problem in a specific way, as in Gilovich's study, determines how the problem will be represented. However, a pragmatic explanation for these findings cannot be dismissed: in the experimental situations for which positive findings occur, the participant might be, in effect, asking themselves "why are these (and not other) aspects of the environment being made salient? or why are these terms (such as "blitzkrieg") being employed when other terms would do (see Katz, in press, for an elaboration of this argument). Language might work in these experimental situations by encouraging thought processes that would not work spontaneously in more normal communicative situations.

Linguistic determinism without linguistic relativity.   The Whorfian hypothesis has emphasized the differences between languages. But as Jackendoff (1977) and many other linguists and psycholinguists would argue today, all human languages show a basic and deep commonality (see Pinker, 1994, chap. 4 for a good review). Specific languages differ along a set of parameters, such as whether the head of a phrase comes before or after its arguments, but all languages will have phrases with heads and arguments.

Bickerton (1990, 1995) accepts the basic commonality of all human languages but goes a controversial step further. Language, he avers, is not a mere communication device but rather evolved as a representational system, not as a communication device. He makes the distinction between sensory-based models of the world (Primary Representational System, PRS), which is limited to "on-line" thinking, thinking based on events and objects in the here and now, and a Secondary Representational System (SRS), a model of the world that works "off-line." The SRS is language-based, so that concepts are represented lexically, and thinking, using lexical items, is driven by a syntax machine. Some nonhuman animals, and humans in special cases, such as with brain damage, do think via the PRS, but only adult humans, he argues, can think via the SRS.

For the present purposes, Bickerton's position leads to the argument that most of what we would consider human thought is based on the principles underlying language. For instance, Bickerton (1990, chap. 8) points out various constraints on human thought such as causal primacy ("when x happens, y happens" is construed as "x causes y to happen") and identification (any event is interpreted as an action with a causal agent), both of which can be tied to the role of an agent in syntax. Thus, the nature of what we most commonly think of as thought is based on universal features of language.

It should be noted that Bickerton's position is controversial. He frames his argument in an evolutionary perspective that has been questioned by others, who have speculated on the evolution of language (e.g., Pinker, 1994). His argument that off-line, syntax-driven SRS thinking is inextricably linked to language has been challenged by those who argue for a multiplicity in forms of off-line thinking. For instance, Jackendoff (1992) argues for a form of musical thinking that is nonlinguistic but is certainly off-line (to use Bickerton's terminology), driven by a syntax-like machine.

Finally, Bickerton's claim that off-line thinking *is* language-based flies in the face of those who argue that the language of Thought (what some have labeled "mentalese") is different from the language of Language. The arguments for and against the proposition that there is a distinct language of thought has been fought totally on rational grounds, with neither side willing to concede any ground to the other. If Bickerton is correct and the language of thought can be reduced to the structure of language, then, in a sense, we would have linguistic determinism for thought. But because the language system being discussed is about shared properties of all natural languages, determinism would not be reflected in linguistic relativity: presumably all cultures should have the same (language-based) constraints on thinking. If those who argue for mentalese as separate from language are correct (e.g., Pinker, 1994), then we are once again faced with the ancient problem of describing the interface between thought and language.

FIGURATIVE LANGUAGE AND THOUGHT

In my review of language and thought there was little said about *figurative* language and thought, mainly because in each case the arguments advanced did not distinguish between figures of speech and language in general. In fact, the distinctiveness of figurative and so-called literal language has long been assumed, and only recently have some questioned the need for the distinction.

Is Figurative Language Different from "Literal" Language?

A basic question that pervades the study of figurative language is its status as "normal" or "special." Such language might be common, but is it basic or somehow secondary? Many theorists have distinguished between normal or standard language and nonnormal, nonstandard language. This distinction has in some instances been defined by cultural values, such as those in which the speech exhibited by a dominant group, such as men, is standard and that exhibited by subservient groups (such as women) is considered abnormal (see, for instance, Kramer, 1977). The distinction emphasized here is between standard speech and nonstandard speech that presumably is more basic and crosscuts cultural value systems, namely between literal (standard) speech and figurative (nonstandard) speech.

The distinction between literal and nonliteral language has implications for the distinction between language and thought. And the distinction between language and thought has implications for the distinction between literal and figurative language. In general, one issue is whether normal language might be mediated by a set of rules (language modules) that makes minimal contact with general cognitive structures, whereas nonstandard language requires input from the more general (i.e., not language-specific) cognitive system. For instance, are inferences, knowledge of the world, pragmatic factors required for the comprehension of nonstandard language in a way that is not required for standard ("literal") language?

Consider, for instance, the argument made by some, presented earlier, that syntactic analysis might proceed independent of general knowledge structures. As such, the request implicit in a sentence such as "Can you please close the window?" would not be apparent from syntactic analysis alone and requires more general knowledge. But this might not be true of other sentences, such as "The mailman bit the dog," in which who did what to whom is, arguably, available from syntax alone.

Lakoff (1993) nicely reviews what he calls the classical assumptions underlying our understanding of language. With some modifications, they are as follows:

1. All conventional language is literal; none is metaphorical.
2. All subject matter can be comprehended literally, without metaphor; all definitions in the lexicon of a language are literal.
3. Only literal language can be true or false.

From this perspective, metaphor and other figures of language are not basic or intrinsic to language but, although used frequently, somehow abnormal. The tradition that metaphor is "abnormal" is usually attributed to Aristotle (see Ortony, 1993), who was left then with the problem of explaining why they exist. The classic explanation is that, because metaphors (and other tropes) cannot be fundamental to language, they must be an ornamental (optional) way of describing a situation that can be described in literal terms. In essence, figures of language would serve some pragmatic, not semantic, functions.

More recent theorists have elaborated on some of the functional roles played by this "stylistic" preference. Metaphor, for instance, has been described as being compact, efficient, and vivid (see Ortony, 1975), and these properties can serve to increase memorability (e.g., Whitney, Budd, and Mio, 1996); convey a falsehood by obscuring dissimilarities and emphasizing less important similarities (Katz, 1996a); and signal social information, such as social class (Katz, 1996a).

Other figures of speech can also have pragmatic force. Indirect requests, for instance, are associated with social status inasmuch as those with less status are more likely to express a request indirectly and those with higher status are more likely to do so directly (Holtgraves, 1994). And, in a similar way, irony depends not only on what is said but on who says it. Katz and Pexman (1997) have shown that the exact same phrase can be understood as metaphor or as irony, depending on who uttered it (e.g., a priest or a comedian). Dews and Winner (1995) have demonstrated that one social function of irony is to "tinge" meaning. That is, the literal sense of an expressed positive statement (such as "You sure are beautiful" when intending the ironic opposite) or of an expressed negative statement (such as "You are really bad" when intending an ironic compliment) plays a role in comprehension. Thus, the negatively stated compliment is perceived as less complimentary, and the positively stated insult is perceived as less negative than the direct literal counterparts.

The indication that figures of speech have pragmatic force does not, of course, say anything about the claim that such tropes are, at base, represented literally. After all, so-called literal language also served pragmatic functions!

Moreover, as Ortony (1975) pointed out, metaphors may not only be nice, they may in fact be necessary in many situations. That is, metaphor might be intrinsically related to the human ability to invent new—and meaningful—concepts that might not be explicable by recourse to some more basic literal description (e.g., "black holes," or "transformer toys"). So one might argue that metaphor might play a central role in translating thought, especially novel thought, into language (see Ortony, 1975). If this position is correct, then metaphor is serving a function that cannot be served by literal language.

If metaphors (and other figures of speech) are not basic how does one go from the expressed meaning to the intended meaning?

This question has been at the center of most of the psycholinguistic research into figurative language (see Katz, 1996b). And from this perspective arises what Glucksberg (1991) has labeled the "standard pragmatic theory," namely, that one initially attempts to understand a trope in its literal sense and only if that fails does one attempt a nonliteral interpretation. Thus, the theory argues that the processing of literal meaning is obligatory and that a nonliteral reading occurs only if a literal reading is defective.

If one takes the usual assumption that during comprehension one processes one word at a time, adding each word to create a syntactically meaningful structure, then we face at least two basic problems, if one assumes that the structures so constructed are based on literal meaning. The recognition problem is in identifying that the nonliteral sense is intended; this is especially problematic if a valid literal interpretation is plausible. The comprehension problem is in describing a psychologically real algorithm that permits one to compute the sense of the trope being *conveyed* by the expression but not being *stated* by it.

On the recognition problem.   One can dissociate recognition from computation. For instance, when my daughter Meredith was about five years old, she asked me to buy something that I thought looked more valuable than it actually was. Perhaps foolishly I expressed my opinion proverbially: ''The grass is greener on the other side.'' She looked at me and told me, ''I know that you are using an expression. What does it mean?'' In effect, Meredith had solved the recognition, but not the computation, problem. In fact, my informal observation is not unique. Winner (1988) reports that, in general, children recognize that a nonliteral usage is occurring even before they know what is being conveyed.

It should be noted that a recognition problem exists only if the processing system is looking for literal meaning. Given that, the question becomes: how does the processing apparatus ''know'' that a nonliteral meaning is being expressed? Most explanations have centered around the idea that the speaker somehow marks nonliteral usage. Several of these markings have been identified at the level of the trope itself. Empirical evidence indicates a number of heuristic cues that invite a nonliteral interpretation. For instance, with items of the form X is a Y (such as ''My car is a lemon'' or ''My cat is a Persian''), a metaphorical reading is more likely to occur when the predicate violates ''literal'' category membership (Glucksberg and Keysar, 1990), when the predicate is concrete and easy to image (Katz, Paivio, Marschark, and Clark, 1988), when the constituents being compared are semantically related and the sentence is rated as easy to comprehend (see Katz et al., 1988). Torreano and Glucksberg (1996) have shown also that the metaphoricity of a sentence is directly related to the degree to which the verb is used in thematically unusual ways. Kreuz (1996) argues that ironic usage is also invited by a set of heuristic devices, such as hyperbole (e.g., ''Boy, he is sure the best friend in the universe'') and the use of tag questions (e.g., adding, ''isn't he?'' to the previous example).

Another source of recognition arises from the context in which the trope is embedded. Figures of speech arise in an ecology: the preceding discourse, environmental events, and the like. Almost all of the relevant research has examined discourse context, and almost all comments relevant to the recognition problem argue that contextual information aids in facilitating a nonliteral interpretation. The specifics differ.

Some have argued that both the literal and nonliteral senses of a trope are computed in parallel, if both are contextually plausible (e.g., Keysar, 1989; Titone and Connine, 1994). In line with this, Gildea and Glucksberg (1983) have shown, by manipulating primes types, and others by manipulating instructions or expectancies (Alonzo-Quecty and de Vega, 1991; Gregory, 1993), that a context that activates properties informative about the topic is sufficient to trigger immediate comprehension, regardless of literality. Onishi and Murphy (1993) have argued that the nature of the context is especially important because it is easier to achieve coherence with the literal than with figurative usage due to the semantic similarity in literal items. That is, with figurative language (but not with literal language) one has to somehow mark the text to maximize achieving coherence; if marking is done well, one should be able to process the figurative use as rapidly as the literal use. Presumably, differences in processing speed between literal and figurative usages would be more noticeable as the context becomes progressively less marked. Tests of this hypothesis are still required.

On the computation problem. In essence, the two-pronged argument goes as follows: if the basic processing of language is literal, then one should not compute a nonliteral interpretation if a literal counterpart is available, and if one is not available, then there should be a cost (in processing speed) in coming up with an appropriate nonliteral interpretation. That is, the interpretive process is set for literal meaning and *only* when that fails does the processing system look for a contextually plausible nonliteral interpretation.

Both prongs of the argument have been tested extensively. The first, that nonliteral processing is optional (whereas literal processing is obligatory), has been tested using Stroop-like tasks. Arguably, the nonliteral interpretation of a sentence should not interfere with the processing of the literal meaning option *unless,* in contrast to predictions of the standard pragmatic theory, the nonliteral meaning automatically becomes available at about the same time as the literal sense. In fact, interference effects have been observed with both familiar metaphors (e.g., Glucksberg, Gildea, and Bookin, 1982) and with items in which the nonliteral interpretation is determined only by the context (Keysar, 1989). These data have been interpreted as showing that extracting nonliteral meaning is as obligatory as extracting literal meaning. The picture probably is somewhat more complicated. There is some evidence that familiarity of the nonliteral expression plays a role in whether or not literal meaning is given processing priority (e.g., Blasko and Connine, 1993). And, even with highly familiar items, some processing priority of literal meaning has been shown—with idioms for example (Cacciari and Tabossi, 1988; Needham, 1992).

The second prong of the argument, that nonliteral meaning occurs only after a failure to find a contextually appropriate literal sense, and hence that nonliteral comprehension should take longer to occur than literal comprehension, has also been disproved, at least when the trope is placed in an appropriately elaborated context, for example, with metaphor (Ortony, Schallert, Reynolds, and Antos, 1978b; Shinjo and Meyers, 1987), with idioms (Gibbs, 1980), or with proverbs

(Kemper, 1981). Thus, one is as quick at comprehending nonliteral as literal sentences. Presumably the equivalency in processing of literal and nonliteral meaning depends on a set of contextual factors, such as the elaboration of background information (e.g., Ortony et al., 1978a) and the forewarning of nonliteral usage by marking the text (e.g., Onishi and Murphy, 1993). In any event, the data clearly indicate that nonliteral can be processed as rapidly as literal meaning.

On literal and nonliteral language.   This discussion presumes that there is a basic distinction between literal and nonliteral language. Assuming no distinction between literal and nonliteral meaning has far-reaching implications for both theory and experimentation. For instance, a recognition problem does not exist if the processing system is not obligated to seek an initial literal interpretation, and one need not expect a slowing in processing speed for so-called nonliteral sentences.

At one level, the argument has been rational: identifying a set of criteria by which the two can be distinguished. Such attempts have for the most part been unsuccessful. As Gibbs (1994) and others have pointed out, the term ''literal'' itself has several different meanings. Literal has been contrasted with the poetic, with nonconventional usage, with context-based meaning, and with language in which ''truthfulness'' or ''falseness'' cannot be ascertained. Gibbs (1994, see especially chap. 2) has argued persuasively that ''[t]here is only a remote chance that any principled distinction can be drawn between figurative and literal language'' (p. 78).

Others (e.g., Dascal, 1987; MacCormac, 1985) are more optimistic. Mac-Cormac, for instance, argues that there might not be a set of sufficient and necessary characteristics that distinguish the literal from the nonliteral. But then again, there does not appear to be such a set for other categories, such as ''being human,'' yet we can readily identify humans from nonhumans. His answer is to interpret the distinction of literal and nonliteral as a fuzzy concept and consideration of metaphorizing as a problem in understanding fuzzy sets. In any event, the theoretical distinction between literal and nonliteral language that has been the assumption for so long cannot be taken for granted.

In parallel to the rational argument for or against distinguishing between literal and nonliteral language, there has been empirical evidence that a *process* explanation based on the distinction is not required. As noted above, the received wisdom nowadays (e.g., Glucksberg, 1991) is that the speed with which one interprets a sentence does not seem to depend on whether or not it is literally true, and access of nonliteral meaning does not appear to be based on an initial failure to find literal meaning.

On the locus of metaphorical speech.   The traditional explanation has placed metaphor as a linguistic phenomenon explained by language-based principles. In more recent years, probably the majority of theorists has placed meta-phor as a cognitive or conceptual phenomenon. As Lakoff (1993, p. 203) puts it: ''[T]he word 'metaphor' has come . . . to mean 'a cross-domain mapping in the conceptual system.' The term 'metaphorical expression' refers to a linguistic expression (a word, phrase, or sentence) that is the surface realization of such a cross-domain mapping (this is what the term 'metaphor' referred to in the old theory).'' By ''old theory,'' Lakoff means the traditional language-based expla-nations.

Metaphor as a linguistic problem

Semantic approaches.   The classic explanation places metaphor as a linguistic problem: namely, the semantic problem of stretching meaning so that a literally based term acquires a nonliteral interpretation. This tradition has been attributed to Aristotle, who describes metaphor as a problem in transference of meaning, or giving a thing a name that belongs to something else. Metaphor is thus deviant from literal usage because a name is applied to an object to which it does not literally belong. Some have called this the substitution theory (e.g., see Ortony, Reynolds, and Arter, 1978a). Assumedly, the process involved finding a simi-larity between otherwise disparate things, similar to analogy.

In the twentieth century several variants in general fall within the Aristotelian tradition, in understanding how people can find similarity in dissimilar objects or events. In contrast to the classic argument of substitution, several models posit that, in good metaphors, the juxtaposition of topic and vehicle produces a new meaning that transcends the meaning of either topic and vehicle alone. That is, the act of metamorphizing creates (and does not find a preexisting) similarity between metaphor topic (the subject being discussed) and vehicle (the term being used to describe the topic metaphorically).

Various comparison models have been suggested, based on semantic features associated with topic and vehicle terms. For instance, Cohen (1993) argues that metaphor interpretation proceeds by canceling semantic features of the vehicle inconsistent with the topic, the remaining features being the basis for similarity. And MacCormac (1985, ch. 4) argues that semantic markers can be represented as fuzzy sets and that, adopting the notion of fuzzy set, one can actually en-compass the combination of contrasting or even contradictory markers. Black (1993), in his interaction position, argues that a metaphor has two distinct sub-jects: a principal and subsidiary one. The subjects should be thought of as a system of things. In metaphor one applies to the principal subject a system of implications associated with the subsidiary subject. For instance, in the metaphor ''that man is a wolf,'' a family of associations common to ''wolf'' (subsidiary subject) are used as a filter with which to understand ''that man,'' the principal subject.

Psychological models within this general tradition have been mostly modest, attempting to demonstrate the importance of semantic features as psychologically real instruments of metaphoric comprehension. For instance, Malgady and Johnson (1980) have demonstrated that one can predict those sentences rated as easy to understand and as good metaphors by the number and saliency of properties that metaphoric topic and vehicle share. Ortony (1979; Ortony, Vondruska, Foss, and Jones, 1985) proposed, and provided some empirical evidence for, a model that addressed a basic inadequacy of simple overlap models: namely, the inability to explain the asymmetry in meaning produced when topic and vehicle are reversed, such as when one compares "that man is a wolf" with "that wolf is a man."

Ortony and his colleagues addressed the asymmetry problem by proposing that the meaning of metaphor derives from semantic features shared by topic and vehicle; relevant features are highly salient for the the vehicle but not for the topic. That is, in the metaphor "that man is a wolf," salient features of "wolf" (such as wild, predatory) are mapped onto the same characteristic associated, albeit nonsaliently, with "men." Reversing the topic and vehicle will lead to different mappings. Ortony argues further that the imbalance in saliency characteristic of metaphor is not found with literal sentences, a position that has been attacked by those who argue that symmetry of reversals is independent of literalness (see Glucksberg and Keysar, 1990).

The saliency imbalance model has also been attacked by Gentner (cf., Gentner and Clements, 1988). Gentner argues that one maps from vehicle to topic domains in ways that maintain systems of relations and that the choice of which relations to map is governed by a principle of systematicness. In empirical tests of her model, Gentner has demonstrated that relational characteristics are better predictors of judged metaphoricity or of metaphor aptness than are simple descriptive features. Moreover, when tested on her database, her model was more predictive than was the imbalance model.

Finally, there are models based on the representation of words' multidimensional semantic space (see Katz, 1992, for a review). In general, these models argue that words that are semantically similar to one another are "closer" in proximity in semantic space. In the most articulated of these models, Tourangeau and Sternberg (1981) posit that on presentation of a metaphor (e.g., "Clinton is a cream puff") higher order domains, such as "world leaders," "food," are activated in semantic space and that a vector is constructed from the instance in the source domain to the parallel location in the target domain. In essence, as Aristotle suggested, they argue that metaphorizing involves constructing an analogy (i.e., Clinton is to politicians as cream puffs are to a specific type of food). The model predicts that the ease of comprehension depends on the similarity of the characteristics of the domains, whereas aptness depends on the dissimilarity between domains. Empirical findings have in general provided positive but weak support for the model (see Katz, 1989; Trick and Katz, 1986).

None of the various psychological models discussed above would claim to capture all of the characteristics of metaphor, or, even within the limited domains studies, to account for most of the variance in the empirical tests of the model. Moreover, each class of model is subject to some basic theoretical problems. For instance, comparison models depend on mapping preexisting semantic features, though likely such features emerge often only in the context of metaphoric juxtaposition (e.g., see Camac and Glucksberg, 1984; Tourangeau and Rips, 1991), as might be suggested by interaction theories. However, interaction theory itself is problematic. For instance, interaction presumes that the primary and subsidiary subjects have a reciprocal effect on one another, yet an extensive psychological literature indicates that the two aspects of metaphor play quite different roles in metaphor comprehension.

Nonsemantic models. In contrast to linguistic models that place the processing load with the meaning of words, the emphasis here is with use. A contrast is made between what the word(s) means literally and what the speaker intends to convey by use of those words. Searle (1993) argues that the basic problem is going from an utterance "S is P" to an intended meaning "S is R." In literal language he avers "S is P" = "S is R" and does not require any information except the rules of language, awareness of the conditions under which the utterance was made, and knowledge of the common ground shared by those in communication. When one is speaking metaphorically, however, additional information is required to recover speaker meaning.

Searle (1993) and others (e.g., Bach and Harnish, 1979) argue in essence that to understand metaphor, one has to be especially sensitive to the context in which the utterance was used and that comprehension depends on basic cognitive processes, such as inferential thinking, to derive a speaker's meaning. For example, Searle (1993) argues the following:

1. Look for speaker meaning that differs from sentence meaning if the sentence is defective when taken literally.
2. Try to find ways that S might be like P by generating salient, well-known, and distinctive features of P that can be used as candidates for R.
3. Check to see which of the generated candidates for the value of R are possible likely properties of R.

These models depend on the distinction between literal and nonliteral language; they also assume that the processing of metaphor depends upon recognizing that "S is P" is defective as a literal statement. In addition, the models give a primary role to inferential (cognitive) factors in metaphor comprehension. As pointed out before, there is empirical evidence that casts this explanation in doubt: for instance, the failure to find a processing difference between literal and nonliteral statements or evidence that comprehension depends on a prior recognition of sentential defectiveness. Moreover, as Cohen (1993) points out, there is a difference between metaphor and speech acts in general that makes it unwise to classify metaphor as a type of speech act. For instance, if Tom says "I am sorry," the speech act might be one of apologizing. However, if I were to say "Tom said that he was sorry," I am not apologizing, merely reporting Tom's comments. That is, the speech act is overridden. In contrast, if Tom said "That neighbor is an evergreen tree," the description could be understood only by someone who can derive a metaphorical interpretation. If I were to say "Tom said that the neighbor is an evergreen tree," understanding still depends on making sense of the metaphor. That is, metaphor is not overridden, as the speech act of apologizing had been. Cohen (1993) takes this to mean that "metaphorical meaning inheres in sentences, not just speech acts" (pp. 59–60).

Metaphor as a cognitive, not merely linguistic, activity. Saddock (1993) makes the argument succinctly. Metaphor is not a linguistic problem at all because the mechanisms underlying metaphor exist independently of language. This position is also the motivation for the distinction between metaphor and metaphoric expression made by Lakoff (1993), as quoted earlier. Of the various sources that point to a cognitive locus for metaphor, only some will be reviewed here.

Nonlinguistic metaphor. Two examples will be provided: pictorial metaphor and synesthesia. Kennedy (1996) in his review of 15 years of research, demonstrates that pictures can be either literal or metaphorical; an example of the latter is when lines are employed to indicate pain or speed. Of immediate interest, Kennedy has found that blind individuals with virtually no experience with pictures can figure out what these "pictorial metaphors" mean in raised line drawings.

In synesthesia, perceptual stimuli presented in one modality (e.g., as sound) consistently map to another modality (e.g., as a visual analog). Marks (1996) gives a pertinent review of this literature. Among the aspects of this phenomenon is that cross-modal mapping is evident in some cases soon after birth, that is, well before the development of language.

Linguistic analyses. Once again, only a small subset of the evidence will be presented here. The classic work here was by Lakoff and Johnson (1980), who demonstrated that much of conventional language is governed by mappings of one conceptual domain (e.g., love) in terms of another conceptual domain (e.g., journeys). As an example, in the LOVE IS A JOURNEY conceptual metaphor, the correspondences would include the lovers = travelers, the love relationship = vehicles, the lovers' goals = destinations, and the like. Thus, many diverse expressions can be understood as surface manifestations of a basic (or set of basic) conceptual mapping(s) or metaphor(s). For example, the conceptual metaphor, THE MIND IS A CONTAINER, allows us to understand the relationship between quite different linguistic expressions, such as "He has a closed mind," "He is empty headed," "He blew his top," and the like. Moreover, given a conceptual metaphor, we can understand the inferences people are likely to draw because we can reason about LOVE, (or about MINDS) using the knowledge that we use to reason about JOURNEYS (or CONTAINERS). Thus, we have a mechanism that permits us to understand novel extensions of conventional metaphor.

The recognition of conceptual metaphor has had a great impact on our understanding of metaphor and of the assumptions underlying our understanding of metaphor. For instance, Lakoff (1993) and others (see Gibbs, 1994) argue that even so-called literal meaning depends on basic conceptual metaphors and have shown that concepts, idioms, proverbs, poetry, polysemy, and other linguistic phenomena are grounded in nonlinguistic conceptual mappings.

Within this tradition, attempts continue in understanding the constraints on conceptual mappings. Some have been described in detail: mappings are at a superordinate level; mappings preserve the cognitive topology of the source domain (e.g., CONTAINERS) in a way that is consistent with the inherent structure of the target domain (e.g., MINDS), surface expressions often reflect multiple conceptual mappings and mappings might be embedded within a hierarchical structure (see Lakoff, 1993, for a brief review).

Empirical evidence for conceptual metaphor has usually come from judgment tasks, not from on-line measures. As such, one might argue that conceptual metaphors are not automatically engaged during the act of comprehension (e.g., see Glucksberg, Brown, and McGlone, [1993], though Gibbs [1994] presents data that suggest they might act on-line, at least in some conditions).

The evolutionary evidence. As far as has been determined, *Homo sapiens* is the only species with full language abilities, though some have argued that nonsyntactic proto-language might be present in other primates and might have been present in our evolutionary ancestors (see Bickerton, 1990). If metaphor is routed in the conceptual system, and not just in language, then perhaps metaphoric-like activity might be observed in our nonhuman, nonlinguistic genetic relatives.

The logic goes as follows: if closely related animals (but not more distant ones) exhibit similar behaviors, then one can infer that the common ancestor of the related animals possessed the genetic capabilities that underlie those behaviors. With respect to language, if one were to find a closely related species to ours that employed, for example, syntactic-like communication, then one might infer that our present language syntactic abilities can be traced, genetically, to a common ancestor that possessed proto-syntactic abilities. Based on genetic evidence (see Byrne, 1995), humans are most closely related to chimpanzees (separating from a common ancestor about 6 million years ago) and gorillas (separating into distinct lineages about 7.5 million years ago). In fact, humans share perhaps as much as 99% of our genetic material with the chimpanzee (Bickerton, 1990), though obviously that small difference has had enormous evolutionary consequences.

Examination of the comparative evidence clearly supports the contention that our closest nonhuman relatives do possess the cognitive elements necessary for metaphor. As Dingwall (1988) puts it in his review of the literature: "If one constructs a list of man's putatively unique behaviour patterns, one finds that almost without exceptions these have precursors in the behaviour of the great apes. . . . The great apes display tool use and construction, cooperative hunting and food sharing . . . [as well as] bipedal locomotion and social organization" (p. 284). Further, Dingwall suggests:

> If cognitive abilities alone could assure human-like communicative behaviour, it should be manifest. General learning, self-recognition, symbolic play, 'art,' insight learning, counting, maze running, relationship problems, categorization, cross-modal transfer and even the construction of australopithecine-like tools . . . do not lie beyond the abilities of the great apes." (p. 286)

More recent work has shown further that our closest nonhuman relatives also possess the fundamentals necessary for metaphoric communication: a theory of mind and the ability to deceive by what is uttered (see Byrne, 1995). These are preconditions that must certainly underlie pragmatic aspects of language. Consider, for instance, when one speaks ironically: to understand the intent, one has to understand that the statement is not meant as a description but as a comment or evaluation on the utterance. And if irony has both a privileged audience that is meant to recognize the irony and a nonprivileged audience that is the target of the barb, then those in the "know" must recognize the deceit and the aim of the speaker. Similar analyses can be made for many instances of indirect request, in which the social role of the participants in communication become so important (e.g., Holtgraves, 1994).

In general then, the evidence is that, at a cognitive level, humans and our great ape relatives share abilities necessary (though not sufficient) for metaphor and metaphoric expression. If, as some argue (e.g., see Walker and Shipman, 1996), true speech did not emerge until the evolution of *H. sapiens,* then the cognitive locus for metaphor was present long before the emergence of syntax or, in Bickerton's (1990) terms, the secondary representational system.

CAN METAPHOR INFORM US ABOUT
LANGUAGE-THOUGHT RELATIONS?

In the initial section of this chapter, I reviewed some of the posited relations between thought and language and some of the data brought to bear on the question. In the previous section, I reviewed some of the literature on metaphor. In this final section, I review some of the implications that the metaphor literature might have for our understanding of language-thought relations in general.

On the functional independence of language and thought. The question is the extent to which some language processing occurs independently of more general cognitive processes. The modular hypothesis argues for specialized processing units dedicated to performing language-related function and uninformed by higher-level cognitive processes. Interactive models posit that cognitive processes play a role even in the earliest stages of language comprehension, such as lexical look-up and syntactic analysis. If metaphor is a property of cognition (and not of language), as Lakoff (1993) and others argue, and if nonliteral language is processed as rapidly as literal language, as many argue (e.g., Glucksberg, 1991), then interactive models of language would fit the data better.

What types of experimental evidence would be useful here? One source might be to examine social factors that presumably play a role in our understanding of irony, indirect requests, and other forms of so-called nonliteral language. One such source would be the social role of the agent who utters the trope. Consider a statement such as "Children are precious gems," uttered by either a priest or a comedian. From the modular perspective, speaker occupation should not play an early role in comprehension, whereas interactive models could easily accommodate how such information might be used. Katz and Pexman (1997) have shown that such information is used in judgment tasks: a metaphor can be treated as irony if spoken by a person associated with ironic use, such as a comedian. Penny Pexman, Todd Ferretti, and I are now testing to see if the effect of occupation emerges during on-line reading, with initial positive findings (e.g., Pexman, Ferretti, and Katz, 1997). There is some (albeit weak) other evidence that social roles act on-line: Holtgraves (1994) examined social roles (e.g., boss, worker) on-line for indirect requests and found the expected results that this information was used early in the comprehension process.

A second source of information would be to examine grammatical aspects of metaphor. Most of the research to date, following a suggestion by Max Black, has examined nominal metaphors of the sort, "X is a Y" (e.g., "Men are wolves"). Many metaphors are not joined in that way but are linked via grammar. Consider, for instance, "The ship plowed the sea," in which the linking is between the action of a ship and the plowing of a field, with the associated linkages to growth, civilization, fertilization, and the like. Torreano and Glucksberg (1996) has demonstrated that rated metaphoricity is a function of the "distance" of the linkage. Thus "The idea flew across town" is perceived as more metaphorical than "The boy jumped on his bike and flew across town" which, in turn, is perceived as more metaphorical than the literal, "The bird grabbed the worm and flew across town." Torreano and Glucksberg also varied specificity of linkage (e.g., the verb "flew" versus the more general verb, "traveled") and found that generality also was important.

In essence, what Torreano and Glucksberg varied, within each level of verb specificity, was the nature of the agent. Recall that a version of this manipulation has played an important role in studies that have tested modularity, namely varying the animacy of the agent. For instance, some have argued that people use the animacy/inanimacy of the initial noun to determine (pragmatically) whether or not the noun is acting as the agent of a temporarily ambiguous sentence. The answer to this issue is still controversial (see, for instance, Clifton, 1993). The relevance of these manipulations to metaphorical usage has not been considered in the mainline psycholinguistic literature, though it is clear that manipulating the context to make the initial noun the agent (via metaphor) is an obvious way to help resolve the issue—and would be a source of evidence about the immediacy of metaphoric (versus literal) usage in syntax resolution.

On language determining thought.   Recall the Whorfian hypothesis that language plays an essential role in determining the nature of thought. As shown earlier, few today hold to that hypothesis, although there is a recent renaissance of support and some evidence that language plays some roles in specific cognitive tasks. Methodologically, Whorf used differences in linguistic expression to conclude that there were corresponding differences on conceptualization. This methodology is not unique, and later theorists have employed variants of it, with the argument now being that one can get insight into the thought patterns of various groups by understanding their language. In essence, this is the strategy employed by Lakoff and Johnson (1980), Jackendoff (1992), and other linguists.

Consider for a moment an example from Jackendoff (1992): many verbs and prepositions appear in two or more semantic fields and do so in a lawful manner. Thus, the verb "go" and prepositions "from" or "to" can be found in the domain of spatial relations ("The bird went from the ground to the tree," "The bird is in the tree"), the domain of possession ("The inheritance went to Philip," "The money is Philip's"), the domain of property ascription ("Harry went from elated to depression," "Harry is depressed"), and so on. In each case a lawful relation holds in which the "go" verb expresses a change of some sort, with the "be/is" sentence representing the terminal state of the change. Jackendoff uses examples of this sort to characterize the conceptual structure underlying use of language in different domains.

But where do the conceptual structures themselves come from? One possibility is that the conceptual relations are basic and are grounded in experience, as Lakoff and Johnson (1980) argue in a somewhat different context. Thus, in the prior example, in the spatial domain one might experience pouring a liquid into a container and see that more liquid in the container is related to height and thus a conceptual mapping of MORE IS UP: LESS IS DOWN. This conceptual metaphor would be the basis for our understanding (or manifestations) of a host of linguistic expressions (e.g., "My pay has just gone up," "Unemployment is down"). From this perspective, metaphor involves the mapping of a linguistic expression onto a conceptual structure. Moreover, if Lakoff (1993) is correct, then all cultures will experience "more" with "up," though all might not develop a conceptual metaphor. The theory predicts that no culture will make the opposite mapping (LESS IS UP) because that relation is not grounded in experience.

The modern emphasis has given priority to the conceptual structure, not to the linguistic input, unlike Whorf, who used the opposite emphasis. But are we in a chicken-and-egg game here? What if language is itself a source of experiential knowledge? We then have language involved in the creation of conceptual relations that then play a role in motivating our understanding of linguistic input. In fact, some have argued that conceptual structures, such as schemata or mental models, might be based, at least in part, on linguistic input (e.g., Banks and Thompson, 1996). Thus, one could argue that we have a variant of linguistic determinism, to the extent that language plays a role in determining the creation of conceptual mappings.

One could argue further that metaphor might be an ideal natural laboratory where one could study linguistic effects on cognition because, as many have noted, metaphor not only illuminates, it conceals. A good metaphor emphasizes similarity relations and deemphasizes the dissimilarities. Thus, someone who states, as some did during the Iranian invasion of Kuwait, "Sadam Hussein is a modern Hitler," emphasizes certain relations and associations, such as violations of human rights, military aggressiveness, and brutality, but deemphasizes the differences between a European superpower and a Third World nation and the consequent implications for worldwide involvement.

There is a tradition, largely in applied cognition, that tacitly takes the neo-Whorfian position that I have just outlined. That is, the linguistic expressions used by a person provide insights into (and perhaps determine) the conceptual world that motivates a person. I am reminded by a story told to me by an anthropologist colleague who did his field work among the Innuit. Some of the first Europeans who came into contact with the groups that he studied had been missionaries, who took it upon themselves to translate the Bible for the Innuit. But they had difficulty with the recurring image of the shepherd with his flock because the culture consisted of nomadic hunters. In any event, the missionaries decided to use as an acceptable alternative the phrase, "The hunter with his dog team.'' As my colleague noted, the relationship is not apt because under duress the hunter will beat, or even eat, the dogs, and the concept of God that was conveyed was one of a masterful cannibal.

I take the example as neo-Whorfian in the sense that the experience of the Innuit was linguistic and, once mapped onto existing conceptual structures, influenced subsequent processing of information from the new (religious) domain. One need not go to exotic cultures to find other examples. For instance, in Katz and Mio (1996, sect. 2 and 3) there are chapters in which metaphors play an important role in understanding the conceptual structures of people in psychotherapy, divorce mediation, understanding of medical terms, and, in a more general sense, political discourse.

On the computational question: A cautionary note.   Several contrasts were presented in the earlier sections: modular versus interactive models of language, language determining thought versus merely expressing it, the necessity versus nonnecessity of making a distinction between literal and nonliteral language, metaphor as cognition versus metaphor as language. In most cases, the arguments and experiments have emphasized the constraints that any relevant theory would have to incorporate. In this final section, I address the implications that arise from realizing these constraints in psychologically real models of language processing.

One can take the standard pragmatic model discussed earlier as an example of such a plausible model. The constraints necessary to implement this model would include the following: (1) a distinction between literal and nonliteral language, (2) processing priority of the literal, (3) description of conditions under which the literal fails, and (4) the type of inferential processing that permits the recovery of an intended speaker's meaning. Even if one could model these constraints computationally, the model would not be psychologically real because, as also discussed before, tests of this model have demonstrated that several links in this sequence do not appear to be necessary for the understanding of nonliteral language.

As Martin (1996) has pointed out, in general traditional artificial intelligence (AI) computational models of language processing are inadequate as they fail to handle nonliteral language. At one level this might suggest that literal language can be handled one way (via the compositionality principle) whereas nonliteral language requires different rules of processing. The exception to this is context-based models. In such models prior discourse context is given the prominent role in suggesting plausible representations for a target sentence. This approach is valid for literal and nonliteral alike and is consistent with the data reviewed earlier, which indicates that (1) given sufficient discourse context, the speed with which one processes a nonliteral target is as rapid as that found with a literal target, and (2) any information that activates properties informative about a topic is sufficient to trigger immediate comprehension, regardless of topic literality. Despite being in the mainstream of much of the current psycholinguistic research, these models are mute on several basic questions of importance to our understanding of figurative language. What makes some metaphors so apt and others so mundane, some sarcastic comments so biting and others mild, some indirect requests so transparent and others not? And what about the systematicity described by Lakoff and Johnson and others, namely, that diverse expressions, both literal and nonliteral, are often linked by core conceptual metaphoric mappings?

In contrast to context-based models, two other classes of AI models have emerged in recent years as concrete implementations of nonliteral language (Martin, 1966). Each of the two classes of models has started from a different set of theoretical assumptions and consequently have adopted different perspectives on the basic problem the model has to solve. If one assumes that metaphor is a matter of language (and not cognition), the problem is one of stretching meaning so that a concept comes to mean something new. If one assumes that conceptual metaphors play the critical role in processing, then the problem becomes one of elaborating upon the nature of the core structure and how input is mapped into it. The success or failure of these attempts in AI can, in principle, tell us whether or not the approach is theoretically possible at all. And the differences between models can be informative about how the various approaches explain similar phenomena. As an example, let us contrast approaches that assume metaphor is language-based with those that, following Lakoff and Johnson (1980), assume that metaphor is cognitively based.

Metaphor-as-language approaches have followed in the classic assumption that analogical reasoning underlies metaphor comprehension. That is, the task of the metaphor interpreter is to find or create a set of relations linking the topic and vehicle. And from the large number of ways that the concepts can be linked, the problem then becomes one of finding the best of the candidate mappings. Different models apply different mechanisms in generating the underlying analogical relation and in determining suitability of the candidates. Such models do exist and can explain a set of empirical findings (e.g., Gentner, 1983; Indurkhya, 1987). At one level the successful implementation of metaphor-as-language models indicates that one cannot dismiss this theoretical approach as unrealistic. Moreover, these models have the advantage of explicitly describing the principles that underlie metaphor aptness.

Models that follow the metaphor-as-cognition approach assume that there are a set of core conceptual metaphors and that the task of comprehension is to first make a match of input with one of these conceptual metaphors and then, via a set of rules, to translate that metaphor into a form that takes into account the constraints of the surface input. Computer models of this sort have differed in the number of conceptual metaphors necessary to handle language. Moreover, there is at present no mechanism in these models that simulates human judgments of metaphor aptness. Nonetheless, the successful implementation of models built on core conceptual metaphors argues for the viability of this approach.

It should be noted that in implementing the theoretical constraints inherent in a model, the programmers had to make explicit decisions that are not explicit in the psychological or linguistic literature on which they are based. Thus, one can acknowledge the need for conceptual metaphors but face very real implementational problems, such as that found in the trade-off between elaborating representational information or processing power. This contrast can, in fact, be found in the literature on implementing Lakoff and Johnson's conceptual metaphor position. If one assumes that only a few core metaphors exist (i.e., representational information is low), then the processing load is taken up by increasing the operators that work on the information; in contrast, if one has a very enriched set of conceptual metaphors, then one requires less from the mental operators. From a psychological perspective, the various models in the literature point out the leap from theoretical constraints to psychologically real implementations of these constraints.

And now the cautionary concluding note. In the literature reviewed in this chapter, different perspectives on the language-thought issue were outlined. In many cases there is no consensus on the basic commitments required for theorizing about nonliteral language, or even on whether nonliteral language is a separate problem from literal language. Even when there is an agreement, such as a commitment to metaphor as a matter of cognition and not of language, as pointed out previously, this commitment does not necessarily lead to a single psychologically real processing model.

The empirical literature becomes difficult if not impossible to interpret without the link from theoretically motivated constraints to psychologically real implementation of these constraints. Consider the implication of this state of affairs for one recent study. Recall the study by Glucksberg et al. (1993) mentioned earlier: they failed to find evidence that conceptual metaphors are automatically engaged during idiom comprehension. But what does this finding indicate? Not knowing how the idea of conceptual metaphors is actualized, one can suggest several possibilities. One can take it, as in fact Glucksberg et al. did, as an indication that conceptual metaphors do not play an early and primary role in language processing. However, one can also interpret the data as indicating that the conceptual representation consists of only a few core metaphors and that much subsequent processing is necessary to go from the basic conceptual metaphors to other more derived forms. Or one can take it to show that conceptual metaphors do not exist as prestored representations, as the metaphor-as-language models suggest. Indeed, the AI models based on analogical reasoning can offer a radically different explanation for the systematicity that has been used as evidence for the necessity of conceptual metaphors. In this last case, the finding that quite different surface expressions share a basic meaning commonality can be attributed to the fact that the analogical solutions, computed independently for each surface expression, are quite similar.

REFERENCES

Alonzo-Quecty, M., & de Vega, M. (1991). Contextual effects in a metaphor verification task. *European Journal of Cognitive Psychology, 3,* 315–341.

Altmann, G., & Steedman, M. (1988). Interaction with context during human sentence processing. *Cognition, 30,* 191–238.

Au, T. Kit-Fong. (1983). Chinese and English counterfactuals: The Sapir-Whorf hypothesis revisited. *Cognition, 15,* 155–187.

Bach, K., & Harnish, R. (1979). *Linguistic communication and speech acts.* Cambridge, MA: MIT Press.

Banks, W., & Thompson, S. (1996). The mental image of the human body: Implications of physiological mental models for our understanding of health and illness. In J. Mio & A. Katz (Eds.), *Metaphor: Implications and Applications* (pp. 99–126). Mahwah, NJ: Erlbaum.

Berlin, B., & Kay, P. (1969). *Basic color terms: Their universality and evolution.* Berkeley: University of California Press.

Bickerton, D. (1990). *Language and species.* Chicago: University of Chicago Press.

Bickerton, D. (1995). *Language and human behavior.* Seattle: University of Washington Press.

Black, M. (1993). More about metaphor. In A. Ortony (Ed.), *Metaphor and thought.* 2nd ed. (pp.19–41). Cambridge: Cambridge University Press.

Blasko, D., & Connine, C. (1993). Effects of familiarity and aptness on metaphor processing. *Journal of Experimental Psychology: Learning, Memory and Cognition, 19,* 295–308.

Bloom, A. (1981). *The linguistic shaping of thought: A study in the impact of language on thinking in China and the West.* Hillsdale, NJ: Erlbaum.

Brown, R. (1976). Reference—In memorial tribute to Eric Lennenberg. *Cognition, 4,* 125–153.

Brown, R. (1977). In reply to Peter Schonbach. *Cognition, 5,* 185–187.

Brown, R., & Lennenberg, E. (1954). A study in language and cognition. *Journal of Abnormal and Social Psychology, 49,* 454–462.

Burgess, C., & Chiarello, C. (1996). Neurocognitive mechanisms underlying metaphor comprehension and other figurative language. *Metaphor and Symbolic Activity, 11,* 67–84.

Byrne, R. (1995). *The thinking ape: Evolutionary origins of intelligence.* Oxford: Oxford University Press.

Cacciari, C., & Tabossi, P. (1988). The comprehension of idioms. *Journal of Memory and Language, 27,* 668–683.

Camac, M., & Glucksberg, S. (1984). Metaphors do not use associations between concepts, they are used to create them. *Journal of Psycholinguistic Research, 13,* 443–455.

Carmichael, L., Hogan, H., & Walter, A. (1932). An experimental study of the effect of language on the representation of visually perceived form. *Journal of Experimental Psychology, 15,* 73–86.

Carroll, J., & Casagrande, J. (1958). The function of language classification in behavior. In E. Maccoby, T. Newcombe, & E. Hartley (Eds.), *Readings in social psychology,* 3rd ed. (pp. 18–31). New York: Holt, Rinehart, and Winston.

Chiarello, C., Burgess, C., Richards, L., & Pollock, A. (1990). Semantic and associative priming in the cerebral hemispheres: Some words do, some words don't . . . sometimes, some places. *Brain and Language, 38,* 75–104.

Chomsky, N. (1965). *Aspects of the theory of syntax.* Cambridge, MA: MIT Press.

Clifton, C. (1993). Thematic roles in sentence parsing. *Canadian Journal of Experimental Psychology, 47,* 222–246.

Cohen, L. J.(1993). The semantics of metaphor. In A. Ortony (Ed.), *Metaphor and Thought,* 2nd Ed. (pp. 58–70). Cambridge: Cambridge University Press.

Damasio, A., & Damasio, H. (1992). Brain and language. *Scientific American, 117,* 1258–1260.

Dascal, M. (1987). Defending literal meaning. *Cognitive Science, 11,* 259–281.

Denny, J. P. (In press). Evaluating Whorf's Algonquian studies. *Anthropological Linguistics.*

Dews, S., & Winner, E. (1995). Muting the meaning: A social function of irony. *Metaphor and Symbolic Activity, 10,* 3–19.

Dingwall, W. (1988). The evolution of human communicative behavior. In F. Newmeyer (Ed.), *Linguistics: The Cambridge survey.* vol. 3. *Language: Psychological and biological aspects* (pp. 274–313). Cambridge: Cambridge University Press.

Dinneen, F. (1967). *An introduction to general linguistics.* New York: Holt, Rinehart, and Winston.

Ferreira, F., & Clifton, C. (1986). The independence of syntactic processing. *Journal of Memory and Language, 25,* 348–368.

Fishman, J. (1960). The systematization of the Whorfian hypothesis. *Behavioral Science, 5,* 323–339.

Fodor, J. (1983). *The modularity of mind.* Cambridge, MA: MIT Press.

Frazier, L. (1987). Sentence processing: A tutorial review. In M. Coltheart (Ed.), *Attention and performance, 12: The psychology of reading* (pp. 559–586). London: Erlbaum.

Frazier, L., & Rayner, K. (1982). Making and correcting errors during sentence processing: eye movements in analysis of structurally ambiguous sentences, *Cognitive Psychology, 14,* 178–210.

Gardner, H. (1983). *Frames of mind.* New York: Basic Books.

Gentner, D. (1983). Structure mapping: A theoretical framework for analogy. *Cognitive Science, 7,* 155–170.

Gentner, D., & Clements, C. (1988). Evidence for relational selectivity in interpreting analogy and metaphor. In G. Bower (Ed.), *The psychology of learning and motivation,* vol. 22 (pp. 307–358). New York: Academic Press.

Gibbs, R. (1980). Spilling the beans on the understanding and memory for idioms in conversation. *Memory and Cognition, 8,* 449–456.

Gibbs, R. (1994). *The poetics of mind.* Cambridge: Cambridge University Press.

Gick, M., & Holyoak, K. (1980). Analogical problem solving. *Cognitive Psychology, 12,* 306–355.

Gick, M., & Holyoak, K. (1983). Schema induction and analogical transfer. *Cognitive Psychology, 15,* 1–38.

Gildea, P., & Glucksberg, S. (1983). On understanding metaphor: The role of context. *Journal of Verbal Learning and Verbal Behavior, 22,* 577–590.

Gilovich, T. (1981). Seeing the past in the present: The effect of associations to familiar events on judgments and decisions. *Journal of Personality and Social Psychology, 40,* 797–808.

Glucksberg, S. (1991). Beyond literal meanings: The psychology of allusion. *Psychological Science, 2,* 146–152.

Glucksberg, S., Brown, M., & McGlone, M. (1993). Conceptual metaphors are not automatically accessed during idiom comprehension. *Memory and Cognition, 21,* 711–719.

Glucksberg, S., & Danks, J. (1968). Effects of discriminative labels and nonsense labels upon availability of novel function. *Journal of Verbal Learning and Verbal Behavior, 7,* 72–76.

Glucksberg, S., Gildea, A., & Bookin, H. (1982). On understanding nonliteral speech: Can people ignore metaphors? *Journal of Verbal Learning and Verbal Behavior, 21,* 85–98.

Glucksberg, S., & Keysar, B. (1990). Understanding metaphorical comparisons: Beyond similarity. *Psychological Review, 97,* 3–18.

Gregory, M. (1993). Metaphor comprehension: From literal truth to metaphoricity and back again. *Metaphor and Symbolic Activity, 8,* 1–21.

Grice, H. (1975). Logic and conversation. In P. Cole (Ed.), *Syntax and semantics.* vol. 9 *Pragmatics* (pp. 113–127). New York: Academic Press.

Heeschen, C. (1985). Agrammatism versus paragrammatism: A fictitious opposition. In M. Kean (Ed.), *Agrammatism* (pp. 207–248). New York: Academic Press.

Heider, E., & Olivier, D. (1972). The structure of color space in naming and memory for two languages. *Cognitive Psychology, 3,* 337–354.

Hellige, J. (1990). Hemispheric asymmetry. In M. Rosenzweig & L. Porter (Eds.), *Annual review of psychology.* vol. 41 (pp. 55–80). Palo Alto, CA: Annual Reviews, Inc.

Hill, J. (1988). Language, culture and world view. *Linguistics: The Cambridge survey.* vol. 4. *Language: The socio-cultural context* (pp. 14–36). Cambridge: Cambridge University Press.

Holtgraves, T. (1994). Communication in context: Effects of speaker status on the comprehension of indirect requests. *Journal of Experimental Psychology: Learning, Memory and Cognition, 20,* 1205–1218.

Indurkhya, B. (1987). Approximate semantic transference: A computational theory of metaphors and analogy. *Cognitive Science, 11,* 445–480.

Jackendoff, R. (1977). *X-bar syntax: A study of phrase structure.* Cambridge, MA: MIT Press.

Jackendoff, R. (1992). *Languages of the mind: Essays on mental representation.* Cambridge, MA: MIT Press.

Johnson, D. (1972). *A systematic introduction to the psychology of thinking.* New York: Harper and Row.

Katz, A. (1992). Psychological studies in metaphor processing: Extensions to the placement of terms in semantic space. *Poetics Today, 13,* 607–632.

Katz. A. (1996a). On interpreting statements as metaphor or irony: Contextual heuristics and cognitive consequences. In J. Mio & A. Katz (Eds.), *Metaphor: Pragmatics and applications* (pp. 1–22). Hillsdale, NJ: Erlbaum.

Katz, A. (1996b). Experimental psycholinguistics and figurative language: circa 1995. *Metaphor and Symbolic Activity, 11,* 17–37.

Katz, A. (In press). Pragmatic psycholinguistics as a framework for the evaluation of creativity. In M. Runco (Ed.), *Critical creative processes.* Cresshill, NJ: Hampton Press.

Katz, A., & Mio, J. (Eds.).(1996). *Metaphor: Pragmatics and Applications.* Hillsdale, NJ: Erlbaum.

Katz, A., Paivio, A., Marschark, M., & Clark, J. (1988). Norms for 204 literary and 260 nonliterary metaphors on 10 psychological dimensions. *Metaphor and Symbolic Activity, 3,* 191–214.

Katz, A., & Pexman, P. (1997). Interpreting figurative statements: Speaker occupation can change metaphor to irony. *Metaphor and Symbolic Activity, 12,* 19-41.

Kawamoto, A. (1993). Nonlinear dynamics in the resolution of lexical ambiguity: A parallel distributed processing account. *Journal of Memory and Language, 32,* 474–516.

Kemper, S. (1981). Comprehension and the interpretation of proverbs. *Journal of Psycholinguistic Research, 10,* 179–198.

Kennedy, J. (1996). Metaphor in tactile pictures for the blind: Using metonomy to evoke classification. In J. Mio & A. Katz (Eds.), *Metaphor: Pragmatics and applications* (pp. 215–230). Hillsdale, NJ: Erlbaum.

Keysar, B. (1989). On the functional equivalence of literal and metaphorical interpretations in discourse. *Journal of Memory and Language, 28,* 375–385.

Kimura, D. (1993). *Neuromotor mechanisms in human communication.* Oxford: Oxford University Press.

Kittay, E., & Lehrer, A. (1981). Semantic fields and the structure of metaphor. *Studies in Language, 5,* 31–63.

Kolk, H., Van Grunsven, M., & Keyser, A. (1985). On parallelism between production and comprehension in agrammatism. In M. Kean (Ed.), *Agrammatism* (pp.165–206). New York: Academic Press.

Kramer, C. (1977). Perceptions of male and female speech. *Journal of Social Psychology and Personality, 32,* 151–161.

Kreuz, R. (1996). The use of verbal irony: Cues and constraints. In J. Mio & A. Katz (Eds.), *Metaphor: Implications and applications* (pp. 23–38). Mahwah, NJ: Erlbaum.

Lakoff, G. (1993). The contemporary theory of metaphor. In A. Ortony (Ed.), *Metaphor and thought,* 2nd ed. (pp. 202–251). Cambridge: Cambridge University Press.

Lakoff, G., & Johnson, M. (1980). *Metaphors we live by.* Chicago: Chicago University Press.

Lanham, R. (1991). *A handlist of rhetorical terms.* Berkeley: University of California Press.

Lantz, D., & Stefflre, V. (1964). Language and cognition revisited. *Journal of Abnormal and Social Psychology, 69,* 472–481.

Lehrer, A. (1978). Structures of the lexicon and transfer of meaning. *Lingua, 45,* 95–123.

Lennenberg, E., & Roberts, J. (1956). *The language of experience.* Bloomington: Indiana University Press.

Linbarger, M., Schwartz, M., & Saffran, E.(1983). Sensitivity to grammatical structure in so-called agrammatical aphasics. *Cognition, 13,* 361–392.

Lucy, J. (1992). *Grammatical categories and cognition.* Cambridge: Cambridge University Press.

MacCormac, E. (1985). *A cognitive theory of metaphor.* Cambridge, MA: MIT Press.

Malgady, R., & Johnson, M. (1980). Measurement of figurative language: Semantic feature models of comprehension and appreciation. In R. Honeck & R. Hoffman (Eds.), *Cognition and figurative language* (pp. 239–258). Hillsdale, NJ: Erlbaum.

Maratsos, M., & Matheny, L. (1994). Language specificity and elasticity: Brain and clinical syndrome studies. In L. Porter & M. Rosenzweig (Eds.), *Annual review of psychology.* vol. 45 (pp. 487–516). Palo Alto, CA: Annual Reviews, Inc.

Marks, L. (1996). On perceptual metaphors. *Metaphor and Symbolic Activity, 11,* 39–66.

Martin, J. (1996). Computational approaches to figurative language. *Metaphor and Symbolic Activity, 11,* 85–100.

Miller, G., & McNeil, D. (1969). Psycholinguistics. In G. Lindzey & E. Aronson (Eds.), *The handbook of social psychology,* vol. 3. Reading, MA: Addison-Wesley.

Needham, W. (1992). Limits on literal processing during idiom interpretation. *Journal of Psycholinguistic Research, 21,* 1–16.

Onishi, K., & Murphy, G. (1993). Metaphoric reference: When metaphors are not understood as easily as literal expressions. *Memory and Cognition, 21,* 763–772.

Ortony, A. (1975). Why metaphors are necessary and not just nice. *Educational Theory, 25,* 45–53.

Ortony, A. (1979). Beyond literal similarity. *Psychological Review, 86,* 161–180.

Ortony, A. (1993). Metaphor, language and thought. In A. Ortony (Ed.), *Metaphor and thought,* 2nd ed. Cambridge: Cambridge University Press.

Ortony, A., Reynolds, R., & Arter, J. (1978a). Metaphor: Theoretical and empirical research. *Psychological Bulletin, 85,* 919–943.

Ortony, A., Schallert, D. Reynolds, R., & Antos, S. (1978b). Interpreting metaphors and idioms: Some effects of context on comprehension. *Journal of Verbal Learning and Verbal Behavior, 17,* 465–477.

Ortony, A., Vondruska, R., Foss, M., & Jones, L. (1985). Salience, similes, and the asymmetry of similarity. *Journal of Memory and Language, 24,* 569–594.

Paivio, A., & Begg, I. (1981). *Psychology of language.* Englewood Cliffs, NJ: Prentice-Hall.

Pederson, E. (1994). *Language as context, language as means: Spatial cognition and habitual language use.* Nijmegen: Max Planck Institute for Psycholinguistics, Cognitive Anthropology Research Group, Working paper no. 26.

Pexman, P. Ferretti, T., & Katz, A. (1997). *Reading figurative statements: The role of contextual constraints in on-line processing.* Presented at meeting of Canadian Psychological Association, Toronto, June.

Pinker, S. (1994). *The language instinct.* New York: W. Morrow and Co.

Poizner, H., Klima, E., & Beluga, U. (1987). *What the hands reveal about the brain.* Cambridge, MA: MIT Press.

Pollio, H., Smith, M., & Pollio, M. (1990). Figurative language and cognitive psychology. *Language and Cognitive Processes, 5,* 141–167.

Rayner, K., Carlson, M., & Frazier, L. (1983). The interaction of syntax and semantics during sentence processing: Eye movements in the analysis of semantically biased sentences. *Journal of Verbal Learning and Verbal Behavior, 22,* 358–374.

Roberts, R., & Kreuz, R. (1994). Why do people use figurative language? *Psychological Science, 5,* 159–163.

Saddock, J. (1993). Figurative speech and linguistics. In A. Ortony (Ed.), *Metaphor and thought,* 2nd ed. (pp. 42–57). Cambridge: Cambridge University Press.

Schaff, A. (1973). *Language and cognition.* New York: McGraw-Hill.

Scribner, S. (1977). Modes of thinking and ways of speaking: Culture and logic reconsidered. In P. Wagon & P. Johnson-Laird (Eds.), *Thinking.* Cambridge: Cambridge University Press.

Searle, J. (1993). Metaphor. In A. Ortony (Ed.), *Metaphor and thought,* 2nd ed. (pp.83–111). Cambridge: Cambridge University Press.

Shinjo, M., & Myers, J. (1987). The role of context on metaphor comprehension. *Journal of Memory and Language, 26,* 226–241.

Swinney, D. (1979). Lexical access during sentence comprehension: Reconsideration of context effects. *Journal of Verbal Learning and Verbal Behavior, 18,* 645–659.

Tabossi, P., & Zardon, F. (1993). Processing ambiguous words in context. *Journal of Memory and Language, 32,* 359–372.

Tarban, R., & McClelland, J. (1988). Constituent attachment and thematic role expectations. *Journal of Memory and Language, 27,* 597–632.

Titone, D., & Connine, C. (1994). *Taking on semantic commitments: Processing semantically non-decomposable and decomposable idioms.* Poster presented at the 8th Annual CUNY Conference on Human Sentence Processing.

Torreano, L., & Glucksberg, S. (1996). *When are verbs metaphorical? The role of selection restriction violations.* Paper presented at 37th Psychonomic Society Meeting, Chicago, November.

Tourangeau, R., & Sternberg, R. (1981). Aptness in metaphor. *Cognitive Psychology, 13,* 203–244.

Tourangeau, R., & Rips, L. (1991). Interpreting and evaluating metaphors. *Journal of Memory and Language, 30,* 452–472.

Trick, L., & Katz, A. (1986). The domain interaction approach to metaphor processing: Individual differences and metaphor characteristics. *Metaphor and Symbolic Activity, 1,* 185–213.

Trueswell, J., Tanenhaus, M., & Kello, C. (1993). Verb-specific constraints in sentence processing: Separating effects of lexical preference from garden paths. *Journal of Experimental Psychology: Learning, Memory and Cognition, 19,* 528–553.

Vygotsky, L.(1962). *Thought and language.* Cambridge, MA: MIT Press.

Walker, A., & Shipman, P. (1996). *The wisdom of the bones.* New York: Knopf.

Whitney, P., Budd, D., & Mio, J. (1996). Individual differences in metaphoric facilitation of comprehension. In J. Mio & A. Katz (Eds.), *Metaphor: Implications and applications* (pp. 203–214). Mahwah, NJ: Erlbaum.

Whorf, B. (1956). *Language, thought and reality: Selected writings of Benjamin Lee Whorf.* Cambridge, MA: MIT Press.

Winner, E. (1988). *The point of words: Children's understanding of metaphor and irony.* Cambridge, MA: Harvard University Press.

CHAPTER 2

Figure

Mark Turner

THE CLASSICAL FOUNDATION

The classical Greek word σχῆμα (*schema*) had a range of commonplace meanings that cluster around a central prototype: a *schema* is a pairing of two patterns at unequal levels. The steps of a dance are a *schema* of the dance. A stately bearing is a *schema* of a dignified character. Human dress is a *schema* of the human body, and a fashion of dress is a *schema* of an aspect of the body. Posture is a *schema* of attitude. The imperative mode of the verb is a *schema* of command. Plato called the concrete circle traced in the sand a *schema* of the single, transcendent, and metaphysically prior ideal circle. Aristotle reversed the direction of abstraction, preferring to see abstract mental forms as epistemological *schemata* of concrete realities they represent.

Schema became a technical term of Greek rhetoric, used prototypically to signify a conventional pairing of a form and a meaning or, more broadly, a form and a conceptual pattern. To know a language, one must know its *schemata*. In practice, *schema* often designated the formal half of a form-meaning pair, the way ''daughter'' designates one half of the pair it signifies.

Greek names for schemata sound foreign, but the patterns and pairings they signify are familiar elements of thought and language. For example, we often understand a complex event as consisting of steps, and we conventionally express this conceptual pattern in the linguistic pattern found in ''sex leads to pregnancy and pregnancy leads to children'' or ''fear brings paralysis and paralysis brings failure.'' The pairing is the schema *climax* (Greek for ''ladder''). For a second example, we often understand two elements as standing in symmetric relationship, and we conventionally express this conceptual pattern in the linguistic pattern found in ''James accuses Paul and Paul accuses James''

FIGURE **45**

or "electricity induces magnetism and magnetism induces electricity." The pairing is the schema *antimetabole* (Greek for "turning about").

Some schemata, like *antimetabole,* have as their conceptual half a highly abstract set of connections between elements, with negligible suggestion of the categories to which these elements might belong. Their abstract conceptual pattern fits many different kinds of specific scenes and even many different abstract meanings. Consider, for example, "electricity induces magnetism and magnetism induces electricity." To be sure, its *words* concern electromagnetism and causation, but its *antimetabole figure* does not: the formal pattern of the figure is a doubled expression that includes A and B in its first half and their transposition in its second, while the paired conceptual pattern of the figure is symmetric relation between A and B. Obviously, this conceptual pattern provides no suggestion of the categories to which A and B belong. We can apply it, at least in principle, to any kind of A and B.

Other schemata have, in contrast, a kind of conceptual pattern that is much more specific, namely, a conceptual frame that is conventional and that models a common and rich human scene. For example, there is a basic human scene in which someone cries out from an access of emotion; the conceptual frame modeling that scene is paired with the form *exclamation* and with specific lexical exclamations, such as "O!" "Alas!" "Damn!" and "God!" This pairing is the schema *ecphonesis.* There is a basic human scene in which emotion paralyzes a speaker; the conceptual frame modeling that scene is paired with a particular linguistic form—an abrupt halt in the middle of a clause and the replacement of its expected conclusion with silence, a gesture of incapacity, an expressive vocal sound, tears, or a verbal derailment such as "Forgive me," "I cannot go on," or "It's just too terrible." This pairing is the schema *aposiopesis.*

Rhetoricians of classical antiquity began the inquiry into the kinds of schemata, the mechanisms of schemata, and the network of relations between schemata. They left us foundational taxonomies, subtle analyses, and Greek names like *antithesis* and *parenthesis,* a few of which have survived into English, although our word for *schema* itself as a technical term in rhetoric comes from the Latin word chosen as its equivalent by Roman translators and adaptors: *figura,* the root of our "figure."[1]

Unfortunately, Greek and Hellenistic rhetorical and linguistic inquiries into schemata or figures have been lost. The earliest surviving document that presents an extensive treatment of figures is the pseudo-Ciceronian *Rhetorica ad Herennium,* dating from the first century B.C., which lacks the seriousness of theoretical inquiry we find in Aristotle on metaphor or Longinus on style. It is a pedagogical manual.

Nonetheless, works of the sort to which the *ad Herennium* belongs show that classical rhetoricians had anticipated some of the most influential discoveries about the nature of form-meaning pairs. Often, it is only in retrospect that these anticipations are seen for what they were. For example, in work on conceptual integration, Gilles Fauconnier and I observed that there is an optimality principle leading to the tightening of metonymies under certain conditions (Fauconnier and Turner, in press b). By way of illustration, consider the conventional knowledge that *winter* as a period of time is connected through a chain of metonymies to snow, ice, and whiteness: in some parts of the world (although not where I was raised), the period of winter includes intervals during which the ambient temperature falls below freezing, and during these intervals (which may be infrequent), a body of water such as a lake or pond may freeze over, and precipitation may take the form of snow, whose color is white, or sleet, freezing rain, and so on. Personifications of winter routinely shorten this chain of metonymies, so that ice, snow, and whiteness become part of the immediate concrete form of the personification. In retrospect, it appears that the explicit statement of the metonymy-tightening principle has as one of its specific corollaries the rhetorical figure *metalepsis*. In *metalepsis,* a distant effect is transformed into a feature of its cause. For example, a vehicular speed viewed as risky can be thought of as *breakneck speed*. A situation that makes us comfortable can be thought of as a *comfortable situation.* A man who makes noises we judge to be loud can be thought of as a *loud man*. These are examples of *metalepsis*.

As Jeanne Fahnestock has surveyed in her superb study *Figures of Argument,* research over two and a half millennia into the nature of figure has been confused and uneven, but its anchor is the notion of pairing: ''The goal of a compendium of figures was . . . to define the formal means for achieving certain cognitive or persuasive functions. One or the other arm of this form-function connection could pivot . . . but the central link should still hold.''

Often it failed to hold, when the rhetorician worked on a single pattern, conceptual or formal, instead of on a pairing. Pairing eventually fell to secondary or even incidental place as a principle of the theory of figure. Some major figures—like analogy, allegory, and parable—were often defined as having to do with abstract conceptual patterns but not so clearly with *linguistic* patterns, since their products can be expressed in many forms. Similarly, figures concerned with conventional frames of rich human scenes—reproving an adversary, turning from the audience to address an individual, or pleading for help—were also given definitions of conceptual pattern unpaired with linguistic form, again because their conceptual patterns can be expressed in many forms.

In the other direction, some well-known figures were defined as linguistic forms only. *Zeugma,* for example, has often been defined as the linguistic form in which a single verb governs two or more clauses or groups of words—as in the prosaic ''Henry ran a mile and James two miles'' or the Shakespearean ''Passion lends them power, time means, to meet.''

Yet even in analyses such as these, the implicit pull toward pairing remains

FIGURE 47

strong. *Hyperbole,* expressible in many forms, is typically illustrated with superlative modifiers. *Metaphor,* expressible in many forms, is typically illustrated with bare lexical nouns that prompt for conventional metaphoric meanings ("wolf," "lion," "vixen"). *Metalepsis,* expressible in many forms ("The loud man," "The man is loud," "The loudness of that man is unbearable"), is typically illustrated with an Adjective-Noun form in which the cause is expressed by the noun and the effect (turned into a feature of the cause) is expressed by the adjective, as in "pallid death." *Zeugma,* a purely formal pattern, is typically illustrated with expressions in which the verb applies with remarkably unequal meaning to the governed clauses. In *The Rape of the Lock,* Alexander Pope writes that Queen Anne, "whom three realms obey, / Dost sometimes counsel take, and sometimes tea," and that Belinda's spirit guardians fear she might "stain her honour, or her new brocade . . . Or lose her heart, or necklace at a ball" (canto 3, lines 7–8; canto 2, lines 107–9).

Classical rhetoricians often observe that linguistic patterns prototypically have conceptual anchors. Fahnestock cites several, among them the following: "the author of the *Ad Alexandrum* (attributed to Anaximenes of Lampsakos, 380–320 BCE) distinguishes antithetical thought from antithetical phrasing, marks the possibility of having one without the other, and stresses the need to combine both in the perfect figure" (Fahnestock, in press). Aristotle sees metaphoric expressions as conceptually anchored: although the *Poetics* contains a potentially misleading sentence describing metaphor as the transfer of an *expression* from one thing to another, the context makes it clear that Aristotle sees the linguistic transfer as motivated by a conceptual relation—either of category (genus to species, species to genus, species to species) or of analogy.[2] In his view, the conceptual transfer induces the linguistic transfer. A few paragraphs later, he defines metaphor as conceptual in explaining that metaphor comes from considering (Θεωρεῖν) likenesses: "τὸ γὰρ εὖ μεταφέρειν τὸ τὸ ὅμοιον Θεωρεῖν ἐστιν" (*Poetics,* book 22, chap. 17 [1459a]).

After the Greeks, rhetoric turned principally to applied tasks, chiefly the production of instructional materials, and rhetoricians increasingly ignored the conceptual work of figures. "Figures" came, for the most part, to refer to linguistic forms in lists of related linguistic forms. Fahnestock provides an apt illustration of this degeneration in contrasting Aristotle's analysis of *asyndeton* with the *ad Herennium's* treatment of *asyndeton.* She begins with Aristotle:

At no place in Book III [of the *Rhetoric*] does Aristotle claim that these devices [figures] serve an ornamental or emotional function or that they are in any way epiphenomenal. Instead, Aristotle's somewhat dispersed discussion suggests that certain devices are compelling because they map function onto form or perfectly epitomize certain patterns of thought or argument. A case in point is his account of asyndeton, the elimination of connectives, and its "opposite."

Fahnestock is referring to the following passage in Aristotle: "Furthermore asyndeta have a special characteristic; many things seem to be said at the same time; *for the connective makes many things seem one, so that if it is taken away, clearly the opposite results: one thing will be many*" (Aristotle, *Rhetoric,* book 3, chap. 12 [1413b], translation from Kennedy [1991], p. 256, emphasis added).

Aristotle here analyzes *asyndeton* and its opposite (*polysyndeton*) as two form-meaning pairs that stand in oppositional relation: partitioning (of concepts) is paired with a formal series that omits connectives; in opposition, chunking (of concepts) is paired with a formal series that uses the connective. Fahnestock contrasts Aristotle's analysis of these figures as two related form-meaning pairs with the treatment provided by the author of the *ad Herennium,* who "pays no attention to the specific ideational work of the figure," merely listing *asyndeton* as a verbal ornament.

The classical rhetorical view according to which figures are anchored in conceptual patterns has had considerable effect in modern literary and rhetorical criticism. In 1936, I. A. Richards wrote that metaphor "is a borrowing between and intercourse of *thoughts. . . . Thought* is metaphoric . . . and the metaphors of language derive therefrom" (Richards 1936, p. 94). In the same year, C. S. Lewis wrote that parable—understanding one story by figural projection from another story—belongs not principally to expression and not exclusively to literature but rather *to mind in general* as a basic cognitive instrument (Lewis, 1936, p. 44). In 1945, Kenneth Burke wrote that metaphor, metonymy, synecdoche, and irony have a fundamental role in the discovery of the truth (Burke, 1945, p. 503). As Fahnestock writes, "[Figures] are endemic to the human mind."

Classical rhetoricians also observe that figure is normal and basic in language. The formal halves of the figures treated in the classical tradition are nearly all grammatical; the exceptions are the intentionally ungrammatical forms that are themselves conventionally paired with meanings, as in our expression, "You pays your money and you takes your chances," an example of the figure *enallage.*[3] "That the figures are part of ordinary usage," Fahnestock observes, "has been acknowledged from Aristotle, who notices in the fourth century BCE that 'all people carry on their conversations with metaphors,' to Du Marsais who affirms in the eighteenth century that 'il n'y a rien de si naturel, de si ordinaire et de si commun que les figures dans le langage des hommes' ." Classical rhetoricians frequently included *question* as a figure, and Hermogenes regarded basic subject-noun predication as a figure.[4] Quintilian observes explicitly that the basic definition of "figure" is any form-meaning pair ("forma sententiae") and "therefore in the first and common sense of the word everything is expressed by figures," ("Quare illo intellectu priore et communi nihil non figuratum est") (Quintilian [1921], book 9, chap. 1, sec. 1–12 [Loeb edition, vol. 3, pp. 352–55]). Such observations come close to asserting that the grammar of a

FIGURE **49**

language consists of form-meaning pairs.[5] In Latin, figure is often described as *ornamentum,* but as Vickers (1988, p. 314) and Fahnestock have observed, Latin *ornamentum* means apparatus, instruments, furniture, armaments—the standard equipment needed for a particular activity.

Quintilian's first definition of figure—meaning expressed in form—turns grammar into a branch of figure. Because Quintilian had no ambition to model the entire language, he naturally proposed a less ambitious definition, one that requires a figure to be "artful." He fails to provide any motivation for this distinction or any principle according to which "artful" figures are to be distinguished from the body of constructions that constitute a language, and his followers have failed uniformly on this same point. Yet his requirement that figure be "artful" became criterial. Figure came to be viewed as a special form-meaning pair (or even a form by itself) distinguished as especially effective, artful, refined, elegant, memorable, vivid, unusual, or powerful. Fahnestock observes, "There has never been a satisfactory definition of figurative language that rigorously separates it from an unfigured domain of usage. There never can be such a definition. The minority view that Quintilian set aside was right."

ICONICITY

Some pairings of form and meaning seem essentially arbitrary. There is no apparent compelling cognitive motive to pair the form "apple" with the meaning *apple*. In other languages, the word for *apple* is "pomme" or "malum." Saussure called this lack of motivation "the arbitrariness of the sign." It is worth remembering that "the arbitrariness of the sign" is a limited principle: a "sign" is typically motivated in various ways. It is motivated by human respiratory or articulatory mechanisms and by the sound pattern of the language in which it occurs. Further, as Ronald Langacker has observed, although it may be arbitrary that a word such as "blend" means what it does in English and that the morpheme "-er" means what it does in English, once these form-meaning pairs exist in the language, it is not arbitrary that "blender" means what it does in English. Any particular sign is more or less motivated relative to other constructions in the language.

The most compelling goal in pairing is to mirror the meaning in the form. Often, a meaning has a basic *image schema* that can be mirrored in a form. An image schema is a skeletal image that underlies everyday experience.[6] For example, we have an image schema of moving toward an object. We have an image schema of joining one thing to another. We have an image schema of a path that leads from a source to a goal. We have image schemas of hesitation and advance, of movement from a center to a periphery, of entering or leaving, of enclosing or extracting, of rising or falling, of stopping or penetrating. These image schemas are not exclusively visual. For example, we have an image schema of a rising pitch, of increasing pressure, of a jab to the skin, as well as many image schemas of temporal rhythm. Many of our most important and useful image schemas concern how we structure space and interact with space. Spatial image schemas can be recruited to make sense of abstractions that are not themselves spatial. We can think of time as linear or circular. We can think of solving a problem as "moving toward" a goal along a path. We can think of the reasoning mind as a body "moving in space," which "comes upon" ideas, "looks them over," "picks them up" for examination, "drops" them to look "further afield," and so on. A considerable portion of our reasoning seems to consist of projections of bodily and spatial image schemas onto abstract concepts. We think of events, which have no shape, as having a shape: open-ended or closed, discrete or continuous, cyclic or linear.

Image schemas can also structure expressions. As forms, expression can have image-schematic structure. A sentence, for example, can be thought of as moving linearly to approach a point. A conceptual pattern that has the image-schematic structure of movement along a path to stop smartly at an end can be mirrored in a sentence that follows the same pattern. Here is an example from Clifford Geertz: "[I]f you want to understand what a science is, you should look in the first instance not at its theories or its findings, and certainly not at what its apologists say about it; you should look at what the practitioners of it do" (Geertz, "Thick Description: Toward an Interpretive Theory of Culture," in Geertz, 1973, p. 5).

In the history of rhetoric, it has often been observed, although not in exactly these words, that the image schema of the meaning can be mirrored in the form. Longinus gives the following example: repeated physical striking has an image-schematic structure that can be mirrored by linguistic anaphora, as in: "By his manner, his looks, his voice, when he strikes you with insult, when he strikes you like an enemy, when he strikes you with his knuckles, when he strikes you like a slave" (Longinus [1995], sec. 20, p. 190). Demetrius talks of linguistic forms as "rounded," "disjointed," "hastening towards a definite goal as runners do when they leave the starting-place," "circular," "tense," "periodic," and so on. He observes that thought comes with part-whole structure that can be mirrored in linguistic form (Demetrius [1995], sec. 1.1–2, pp. 295–97). He also observes that we experience syntactic forms image-schematically: "Long journeys are shortened by a succession of inns, while desolate paths, even when the distances are short, give the impression of length. Precisely the same principle will apply also in the case of members [syntactic forms]" (Demetrius [1995], sec. 2.46, p. 331).

The device of matching the form's image schema to the meaning's image schema—known as "iconicity" of form—provides one of the most effective tools of persuasion. Involving members of the audience in the image schema of

FIGURE **51**

the iconic *form* automatically involves them in the basic structure of the meaning, thus moving them part way toward accepting the whole. Kenneth Burke offers an example: "Who controls Berlin, controls Germany; who controls Germany controls Europe; who controls Europe controls the world." Burke says of this *climax,* "By the time you arrive at the second of its three stages, you feel how it is destined to develop—and on the level of purely formal assent you would collaborate to round out its symmetry by spontaneously willing its completion and perfection as an utterance" (Burke, 1950, pp. 58–59). Cooperation with the image schema of the iconic form disposes us to yield to the meaning. Burke says:

> [W]e know that many purely formal patterns can readily awaken an attitude of collaborative expectancy in us. For instance, imagine a passage built about a set of oppositions (*"we* do *this,* but *they* on the other hand do *that*; *we* stay *here*; but *they* go *there*; *we* look *up,* but *they* look *down,"* etc.) Once you grasp the trend of the form, it invites participation regardless of the subject matter. Formally, you will find yourself swinging along with the succession of antitheses, even though you may not agree with the proposition that is being presented in this form. Or it may even be an opponent's proposition which you resent—yet for the duration of the statement itself you might "help him out" to the extent of yielding to the formal development, surrendering to its symmetry as such. Of course, the more violent your original resistance to the proposition, the weaker will be your degree of "surrender" by "collaborating" with the form. But in cases where a decision is still to be reached, a yielding to the form prepares for assent to the matter identified with it. Thus, you are drawn to the form, not in your capacity as a partisan, but because of some "universal" appeal in it. And this attitude of assent may then be transferred to the matter which happens to be associated with the form. (Burke, 1950, p. 58).

SYMMETRY

The kind of symmetry presented by Burke's example is *oppositional, bilateral,* or *heraldic* symmetry. It occurs whenever transposing the opposed elements of something gives us back the "same" thing. For example, in Burke's antithesis, at the conceptual level, transposing all the opposed conceptual elements (*we do this* versus *they do that,* for example) still leaves us with an array of opposed meanings; and at the formal level, transposing all the opposed formal elements on each side of "but" ("we do this" versus "they do that," for example) still leaves us with an expression that consists of conjoined opposed forms. In antithesis, meaning is structured by the image schema *balance about a center,* and the form inherits the image schema of the meaning. Elsewhere, I have analyzed ways in which symmetry provides the basis for some other form-meaning pairs.[7]

Antithesis is only one kind of symmetry. When we recognize that something can be mapped onto itself while preserving essential relations, we perceive that it is symmetric under that mapping. For example, we recognize that rotating a sphere in any direction to any degree about its center leaves us with the identical sphere; the sphere has rotational symmetry.

Formal symmetry in the world is often associated with meaning. For example, an array of forces symmetric about a location is associated with the meaning *equilibrium.* We are disposed to pay attention to the location about which the forces are symmetric since we can maintain equilibrium in the system by preserving formal symmetry about that location. We stand upright to avoid falling over. The *form* (the symmetry of uprightness) is paired with a *meaning* (equilibrium, and hence stability, security, control, and importance); in this case, the pairing is causal. The location about which the form is symmetric is naturally paired with the meaning: *this is the essentially important element.*

Consequently, in classic modes of linguistic and visual representation, the conceptually important element is typically located at the center of formal symmetry. The main altar is not placed in an eccentric spot of the cathedral. Cedric Whitman has analyzed Homer's *Iliad* as constructed according to "ring composition," wherein conceptually important elements occur at centers of formal symmetries.

Additionally, the breaking of formal symmetry in an otherwise formally symmetric background is paired with the conceptual meaning *pay specific attention,* for the following reason. To the extent that some aspect of our world conforms to a background symmetry, we do not have to memorize its details. Given the smallest knowledge about its details, coupled with knowledge of its symmetry, we can complete the pattern without having memorized the details. But we cannot in general tell where that symmetry will break. The breaking of a governing formal symmetry is therefore paired with the meaning *pay specific attention to this important element.* This natural pairing provides a basis for certain principles of figural representation. For example, if, in a Greek vase painting, a central fallen soldier is flanked by a line of identical mourners left and right, all facing him, symmetrically balancing each other, with the exception that the first mourner to the left has fallen to her knees and is reaching out to him, we are disposed to recognize that mourner as the most important element in the relevant cultural frame—*his wife.*

THE XYZ FIGURE

Even though iconicity is the clearest kind of form-meaning pairing, most figures are not essentially iconic. Here, I present a study of the noniconic XYZ figure. My purpose in presenting this case study of one particular figure is to illustrate the conceptual complexity of even very simple figures. This case study will lead

FIGURE **53**

us to ambitious theoretical claims about basic conceptual operations. I sketch a model of those operations. I then draw consequences of that model for thinking about "figurative thought and language."

"Money is the root of all evil" and "Brevity is the soul of wit" illustrate the XYZ figure, which was first noted by Aristotle in the following passage: "As old age (D) is to life (C), so is evening (B) to day (A). One will accordingly describe evening (B) as the 'old age of the day' (D + A)—or by the Empedoclean equivalent; and old age (D) as the 'evening' or 'sunset of life' (B + C)" (*Poetics,* 1457B).

Here, Aristotle announces his threefold discovery—the existence of a conventional mapping scheme at the conceptual level, the existence of a formal pattern, and the existence of a conventional pairing between them. This pairing is the "X is the Y of Z" or XYZ figure.[8] An example of the XYZ figure is "Vanity is the quicksand of reason." The conventional mapping scheme of this figure is quite complicated: X (*vanity*) and Z (*reason*) are to be grouped into a single mental space; Y (*quicksand*) is to be placed inside some different mental space; some unspecified cross-domain mapping is to be found in which Y (*quicksand*) is the counterpart of X (*vanity*); an unmentioned W (e.g., *traveler*) is to be found in the Y (*quicksand*) domain such that W (*traveler*) can be the counterpart of Z (*reason*); X and Y are to be integrated (*vanity-quicksand*); W and Z are to be integrated (*reason-traveler*); the X-Z (*vanity-reason*) relation is to be integrated with the Y-W (*quicksand-traveler*) relation. A great deal—the relevant conceptual domains, their internal organization, W and the other unmentioned counterparts, the nature of the relevant relations, and so on—must be constructed without further formal prompting.

"Vanity is the quicksand of reason" evokes a conceptual mapping that is elaborate and open-ended: reason corresponds to traveling animals, vanity to quicksand, mental activity to motion over a surface, mental focus to visual focus, and so on through a great list.

The products of XYZ mappings can be quite diverse:

Adams Morgan is the Greenwich Village of Washington, D.C.
He's the Babe Ruth of Hungarian kayaking.
Sex is the ancilla of art.
Sex is the poor man's opera.
Children are the riches of poor men.
The wages of sin is death.
"The harlot's cry, from street to street, / Will be Old England's
winding sheet." (Blake)

In "Vanity is the quicksand of reason," the two mental spaces connected by the mapping (the *quicksand* space versus the *reason* space) are radically different: one involves internal personal psychology while the other involves geo-graphical travel. By contrast, in "Adams Morgan is the Greenwich Village of Washington, D.C.," the two mental spaces connected by the mapping share a fairly specific conceptual frame: *city and its neighborhoods*. In "Paul Erdos is the Euler of our century," the mental spaces connected by the mapping share not only a frame (*mathematician*) but many details not standard for that frame: both Euler and Erdos were exceptionally prolific; both lived a long time; both worked in a number of fields; each was eminent but never quite attained the status of a mathematician like Gauss and Newton; and so on. "Erdos is the Euler of our century" seems quite different from "Vanity is the quicksand of reason," but they involve the identical syntactic form paired with the identical pattern of conceptual mapping.

I catalog in *Reading Minds* the ways in which the basic XYZ figure is part of a network of figures. In particular, other syntactic forms can evoke the same XYZ scheme of conceptual mapping. First, there is a more general construction in which nouns Y and Z are connected by any relational preposition, as in "The bar in America is the road *to* honor."

Second, the form NounPhrase-of-NounPhrase contained in the XYZ figure is itself a prompt to perform the XYZ cognitive mapping; it lacks only the explicit instruction for choosing X. For example, in "quicksand of reason," "quick-sand" and "reason" point to elements in different spaces; we are to connect these spaces by a cross-space mapping.

Third, depending on the meaning paired with Y, the XYZ form is related to either the $XY_{adjective} Z$ form or the $XZ_{adjective} Y$ form, as follows. When the Y in an XYZ conceptual pattern is a commonplace transformation of one thing into another, its form may be $XY_{adjective} Z$, so "Language is the fossil of poetry" may be expressed as "Language is fossil poetry." When the Y-W conceptual relation is a part-whole frame relation, the form may be $XZ_{adjective}Y$, so "Las Vegas is the Monte Carlo of America" may be expressed as "Las Vegas is the American Monte Carlo."

Fourth, the full form of the XYZ figure has a corollary Z-Y compound noun form: "disc jockey," "road hog," "budget ceiling," "mall rat," "land yacht," "jail bait," and so on.

Fifth, compositions of XYZ forms evoke compositions of conceptual map-ping schemes. Walter Lippman's "Social movements are at once the symptoms and the instruments of progress" is a composed form that evokes a composition of mappings across three mental spaces—one with social movements and pro-gress, a second with symptoms, and a third with instruments—to achieve an integration in which one element is simultaneously a social movement, a symp-tom, and an instrument. In this example, the X-Z-space maps to two other spaces. But in "As poetry is the harmony of words, so conversation is the

FIGURE **55**

harmony of minds,'' it is the Y-space that maps to two other spaces—one having poetry and words, the other having conversation and minds.

Sixth, XYZ conceptual mappings can be evoked by a variety of syntactic forms for identity, as in ''London, that great cesspool into which all the loungers of the Empire are irresistibly drained'' (Arthur Conan Doyle). This example, which I analyze in *Reading Minds* (1991), requires multiple mappings.

The XYZ figure provides a glimpse of the complexity involved in form-meaning pairing. Individual XYZ examples may look straightforward, but on analysis they reveal:

- intricate and systematic conceptual patterns;
- formal patterns paired with these conceptual patterns, to give a group of form-meaning pairs; and
- a relational network of these form-meaning pairs.

CONSTRUCTION GRAMMARS

Contemporary models of form-meaning pairs are known as ''construction grammars.'' A construction grammar models both individual form-meaning pairs and the network of relations in which these pairs stand. Construction grammarians are linguists who have chosen to return to the more traditional view that the grammar of a language consists of a network of form-meaning pairs, which they call ''constructions.'' Charles Fillmore and Paul Kay have collaborated on a sophisticated ''construction grammar.'' Ronald Langacker's ''cognitive grammar'' is a construction grammar. Adele Goldberg, Claudia Brugman, and George Lakoff have individually worked on particular constructions. My early work on the XYZ figure is a study of a construction. Well-known contributors to the emerging field of construction grammar include Gilles Fauconnier, Michael Israel, Daniel Jurafsky, Jean-Pierre Koenig, Suzanne Kemmer, Knud Lambrecht, Laura Michaelis, and Elizabeth Traugott.[9]

Constructions recognized by construction grammarians include traditional clausal patterns, such as the Passive Construction, but also other clausal and phrasal patterns, such as the Resultative Construction (''He hammered it flat,'' ''She kissed him unconscious''), the Ditransitive Construction (''He faxed me a letter''), the Caused-Motion Construction (''John sneezed the napkin off the table''), the Covariational Conditional construction (''The more you think about it, the less you understand it''), the Way Construction (''Peter talked his way into the job''), and so on. In most construction grammar models, morphemes and words are also constructions, as are abstract grammatical categories such as Noun Phrase and Verb Phrase and abstract phrasal and clausal patterns like the

Subject-Predicate construction. Lexical or morphemic constructions include phonological form.

Constructions commonly include pragmatics as part of their meaning. Consider "And they call it puppy love" and "And they say I don't work hard." These are instances of a sentential construction that carries a pragmatics: the speaker is calling the hearer's attention to what the speaker sees as absolute evidence that the reported assertion is absurd. (The construction can be used ironically or in free indirect discourse, but in either case, the construction still evokes this pragmatics, with additional complexity.)

The justifications for construction grammar are essentially identical to those for the original classical rhetorical program of analyzing figures. Construction grammarians typically observe that constructions exist in a language that any grammar of the language must cover but that are not treated by grammars in which constructions are regarded as epiphenomenal. Principles-and-Parameters grammars are the best-known grammars that conflict with construction grammar on this point. In Principles-and-Parameters grammars, constructions are regarded as artifactual consequences of the interaction of (conjectured) principles of a (conjectured) Universal Grammar.

Construction grammarians such as those I named above cite the following kinds of expressions as examples of intricate constructions in the language that are not captured in nonconstruction grammars:

Never will I leave you.
Long may you prosper!
Onward, Christian soldiers!
Am I tired!
Watch it not rain [now that I've bought an umbrella].
Idiot that I am, . . .
Looks like something going on inside.
Be back in a minute.
He didn't give them one page, *not a one.*
Are you going home or *home home*?
It satisfied *my every wish.*
He did not like it *at all.*
Looks like a soup, eats like a meal.
Not that I care.
I live near work, but *lazy me,* of course I drive.
It's time you got married.
You're no Jack Kennedy.
She handed him the towel wet.
He talked his way out of it.
That's my desk you've got your feet on!
This book reads easily.

FIGURE 57

Some historians *have* Jefferson doubting himself at this moment.
I *had* my dog die on me.
He is consultant to the president.
He's completely happy, *James is.*
How about Harry?
Down with Harry!
Smoking or non?
Another one like that, John, and Pow! right in the kisser.
The more, the merrier.
Nice play.
My hero!
You idiot!
What a guy!
Thank you.
Bless you.
Hooray for you.
Been there, done that.
It's amazing, the difference!
Why go to the store?

These constructions are widely judged to be grammatical. Other constructions, by contrast, are grammatical for only a few speakers. From time to time such a restricted construction gradually becomes grammatical for a wider community, to the extent that it becomes part of publicly shared linguistic knowledge. For example, I increasingly hear spoken expressions of the form "The feeling is is that they will head north from the capital," which I heard spoken on the BBC World Service News Summary on October 21, 1996. I do not know for a fact that this news summary was read, but it sounded read, and the news summary is always introduced by one BBC announcer as "read by" a second BBC announcer, as it was in this case. More important, the "is is" sequence in this reading had a prosodic pattern associated with the closing of a subject noun phrase followed by the onset of a verb phrase, rather than a prosodic pattern suitable for a duplicative bauble of a single verb. In this construction, "The feeling is" becomes suitable for subject position, perhaps by recruiting partly from the (already grammatical) construction underlying expressions such as "What the feeling is is that they will head north" or "What the current opinion is, among the press corps, is that the candidate will go negative." Whether the reader finds "The feeling is is" to be theoretically illuminating or aesthetically barbarous, many constructions now regarded by educated speakers as fully grammatical began life as disapproved inventions.

For each of the examples on this list of constructions, a form is paired with a skeletal meaning; the meaning of the expression is not provided exclusively by the so-called meanings of the words, or even by a composition of other constructions; rather, we know the form and know that it prompts us to construct certain kinds of abstract meaning.

Our knowledge of these form-meaning pairs is complex, but we cannot easily or fully articulate what we know intuitively. Obviously, absent an unusual context, we will not be regarded as speaking idiomatic English if we say, "The light bulb crashed its way into being out." But why not? Equally obviously, absent an unusual context, we would not say, "He smoked his way across the Atlantic" to mean that on a transatlantic voyage, he smoked just one cigarette. But why not? Explaining obvious cases such as these is surprisingly difficult, although at first it may seem that there is nothing to explain because they are so obviously "just wrong." Constructions have intricate structure and systematic principles that we know intuitively but not consciously.

Fillmore, Kay, and O'Connor's case study of the "let alone" construction ("I didn't make it to Paris, let alone Berlin") and Kay and Fillmore's case study of the "What's X doing Y?" construction ("What's this bottle of olive oil doing in my wine cellar?") have made it clear that knowing such constructions involves knowing extraordinarily detailed structures. Understanding a simple sentence turns out to be a highly complicated mental event.

Construction grammarians assume responsibility (in principle) for explaining all the constructions in a language, including those that seem peripheral. They also assume responsibility for explaining the network of relations in which these constructions stand. The central assertion of construction grammar is that so-called core components of the language cannot be modeled as the products of interactions among higher-order formal principles. Instead, they, too, need a constructional approach. The machinery needed for modeling the "peripheral" constructions turns out to be indispensable for modeling the "core" constructions.

There is considerable overlap between the classical study of figures and the contemporary study of constructions. The peripheral constructions adduced by construction grammarians as evidence of the indispensability of the constructional approach look like Quintilian's "artful" figures. "Him be a professor?" (the Incredulity Construction) is a noticeable peripheral expression. Among other things, it appears to have a nonfinite form of the verb predicated of a third-person singular pronoun in the objective case. "Such stuff as madmen Tongue and brain not" (*Cymbeline*, act 5, scene 4, line 146) is also a noticeable peripheral expression. It has bare nouns as verbs. The second of these examples made it into the catalog of figures (*anthimeria*) although the first did not, perhaps because it had not yet been invented in classical antiquity when names were bestowed on figures. Construction grammarians and rhetoricians are equally aware of the complexity involved in accounting for such examples and of the ways in which such examples reveal systematic principles and patterns of mean-

FIGURE 59

ing and language that cut across all divisions of discipline, ontogenetic development, mode of expression, and intellectual sophistication.

Construction grammarians and rhetoricians are also similar in their emphasis on clausal, phrasal, and lexical form-meaning pairs. They both slight discourse constructions. Consider as an example of a discourse construction what I will call the "however" construction. If an article begins, "P. However, Q,"—for example, "Many people think Alfred the Great was a great ruler. However, . . ."—readers have expectations about Q. They do not expect, "However, others are uninterested in the entire subject" or "However, I don't want to talk about it." These perfectly unobjectionable English sentences are compatible with common meanings of "however," but they do not fit the "however" discourse construction of argument. We cannot specify where the word "however" will occur in the discourse: it comes after the opening move of the discourse (P), which can be half a sentence or several chapters. Note also that the word "however" is not at all necessary. "Nevertheless" is suitable. So is "I disagree." In fact, if no lexical element of opposition is used, readers may still seek and find a location in the text that seems to separate a P from an opposing Q. They infer that location, but having done so, regard the inference as natural, if they are even aware of having made an inference.

Some constructions are specific to a genre. These genre-constructions have received relatively little attention from construction grammarians and rhetoricians. Consider complimentary closings that introduce the signature on a letter. They form a category of constructions distinguished by fine nuances. In certain ages (such as Jane Austen's) and in certain contemporary social registers (such as the conservative French haute bourgeoisie, who write, for example, "Je vous prie d'agréer, Monsieur le Professeur, les expressions de mes salutations très distinguées" and "Croyez, cher Mark Turner, à mes souvenirs cordiaux et les meilleurs"), this network of constructions involves distinctions so careful that those who hope to assimilate to the proprietary linguistic community often rightly fear that no degree of formal instruction can equip them to use the constructions spontaneously in a way that will not betray their origin.

The most obvious difference between the study of figure and construction grammar is disciplinary: construction grammarians have a disciplinary formation in modern linguists and use the full range of technical instruments evolved in that science. In construction grammar, the model for any particular construction in the language will include grammatical distinctions of various kinds (e.g., verb argument structure, phonological structure) that are examined only incidentally and impressionistically in the study of figure.

Construction grammar has an important advantage over theory of figure in its emphasis on the mechanisms by which constructions are assembled or unified. In the view of construction grammarians, judging an expression to be grammatical is the result of finding a set of constructions that unify in the expression. Construction grammars are "unification-based" grammars: they aspire to model the structural properties, mechanisms, and constraints involved in unification. By contrast, studies of figure rarely consider unification.

Crucially, a construction grammar has a commitment to account (in principle) for the totality of facts of the language. It assumes responsibility for full coverage. This is exactly what Quintilian set aside when he proposed to study only those figures that are "artful."

TRADITIONAL QUESTIONS ABOUT FIGURATIVE LANGUAGE AND THOUGHT

The central concept of a theory of figure as I have sketched it is *pairing* between formal and conceptual patterns. The conceptual half can be a conventionally framed rich scene (as in the figure *aposiopesis,* in which cessation of speech is paired with the rich scene of paralysis induced by emotion). It can be an abstract meaning (as in the figure *question,* in which interrogative forms are paired with the abstract meaning of posing an inquiry). And it can be an even more abstract mapping scheme (as in the XYZ figure).

This view of figure as constructional pairing covers the essential ground, but it leaves unanswered a suite of questions that are often embraced as defining the inquiry into "figurative language and thought":

- Is there a fundamental dichotomy between literal and figurative thought? Is there a fundamental dichotomy between literal and figurative language?
- Is figurative thought mirrored in figurative language? Is figurative thought necessarily paired with linguistic form?
- How do figurative thought and language evolve?
- What is the appropriate relation of an abstract theory of figures to a rich theory of individual figurative events?

The Literal Versus Figurative Dichotomy

In previous work (Turner, 1989, 1991, and 1996b), I offered demonstrations that the commonsense dichotomy between "literal" and "figurative" is a psychological illusion. There is no doubt that some products of thought and language seem literal while others seem figurative. We have reactions, and they are motivated, but these motivations do not come from fundamental differences of cognitive operations. "Literal" and "figurative" are labels that serve as efficient shorthand announcements of our integrated reactions to the products of

FIGURE **61**

thought and language; they do not refer to fundamentally different cognitive operations.

The commonsense dichotomy between "literal" and "figurative" arises from a folk theory concerning thought, reality, and language, or more technically, entities, categories, reference, predication, truth-conditionality, and compositionality. In this folk theory, an entity (this tree outside my window) is a bundle of features (photosynthesis, etc.); a category (tree) is a bundle of criterial features (trunk, limbs, roots, photosynthesis, etc.) shared by its members; common nouns ("tree") refer to categories of objects; verbs ("grow") refer to categories of events; verbs predicate event-features of their subjects ("a tree grows" predicates *grow* of *tree*); adjectives ("big") and adverbs ("slowly") modifying common nouns and verbs assign or remove features (big trees grow slowly); and predication and assignment are compositional in the sense that the meaning and truth-value of any conjunction is just the conjunction of the meanings and truth-values of the components, so that assigning a complex feature is no different from assigning the set of its component features. For example, the subject of "big trees grow slowly" refers to the subcategory of *tree* whose members are additionally *big* (i.e., all objects for which it is true both that "this is big" and "this is a tree"); the verb phrase refers to a subcategory event that has the feature *slowly* along with all the features of the event-category *grow;* and the entire sentence predicates the features of *grow slowly* of the subcategory *big tree*; that is, it adds the features of *grow slowly* to the features of *big tree*. This addition is compositional for both truth-conditions and meaning.

In this folk theory, a connection is true if the state of affairs to which it refers is the case in the world (i.e., it is the case that everything that is both *big* and a *tree* has the complex feature *grows slowly*). It is false if the state of affairs to which it refers is not the case in the real world.

In this view, *The sun is a useful star* predicates of the sun both the feature *useful* and all the features of the category *star*. This predication composes the features of *the sun, useful,* and *star*. The assignment of the complex feature *useful star* is just the composition of the assignments of its component features; all of the component assignments are true (there is a sun with all of its features and it has additionally the feature *useful* and all of the features of *star*), and so their composition is true; the connection is therefore true; the thought is therefore true; and a statement of that thought is therefore true.

"The sun is a planet," in this view, means that it is the case that there is a sun with all its features and that it has all the features of the category *planet*. The thought and expression are therefore viewed as false. (I pass over more sophisticated machinery needed to talk about cases such as "If I were English, I would drink tea instead of coffee.")

In this commonsense folk theory, thought and language operate by truth-conditional composition of features. This is the realm of "literal" thought and language. It is a consequence of this view that there must be a separate kind of thought and language, called "figurative," that uses alternative cognitive operations. The logic that leads to this consequence works as follows: "The sun is a jewel" is just literally false; its literal meaning is a composition of the features of *the sun* and *jewel,* and that composition is not the case in the world. This composition exhausts all the literal meaning and all the literal truth-value the expression can have. Therefore, if "The sun is a jewel" has any alternative meaning or any alternative truth-value, it can do so only by virtue of some different process, of interpretation or of conceptual connection. Because everyone recognizes that "The sun is a jewel" can mean something aside from "the sun exists and it has all of its own features as well as all the criterial features of the category *jewel,*" and because everyone recognizes that "The sun is a jewel" moreover can have (at least something like) positive truth-value, we must conclude that there is some alternative process, some "figurative" process, by which it acquires this alternative meaning and truth-value. "Figurative" here means exactly "not literal."

Clearly, we have different reactions to "The sun is a star" and "The sun is a jewel." We know that an important difference between them is signified when we call the first "literal" and the second "figurative." No question. What is at issue is whether these different reactions indicate fundamentally different cognitive operations in the different cases. I have proposed that the answer is "No."

In my previous work, I have proposed that conceptual connections between two mental arrays strike us differently depending on how those arrays are already related in our category structures. A connection seems literal or figurative (or somewhere in between) not absolutely but in relation to the category structures used to understand it. "A child is a light bulb" asks us to connect mental arrays that are basic level categories, and thus seem figurative. "Parsley is cumin" or "A mug is a glass" or "A steno chair is a rocking chair" asks us to make the same kinds of connections between mental arrays, but in these cases the two mental arrays share a supercategory at or below the basic level (e.g., chair), so we feel that they are literal (but false). In cases such as "Parsley is cumin," the usual claim does not hold that recognizing literal falsity prompts us to recognize "figure" as a way of repairing the falsity. In all these cases, the feeling that something is literal or figurative depends not on special mechanisms of connection but rather on the relative status of the elements connected.

I have also argued that there is another, related influence on judging a connection to be literal or figurative: the degree to which the conceptual connection or the linguistic expression is generatively entrenched. The greatest degree of generative entrenchment for a conceptual connection occurs when it becomes established as a central part of basic category structure: for example, a woman is a human being. But there are other conceptual connections between elements

FIGURE   **63**

in category structures that, although not sufficiently generatively entrenched to seem to belong to our "literal" categories, are nonetheless available to us—a woman is a vessel, for example. Generative entrenchment of mental connection is a graded scale. We connect *wind* to *intentional agent, life* to *drama,* and an object's stasis on a table with the action of *holding* something *up,* all with varying degrees of generative entrenchment. "Life is metabolism," "Life is a performance," "Life is a play," "Life is a cast of dice," and "Life is an isosceles triangle" all ask us to locate conceptual connections that differ in their degree of generative entrenchment in our conceptual systems. Our reactions to these expressions differ accordingly. "Life is metabolism" sounds (to me) literal and definitional; "Life is a play" sounds (to me) halfway between literal and figurative; "Life is a cast of dice" sounds figurative and commonplace; "Life is an isosceles triangle" sounds wildly figurative. It also sounds unintelligible to me, until I finally find a connection: life is like an isosceles triangle; it always has its irregular side.

Consider "I am making intellectual progress." This expression depends on the conceptual connection between *a thinker* and *a person moving in space,* analyzed by Eve Sweetser (1990). When we think about it, this connection does not seem to us to belong to our "literal" category structures—a thinker is not "literally" a traveler. Yet the connection is so entrenched as to be immediately and automatically available from the conceptual domain of *thinking*: no conceptual work is needed to build the connection; the connection to *moving in space* does not need to be activated for new inferential or semantic work. Moreover, connections of this sort typically bring along entrenched grammar and vocabulary: "intellectual progress" follows a standard grammatical pattern for connections in which the adjective comes from the domain to which we wish to refer (*thinking*) while the noun comes from the other domain (*moving in space*). The lexical filling ("intellectual progress") of this grammatical pattern is also highly entrenched. Accordingly, the connection and the expression can strike us as literal.

"Mental journey" strikes us slightly differently. "Intellectual progress" and "mental journey" depend on the identical conceptual connections expressed in the identical phrasal pattern (adjective from the domain referred to, noun from the other domain), but the vocabulary of "mental journey" is somewhat less entrenched. Accordingly, "mental journey" seems a little less literal. The phrase "ethnic cleansing" uses the same grammatical pattern, but the conceptual connections it evokes are much less entrenched, and the vocabulary is less entrenched. It was judged to be highly figurative when first used, but the effect seems to be wearing off with frequent exposure.

Some connections evoked by "figurative" examples might interfere minimally with our category connections and thus be easily assimilated. For example, "A leopard is a tiger with spots instead of stripes" is of course "literally" false and moreover calls explicitly for mental blending that may strike us as figurative. But the connections that we do construct for this expression sit nicely inside our category structure for large mammals, partly because they help us to extend that category structure in ways that do not disrupt it. In contrast, connections evoked by some other "figurative" expressions might be deeply disruptive, with the consequence that their assimilation will be resisted by the conceptual apparatus we already have in place. A surprising expression like "time is the whiteness of the wave," which leads us to form weird conceptual connections that challenge our category structures, may not settle readily into our conventional knowledge. It may remain suggestive, never achieving a stable location. It may not be used up—assimilated and naturalized—as we go through it repeatedly: we may be able to return to it again and again and find it fresh, even powerful, because the connections it suggests cannot be established in our category structures (or perhaps even in our conventional conceptual apparatus) with impunity.

In summary, in my 1989 analysis of the literal versus figurative distinction, I proposed that we feel products to be "literal" or "figurative," that these products arise from the identical cognitive and linguistic mechanisms; but that they evoke different reactions depending on (1) the relative status and degree of entrenchment of the relevant mental arrays in the conceptual structures brought to bear on them, and (2) the degree of entrenchment of the language used for evoking those connections.

Recently, Gilles Fauconnier and I have jointly developed a model of conceptual connection that generalizes and extends my earlier view that "literal" versus "figurative" does not refer to a difference in basic cognitive operations. In the next few pages, I sketch the principles of our model. Subsequently, I draw its implications for the literal versus figurative dichotomy.

In Fauconnier and Turner (1994, 1996, in press a, in press b, and in preparation), Turner and Fauconnier (1995 and in press), Fauconnier (1997), and Turner (1996a, 1996b), Gilles Fauconnier and I have presented our "network model of conceptual integration." The model has additionally served as the basis for Coulson (1995, 1997), Freeman (1997), Grush and Mandelblit (in press) Mandelblit (1995, 1997), Oakley (1995), Ramey (1997), Robert (in press), Sun (1994), Veale (1996), and Zbikowski (1996).[10] The following presentation borrows from these publications.

Conceptual integration (represented in fig. 2-1) is a basic cognitive operation that operates on two input mental spaces to yield a third space, the *blend*. For example, in "Vanity is the quicksand of reason," one input space has *quicksand* while the other has *vanity* and *reason*; the blend has traps for *reason*.

In blending, there is a partial cross-space mapping between the input spaces. In the *quicksand* example, the *traveler* in one input is the counterpart of *reason* in the other input.

FIGURE   **65**

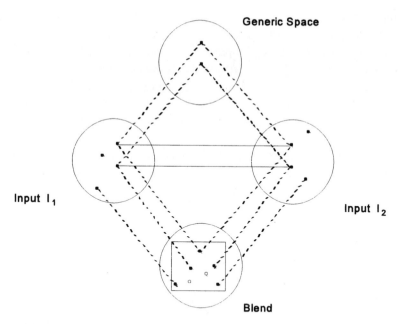

FIGURE 2.1. Conceptual integration.

Perhaps needless to say, the content of the input spaces depends on the do-mains and frames from which they are built. In the movie *Lawrence of Arabia,* there is a scene in the dry heart of the burning desert where quicksand swallows a child whole. Most people I know have this ''dry quicksand frame'' available. Others have only a scientific frame for quicksand, in which it is a combination of sand and water and occurs only where the water table is high, making the scene in *Lawrence of Arabia* impossible. I choose the ''dry quicksand'' inter-pretation to work with.

Partial structure is projected to the blend from the input spaces. The *quick-sand of reason* blend has, from the *quicksand* input, a dangerous trap, namely quicksand, but the blend does not take from the *quicksand* input the knowledge that travelers typically avoid deserts except in the rare instance when they must cross them. From the *reason* input, the blend takes noble and valuable effort but not (for example) vanity as a spur to honorable achievement.

The blend has emergent structure not provided by the inputs. In the *quick-sand of reason* blend, the traveler can be ignorant of the trap even when he is in it.

In addition to the inputs and the blend, conceptual integration involves a *generic space*. The cross-space mapping between the inputs is the content of the generic space. The generic space typically contains an abstract structure viewed as applicable to both inputs. For example, the generic space for ''vanity is the quicksand of reason'' has action (not specified as physical or mental) intended to achieve something, and a difficulty for that action.

In Fauconnier and Turner (in press b), we present a taxonomy of types of integration networks that arise often. This taxonomy depends on the notion of an *organizing frame,* a frame that specifies the nature of the relevant activity, events, and participants. Examples of organizing frames are *man walking along a mountain path, boat sailing along an ocean course,* and *gunslingers at high noon.*

The first type of integration network is a *frame network,* in which all spaces— inputs, generic, and blend—share topology given by an organizing frame. Two of our standard examples of frame networks are ''Debate with Kant'' and ''Regatta.'' In ''Debate with Kant'' (Fauconnier and Turner, 1996), a modern philosopher running a seminar says something like, ''I claim that reason is an autocatalytic somatic complex adaptive system that develops in the individual. Kant disagrees with me on this point. He says it's innate, but I answer that that's begging the question.'' In one input, Kant is thinking and musing and perhaps writing. In the other input, the modern philosopher is thinking and communicating; the generic space has a philosopher working on a question; the blend has Kant and the modern philosopher; moreover, the blend has them debating. All of these spaces have the organizing frame, *philosopher considering a philosophical problem.* The blend has an extension of this organizing frame: *two philosophers considering a philosophical problem and, moreover, debating it.*

In another frame network, ''Regatta'' (Fauconnier & Turner, 1994, Turner & Fauconnier, 1995), a freight-laden clipper ship, *Northern Light,* set the record for an ocean voyage from San Francisco to Boston in 1853, and a modern catamaran is in the process of making that run in 1993. *Latitude 38* reports, ''As we went to press, Rich Wilson and Bill Biewenga [the crew of the catamaran] were barely maintaining a 4.5 day lead over the ghost of the clipper *Northern Light.*''[11] Here, all four spaces have the organizing frame *boat making an ocean voyage.* The blend has an extension of that frame: *two boats making ocean voyages and, moreover, racing as they make them.*

A simpler type of integration network is a *single-framing* network, in which one input is a familiar abstract frame and the other input is a relatively specific situation. If we wish to say that two people—John and James—stand in a certain kin relation, we say something like ''John is the father of James.'' The frame of kin relation is one input; the other input has John and James. In the blend, John is the father of James, and there is a role *father of James.*

In our model, a structure in which all spaces share the topology of a generic space is called a *shared topology network.* Frame networks like ''Regatta'' and ''Debate with Kant'' are of course shared topology networks. But nonframe networks can also be shared topology networks. For example, consider ''On the deficit negotiations, Senate majority leader Bob Dole shot Clinton dead before

FIGURE 67

the President even cleared leather'' (Turner, 1996b). One input has as its organizing frame *gunslingers at a high-noon shoot-out.* The other input has a different organizing frame, *legislative activity.* The network is therefore not a frame network. But these two inputs and the blend all share the topology of *adversarial opposition,* which is also in the generic space. This shared topology makes the network a shared topology network.

A shared topology network is *one-sided* if the inputs have different organizing frames and only one of those frames is projected to organize the blend. For example, a cartoon of Bob Dole and Bill Clinton having a shoot-out evokes a one-sided shared topology network: the frame *gunslingers at a shoot-out* is projected from one of the inputs to organize the blend. The network is therefore one-sided.

Any particular simple metaphoric one-sided network—like the shootout between Dole and Clinton—may have inhering within it a higher-order conventional metaphoric mapping, called by Lakoff and Johnson (1980) a *basic metaphor.* In the case of the *shoot-out* network, the inhering basic metaphor is *opposition is combat.* Such a basic metaphor is highly productive and inheres in many particular constructions of meaning but is itself abstract. It never constitutes an active, complete, on-line construction of meaning. It always requires additional conceptual specification and projection.

A shared topology network is *two-sided* if the inputs are organized by different frames and some topology is projected from both input frames to organize the blend. The metaphor ''Vanity is the quicksand of reason'' is a two-sided network with frame structure projected from both inputs to organize the blend. The projections from the organizing frame of the *quicksand* input are obvious: the blend has a traveler, a path traveled, distance traveled, motion, a potential trap that arrests motion, and so on.

But frame-level projections come from the *reason* input as well. Consider first intentional structure: the reasoner can be unaware of his failure even when his failure is nearly complete. This is projected to the blend, in which the traveler/reason can be unaware of being in quicksand. The traveler/reason can be deluded, viewing himself as perfectly rational, oblivious to the fact that he has in fact long been trapped. This intentional structure conflicts with the frame of the *quicksand* input, in which it is unconventional to be ignorant that one is in quicksand, unconventional to think that one is traveling normally when one's torso is sinking.

Next, consider causal structure from the *reason* input: reasoning can lead to vanity about one's reasoning, which can lead in turn to diminished reason. This structure projects to help organize the blend: in the blend, quicksand/vanity exists for the reasoner but not for the person whose mind is merely wandering, even though they are both travelers. This causal structure conflicts with the organizing frame of the *quicksand* example, in which traveling is not causally related to the existence of quicksand, and in which all travelers in the desert face the same dangers. Additionally, in the *reason* input, the more you have achieved through reason, the more justification you have for being vain; in the blend, the more you have achieved through reason, the more vulnerable you are to being caught in quicksand. But this structure conflicts with the *quicksand* input, where novice travelers should be most vulnerable to quicksand.

Now consider the structure of roles in the *reason* input: there is only one reasoning capacity. The blend follows this structure: the traveler is solitary, or, if not solitary, then accompanied by *unequal* companions (character, memory, etc.). This structure of roles conflicts with the *quicksand* input, where there may be several equal travelers.

Now consider modal structure from the *reason* input: the reasoner does not have the choice of foregoing reasoning while remaining intellectually sophisticated. This projects to the blend: the traveler cannot choose to forego traveling in deserts; traveling/reasoning always presents a certain danger; that danger is in the desert exclusively; so the traveler/reasoner must deal with the desert. This structure conflicts with the *quicksand* input, in which the traveler can avoid the danger by declining to travel through deserts (which can be viewed as uninteresting in any event)—there are many wonderful places one can visit as a sophisticated traveler; one can experience a lifetime of interesting travel without entering a desert; and so on.

In summary, although the frame-level projections to the blend from the *quicksand* input are obvious, there are frame-level projections of intentional, causal, modal, and role structure from the *reason* input to help organize the blend, and these projections conflict with the frame of the *quicksand* input. The blend is in these ways two-sided.

What are the implications of the network model for the literal versus figurative distinction? The network model generalizes my earlier claim that the same conceptual and linguistic operations underlie "figurative" and "literal" examples. Different examples will seem literal or figurative for a number of reasons, including type of network. The type of the network depends partly on the relative status of counterparts in the cross-space mapping between the inputs, a status judged according to the category structures and related conceptual structures brought to bear on them.

For example, a single framing network such as "John is the father of James" has two inputs with the following relative status: one is a familiar abstract frame, while the other is a relatively specific situation with no competing frame. The familiar abstract frame is routinely applied to the conceptual domain (individual human beings) upon which the specific situation is built. This type of integration network usually seems highly literal.

By contrast, if two inputs come from apparently widely different specific conceptual domains, the result is a different type of integration network, namely,

FIGURE 69

a shared topology network, whether one-sided or two-sided. The structure that applies to both of them (i.e., the generic space) is typically highly abstract relative to both of the inputs. Such a case is commonly thought to be figurative (depending, as we will see, on some other gradients of distinction). In particular, highly two-sided shared topology networks, for example, *Vanity is the quicksand of reason,* are typically judged to be highly figurative.

It turns out that even this taxonomy of types of integration networks is too rigid: distinctions between the types are in fact graded, and judgments of literal versus figurative are accordingly graded. Let us consider some examples of grading, taken from *Death is the Mother of Beauty* (1987) and further analyzed in Fauconnier & Turner (in preparation).

As we have seen, "John is the father of James" seems fully literal; there is no competition between organizing frames of the inputs, and the kinship frame is routinely applied to the conceptual domain of individual human beings. "Zeus is the father of Sarpedon"—where Sarpedon is the mortal son of Zeus by a human woman—may strike us as less literal because the kinship frame meets some resistance from the Sarpedon space and the integration is slightly two-sided: from the Sarpedon input, the blend receives the immortality of Zeus; from the kinship input, the blend receives the ego-father relationship but cannot receive the mortality of the father. Yet the role *mother* in the kinship frame does have a standard counterpart in the Sarpedon space, as do various stages of human progeneration involving the mother, and these counterparts are fused in the blend.

A slightly different case is "Zeus is the father of Athena." In Fauconnier & Turner (in preparation), we write, "The blend does not take the frame-level structure *sexual act with a woman that leads to conception and progeneration of an infant.* It takes something more general: the causal link between the parent and the existence of the offspring (although not the immaturity of the offspring), the emergence of the offspring from a container-like body part of the parent, paternal responsibility and protection, and inheritance of attributes."

Let us consider an extended example of two-sidedness—Milton's portrayal of Satan as father in the second book of *Paradise Lost.* I analyze this passage in Turner (1987). The commonplace notion of Satan is already a blend for which a conceptual domain has been elaborated. Satan is a blend of individual human being—thinking, talking, desiring, intending, and so on—and theological ontology. In the theological space, there are eternal features (e.g., evil) as well as nonhuman powers and limitations. Satan is anthropomorphic, but he has theological features and unhuman conditions. The blended domain for Satan is quite elaborated—Satan has like-minded colleagues in the form of a cohort of devils; Satan and the devils form an intricate hierarchical organization of social groups; and so on. This blended domain is entrenched both conceptually and linguistically. Consequently, although the blend is in some ways two-sided, expressions such as "The devil made me do it" or "Get thee behind me, Satan"—or even expressions based on further blending, such as the reference to a child as a "little devil"—do not seem especially figurative.

Milton recruits new structure to the inputs. His purpose is to develop a blend with yet further emergent structure. The result is an integration network that is less entrenched both conceptually and linguistically and that is aggressively, explicitly, and idiosyncratically two-sided. It accordingly strikes us as thoroughly figurative.

Milton activates for the theological space evil, disobedience, sin, death, and their relations, as well as the psychology of the prototypical sinner confronted with spiritual death. He activates for the human space progeneration and kinship relations, especially the role *father.* He adds to the human kinship space a pre-existing blend, of the birth of Athena from the brow of Zeus. In Milton's blend, Satan conceives of the concept of sin; a fully grown woman, Sin, leaps from his brow. Satan is attracted to sin/Sin: he has sex with her. Although he does not know it at the time, his involvement with sin/Sin has a consequence, namely, death—in the blend, Death is the male offspring of Satan's incestuous involvement with Sin. Death rapes his mother, causing her to give birth to a small litter of allegorical monsters.

After Satan has been sent to Hell and has decided to try to escape, he meets two characters at the gates of Hell who have been stationed there to keep him in. They are Sin and Death. He does not recognize them.

I explain in Turner (1987) how the two input spaces—the human space and the theological space—correspond in some ways but not others. Milton chooses to draw from one or the other as it suits his conceptual purposes. In the new vocabulary of the network model, my earlier discussion of Milton's passage analyzes it as a selective, two-sided projection to a blended space. For example, Milton takes from the space of human beings and kin relations Sin's intercession between Death and Satan—father and son—when they are on the brink of terrible combat. By contrast, he takes exclusively from the theological space many central features. For instance, in the theological space, there is a sinful cast of mind that does not recognize spiritual death and mortality as a result of sin and that is at last appalled when it must recognize these consequences. Hence, in the blend, Sin is surprised to have conceived Death, and she finds her son odious. Next, in the theological space, mortality and spiritual death overshadow the appeal of sin and are stronger than sin; acknowledging death devalues sin; willful, sinful desires are powerless to stop this devaluation. Hence, in the blend, Sin is powerless to stop her horrible rape by Death. In the theological space, the fact of spiritual death brings ceaseless remorse and anguish to the sinful mind, and the torments of hell bring eternal punishment. Hence, in the blend, the rape of Sin by Death produces monstrous offspring whose birth, life, actions, and relationship to their mother are impossible for the domain of human kinship:

FIGURE **71**

These yelling Monsters that with ceaseless cry
Surround me, as thou saw'st, hourly conceiv'd
And hourly born, with sorrow infinite
To me, for when they list, into the womb
That bred them they return, and howl and gnaw
My Bowels, thir repast; then bursting forth
Afresh with conscious terrors vex me round,
That rest or intermission none I find.

We see here Milton's skill as a blender. When he takes structure from one input, he is adept at seeking out suitable structure to recruit to the other input, so that the two structures can be given counterpart relations and blended. Children are not prototypically disliked, but Milton can recruit the unusual scenario of disliking a child so he can blend it with horror at recognizing the fact of death. Sons do not typically rape their mothers, but Milton can recruit that horrible scenario so he can blend it with death's effect on sin.

Milton's ingenuity as a blender is best shown, I think, in his recruitment of a particularly vivid medical frame to the input of human kinship. This medical frame is traumatic vaginal birth that physically deforms the mother. In the human space, this disfiguration makes the mother subsequently less attractive. Milton places this newly recruited structure into counterpart relation with something crucial in the theological input—the fact that sin becomes less attractive when death appears as its outcome. The blend is particularly grim:

At last this odious offspring whom thou seest
Thine own begotten, breaking violent way
Tore through my entrails, that with fear and pain
Distorted, all my nether shape thus grew
Transform'd.

My original analysis of Milton's portrayal of Satan as father provided an inventory of its elaborate selective projection, emergent structure, two-sidedness, multiple blending, dynamic recruitment to the inputs of additional structure, maintenance of connections to the inputs, and projection of inferences back to the inputs. But it did not use these terms and did not connect Milton's passage systematically to the many examples of blending in other domains of human thought, language, and action. Less narrowly I presented in *Reading Minds* an analysis of XYZ constructions (like "Vanity is the quicksand of reason") as involving a basic mapping scheme that invokes open-ended conceptual work that leads to emergent structure. I inventoried examples of cross-space mapping, selective projection, and emergent structure, but my analysis of these cognitive operations was incomplete, and my assertion of a broad scope for XYZ mappings was—surprisingly—too modest by far.

These earlier analyses are subsumed by the newer Fauconnier and Turner network model, which gives a much fuller analysis of the cognitive operations involved in conceptual projection, a specification of taxonomies of types of integration networks, a set of optimality constraints on creating them, and a program for demonstrating the general scope of conceptual integration. We have now connected my kinship metaphor and XYZ examples to examples that look ostensibly altogether different—the invention of complex numbers, the operation of grammatical constructions, the evolution of syntax, action slips, category extension, counterfactual argument, and so on.

Although Milton's portrayal of Satan as a father is two-sided, it preserves considerable structure associated with *father* and *birth*. Consider first the paternity of Death. The "father" has human form and speaks human language, is excited by feminine beauty, and has anthropomorphic sex with an anthropomorphic female in a prototypical human scene. There is a birth through a vaginal canal. The son inherits attributes of both father and mother. Father and adolescent son have a conflict over authority. Now consider the paternity of Sin. The father again has human form and speaks human language. There is an offspring in human form, who emerges from a container-like body part and who develops into a sexual being.

Other examples, taken from *Death is the Mother of Beauty,* show a different projection from the space of *father* and *birth*. "Satan, liar and father of lies" does not take anthropomorphic offspring. "The acorn is the father of the oak" takes neither anthropomorphic form nor anthropomorphic progeneration for either father or child. "Thy wish was father to that thought" (Shakespeare) does not take physical distinction for either father or child. Similar two-sidedness appears in "Fear, father of cruelty" (Ezra Pound), "Pain is the father of complaint" (Sidney), "Love's extremity is the father of foul jealousy" (Spenser), and "Pale desire, father of Curiosity" (Blake).

Consider as a final example the XYZ expression, "The Child is Father of the Man" (Wordsworth). The two inputs—father-and-child versus child-growing-to-man—come from the same conceptual domain, human life. But the example seems figurative, for the following reasons. First, the cross-space connections are highly resisted because they run counter to usual categories: *immature child* in the first input has as its counterpart *father* in the second input, and *grown man* in the first input has as its counterpart *immature child* in the second input. Second, the blend must integrate frame-level structure from both inputs in a particularly surprising way. The chronological *child* in the blend takes from the input of father-and-child the relative influence (and even causal role) of the father, but it takes from the input of child-to-grown-man the relative *youth* of the child. The chronological *man* in the blend takes from the input of child-to-man the maturity of the man, but it takes from the input of father-and-child the dependency of the child.

The oddness of its counterpart connections and the extensive two-sidedness of its blend help make Wordsworth's line appear figurative. But the syntax and

FIGURE **73**

mapping scheme of "The Child is Father of the Man" are the same as the syntax and the mapping scheme of "John is the father of Mary." Both evoke a conceptual mapping scheme involving conceptual blending, but "John is the father of Mary" seems absolutely literal.

"Peeled apple" also seems absolutely literal. But as Gagné and Murphy (1996) write:

> Understanding a combined concept involves creating a new concept. For example, a *peeled apple* is no longer just an apple—its features are not entirely identical to those of an apple. A peeled apple is white, not red, and a peeled apple is more likely to be used for baking than is an unmodified apple, and so on. In short, the concept of the head noun is modified in some way by the addition of the modifier. Although one might think that this modification would be a simple process of adding the meaning of the modifier to that of the head noun, this has not turned out to be the case. The interpretation of combined concepts involves an interaction between the two constituents, rather than an additive process. For example, the fact that peeled apples are white is not part of the meaning of *peeled,* but is inferred, based on our interpretation of the entire phrase. Peeled oranges are not white, are not likely to be used in cooking, and so on. Thus, *peeled* cannot be adding the same feature to *apple* and *orange.* (Gagné and Murphy, 1996, p. 80).

From the perspective of the network model, "peeled apple" evokes a single-framing network. One input has a general frame of *peeling* and the other input has *apple*. The two words are prompts for putting together two provisional input spaces. The blend has considerable emergent structure—such as whiteness and association with baking pies—that is not given for the inputs. There is a cross-space mapping connecting, for example, apple to the object being peeled. There is selective projection—we do not project the color of the apple, or peeling with the fingernails, or peeling as a natural process (*do not apply ointment to peeled skin),* and so on. Completion occurs in the blend through recruiting the frame of baking (for example). We show in Turner & Fauconnier (1995) that an example like "peeled apple" is not unusual. Conceptual integration can be seen not only in striking examples such as "land yacht," "jail bait," and "Chunnel," but also in unremarkable examples such as "waterproof," "tamperproof," "foolproof," "child-proof," "talent pool," "gene pool," "water pool," "football pool," "betting pool," "door knob," "radio knob," "house boat," "boat house," and "black bird."

"Fire station," for example, seems entirely literal. But a fire station does not have fire, provide fire, or receive fire; fire is not part of *station* or the category that includes *station*. We have a mental space with *fire* and a mental space with people or equipment stationed at a *station* for a purpose, and we can integrate these mental spaces conceptually into a story in which fire is not a feature of the station or a counterpart of the station. In this story, the equipment and people at the station go to manage fire. *Fire station,* like *peeled apple,* is a single-framing network: the frame of stationing equipment and agents to manage something is applied to the input *fire.* "Fire station" asks us to create this single-framing network. It does so by means of a highly entrenched phrase learned early in childhood. The result is a conventional integration that sits easily in category structures, because we are familiar with categorizing by purpose.

Milton's infernal trinity, *peeled apple,* and *fire station* arise from the same cognitive operation—conceptual integration—but the infernal trinity seems highly figurative while *peeled apple* and *fire station* seem absolutely literal. The counterpart connections in *peeled apple* can be accommodated in our category structures: we already have a way of seeing transformations of objects as categorical subtypes of the object (shriveled apple, rotten apple, etc.). The application of the frame of peeling to the domain of fruits and vegetables is highly frequent and familiar. The phrase "peeled apple" is entrenched both as a pattern ("stewed carrots," "minced onions," etc.) and as a specific item.

Similarly, the counterpart connections in *fire station* can be accommodated in our category structures—the station is set up to deal with *something,* and that *something* has as its counterpart *fire.* In the blend, there is indeed a fire, and the agents and equipment at the station perform the action of dealing with it. This blend may be entirely counterfactual—imagine a fire station as a precautionary element in a chemical plant where no fire ever erupts during the entire existence of the plant—yet the station will be no less fully a "fire station." The single-framing integration network seems entirely literal because we already categorize stations according to what they are designed to manage, because we routinely apply the frame of *station* to the domain of *fire* and to the super-domain of *crisis* or *disaster,* and because the conceptual connections and linguistic forms in "fire station" are entrenched.

By contrast, Milton's infernal trinity is a different type of integration network, highly and aggressively two-sided, explicitly novel in much of its conceptual structure and its linguistic expression. Our judgments of the packages differ, but the basic cognitive operations used to construct them do not.

Let us consider a final suite of connected examples that may help tease apart several aspects of the literal versus figurative distinction. The sentence "President Franklin Delano Roosevelt moved at a quick pace during his first 100 days in office" seems essentially literal to many people. Yet it is grounded in a conceptual blend. One input has Roosevelt's achievements; the other has a person moving along a spatial path toward destinations. In the cross-space mapping, the traveler is the counterpart of FDR. The generic space taken as applying to both inputs has an abstract agent, abstract purposive actions, and an abstract, oriented linear scale whose locations correspond to grades of achievement of

FIGURE **75**

those purposes. In the blend, the linear scale that is the spatial path of one input is fused with the linear scale for measuring achievement in the other input. In the blend, to be farther along the path is to have accomplished more of the relevant purposes. This is a one-sided shared topology network: the frame of the blend is an elaboration of the organizing frame of only one of the inputs, the *travel* input.

Although this network of FDR-as-runner connects two quite different conceptual domains, it can seem literal, for various reasons. First, the basic network of which this is an instance is highly entrenched. It forms what Lakoff and Johnson (1980) call a "basic metaphor." It is constructed repeatedly in many cases that differ only in the specific details of the target input and blend. Just this input of motion along a path toward destinations and this generic space are projected in just this way to many target inputs whose organizing frame is purposive activity. The result in all these cases is just this blend, not counting specific details. New on-line construction of meaning in this case is limited to specific details such as the identity of the agent (FDR), the particular kind of purposive activity (legislation, government), and the interval of time (100 days).

The generic space for this network (agent with purposes and a linear scale of success) is moreover entrenched in its own right, accessible for projection to any purposive activity. Indeed, that generic structure is now entrenched in the frames of various purposive activities themselves, which carry the vestiges of the conceptual integration networks in which they are embedded. In such cases, we do not need to activate the entire network fully and we do not need to perform on-line invention of new projections at the frame level. This integration network (*purposive agent as traveler on a path*) is moreover our standard cognitive instrument for thinking about purposive activity, and it is used with very high frequency. Finally, the vocabulary "move at a quick pace" has historically been projected to the generic space, the conventional frame of the target, and the conventional frame of the blend, and is entrenched there.

We can alter the example, first by using vocabulary more tightly tied to the source input: "FDR *made the dust fly as he sped along* during his first 100 days." Or we can choose vocabulary that evokes a particular scenario for the source: "FDR moved at *full gallop* through his first 100 days." In these cases, we must make the minor but indispensable inference that someone who speeds along while making dust fly or who moves at full gallop in fact moves a far distance over the path.

Further, we can point explicitly to an additional scenario and highlight the existence of a counterfactual blend, as in "If FDR had been a sprinter, he would have won the Olympic gold for his performance during his first 100 days in office." This now seems thoroughly figurative. The type of integration network is unchanged, as are the basic cognitive operations involved, but we have changed the degree of entrenchment of the vocabulary, the amount of on-line blending needed, the familiarity of the scenario as applied to this purposive activity, and the degree of explicit acknowledgment of the blend.

We can also imagine a second and nearly identical conventional blend, "President Clinton has moved at a slow pace during his first 100 days in office." We can make a comparison between these two conventional blends: "FDR moved at a quick pace during his first 100 days; President Clinton by comparison has not." This sets up a counterpart mapping between the two specific blends of FDR-as-runner and Clinton-as-runner. The counterpart mapping connects president/runner to president/runner, FDR to Clinton, and so on. These two blends are both specifications of the more abstract conventional blend *purposive agent as traveler on a path.*

These two blends—FDR-as-runner and Clinton-as-runner—can themselves be input spaces to a new, hyper-blended space, as when we say, two months after President Clinton has taken office, "Clinton was supposed to hit the ground running. He implied that he was going to accomplish as much in his first 100 days as FDR accomplished in his. So far, Clinton has failed completely *to keep pace with* FDR." This is a *frame network:* the organizing frame shared by the two (already blended) inputs, their generic space, and their hyper-blended space is the already blended frame *American president as traveler on a path.* In the hyper-blend, which has both FDR and Clinton, this already blended frame is extended. First, it is extended through composition: although the two paths have been projected from the two inputs to a single fused path in the hyper-blend, the two agents from the two inputs are projected to discrete agents on that single path, so that now we have not one president/runner on the path but two. Second, the blend is additionally extended through completion: the frame of a *race* is used to complete the blend. It brings with it the structure of *keeping pace with, being ahead or behind,* and so on, which is emergent structure unavailable from the inputs themselves.

Although the shared frame of *American president as traveler on a path* is fairly conventional, emergent details of the blend are emphasized ("keep pace with"). This hyper-blend can be made to seem increasingly figurative the more on-line work we require, the less entrenched we make the vocabulary, and the more attention we draw to the blend, as in "At this rate, Clinton's term will be over before he gets anywhere near *the finish line.*" Here, we point directly to the frame of *race,* which is in the hyper-blend. To construct this finish-line hyper-blend, we must do considerable on-line work to conceive of a finish line that corresponds to FDR's degree of accomplishment on his hundredth day in office in the relevant input space of *FDR's first year in office.* Finally, we can guarantee that the blend is forced into consciousness and is thought to be figurative by requiring the construction of a provisional conceptual domain, as in "Clinton is in a race with the *ghost* of FDR."

FIGURE 77

In all of these cases, the conceptual networks are formed using the same cognitive operations. The results seem more or less literal or figurative for various reasons, but not because they have been formed through fundamentally different cognitive operations.

The second traditional inquiry into the literal versus figurative distinction was: *Is figurative thought mirrored in figurative language? Is figurative thought necessarily paired with linguistic form?* Under this account, these questions are misdirected. Typically, languages already possess constructions that can be used to evoke any sort of integration network. "Boat house," "jail house," and "door knob" use compound nouns and existing lexical items to evoke conceptual integrations. So do "land yacht," "fossil poetry," and "jail bait," which seem figurative. "He kicked the ball over the fence" uses existing lexical items in the existing Caused-Motion Construction (Fauconnier & Turner, 1996; Goldberg, 1995), to evoke the blending of (1) a set of unintegrated actions and events (he kicked, his kick made contact with the ball, the ball moved, the trajectory of the ball's motion was over the fence) with (2) the already integrated but abstract Caused-Motion story, in which an agent's action causes an object to move in a direction. I found the following "figurative" example in the *New York Times:* "So far, the people of this small textile town in northwestern Carolina have been unable to pray Mrs. Smith's two little boys home again." This "figurative" example equally uses existing lexical items in the Caused-Motion construction to evoke a similar blend. The cognitive and linguistic operations are the same in the two cases. What varies between them is instead the relative category status of the inputs and the familiarity of applying the Caused-Motion frame to the other domain (*body actions* versus *praying*). We rarely if ever use the intransitive verb "pray" in the three-argument Caused-Motion construction, but when we do, the linguistic operations are no different from those used in "He kicked the ball over the fence." In Fauconnier & Turner (1996), we analyze a sequence of similar Caused-Motion examples that fall at various points on the gradient of the literal versus figurative distinction. In "Junior sped the car around the Christmas tree," "sped" evokes the motion of the object; in "Paul trotted the stroller around the park," "trot" evokes the action of the agent; in "Sarge let the tanks into the compound," "let" evokes causal connection; in "Max carted the drums into the warehouse," "cart" evokes a vehicle used; in "Jane muscled the boxes over the fence," "muscle" evokes the part of the body used for the action; in "The spy Houdinied the drums out of the compound," "Houdinied" evokes someone associated with actions of a certain character. There are no new linguistic constructions in any of these examples, although some seem figurative.

Rarely, new grammar or lexical items do arise under pressure from conceptual blending. In Turner and Fauconnier (1995), we report that page one of *The Atlanta Constitution* of February 17, 1994, carried a header reading "Out on a

Limbaugh," followed by a summary of the story on the inside pages: "Critics put the squeeze on Florida's citrus industry for its $1 million deal with broadcaster Rush Limbaugh." The formal blend of "out on a limb" with "Limbaugh" is driven by a conceptual blend of (1) an agent who climbs out on a limb of a tree with (2) the deal between the Florida citrus industry and conservative radio talk show host Rush Limbaugh. It turns out that conceptual counterparts that are conceptually blended (*limb, Limbaugh*) have formal expressions that are formally blended ("limb," "Limbaugh"). There is emergent formal structure in the blend. "Out on a limb" has an indefinite article with a common noun. "Limbaugh" is a proper surname, not a common noun. Although a proper surname in English can become a common noun for a group of people with that surname ("She's a Kennedy," "She's the poorest Kennedy") or a group of people analogically equivalent to a particular person of that surname ("He's an Einstein"), here "Limbaugh" is not used as a common noun, referring to namesakes or analogs of Limbaugh. Yet it follows an indefinite article. Following an indefinite article is a property of its counterpart formal element, "limb," associated with the other input to the blend. The blend has a new formal element consisting of previously unavailable syntactic structure—indefinite article + proper name.

We often feel that new and deviant language is "figurative"—indeed, "Out on a Limbaugh" is a prototype of a figurative pun. It seems to ask for laughter. But now consider the following example. At the 1988 Olympics in Korea, a boxing match between an Australian contestant and a Korean contestant ended with strange events, including a skirmish that involved officials and coaches. The Australian coach, interviewed at the airport before boarding a plane to leave in disgust, said, as closely as I can recall, "I was hit by the judge; I was tried to be hit by the umpire." We count the second verb phrase as a mistake, but it is not an arbitrary mistake. It follows principles of formal blending under pressure from conceptual blending. The speaker has one input space in which he is the victim or patient of actions. That scene comes with useful syntax, namely the Passive Construction ("I was bit," "I was made to cry," "I was insulted"). The speaker has this scene and this syntax active and wishes to perpetuate them in the minds of the members of his audience. He also has active the set of unintegrated events in which the umpire is an actor and he, the Australian coach, is the umpire's victim or intended victim. In this scene, the umpire tries to do something, and what he tries to do is hit the coach. Had the coach located the verb "assault" as language for this scene, he could have continued to use the Passive Construction with perfectly grammatical parallelism: "I was hit by the judge; I was assaulted by the umpire." But either he did not locate "assaulted" or "assaulted" seemed wrong for some reason, such as inappropriate register or lack of viscerality and vividness. There is other syntax available for this scene, in which the verb phrase is active—"The umpire tried to hit me"—

FIGURE **79**

but it does not evoke so clearly the established abstract scene of passivity that the Australian coach wishes to keep active. The coach wants to prompt for that scene by using the Passive Construction, but he cannot use the syntax of "try" and "hit" in the Passive Construction because "try" as an auxiliary verb does not take the passive form. The coach therefore creates a formal blend—*try* as an auxiliary that takes the passive form—in order to express the conceptual blend. He may have received additional help in constructing this formal blend from existing syntax in expressions such as "This tool was designed to be used by the designer," wherein the designer is the agent of both the action of the designing and the action of using, just as the umpire is the agent of both the action of trying and the (unachieved) action of hitting. "Design" passivizes while "try" as an auxiliary verb does not, but the Australian coach leaves behind that part of the syntactic structure as he gives "try" a new, emergent syntax under pressure from conceptual integration: "I was tried to be hit by the umpire."

"Out on a Limbaugh" and "I was tried to be hit by the umpire" use the same operations of conceptual and linguistic blending, but the first seems figurative and the second seems like a mistake. In "Out on a Limbaugh," at the conceptual level, we have a one-sided shared topology network whose generic space is abstract relative to the organizing frames of the inputs. In "I was tried to be hit," we have something close to a single-framing network, in which a frame of passive victimization is applied to physical actions; moreover, the application of this frame to this conceptual domain is archetypal and routine. The emergent syntax of "Out on a Limbaugh" seems to be planned, while the emergent syntax of "I was tried to be hit" seems to have arisen spontaneously. For reasons such as these, the first seems figurative and the second does not, and the first seems witty and the second seems a little embarrassing. But the basic cognitive and linguistic operations are not different.

Our third traditional inquiry into figurative language and thought was: *How do figurative thought and language evolve?* The short answer is, conceptions and forms that seem figurative evolve in the ways that all thought and language evolve; some products in that evolution seem more or less figurative according to their location on the interacting gradients of distinction, but this interpretation will vary among persons and, moreover, does not indicate a fundamental difference of cognitive operation.

A substantive answer to this question would be a theory of the evolution of conceptual structures and linguistic forms. Such a theory would be highly complicated because human thought and language arise through the interaction of several complex adaptive systems, including biota (all living things through all time; a unit is a gene pool and all its ancestor gene pools); a given gene pool (a unit is a gene); all conceptual systems in all individuals over all time; a conceptual system shared by a community and all the conceptual systems that are ancestors of that conceptual system; a conceptual system within a single individual, and all the conceptual systems that were, in the individual, ancestors of the current conceptual system; human language, all of it, over all historical time; a human language shared by a linguistic community and all the diachronic linguistic structures that are ancestors of that language; and a human language, in an individual, and all the linguistic systems that were, in the individual, ancestors of that current linguistic system.

This list, already paralyzing in its complexity, is actually more complex, for its elements overlap and interact. Modeling thought and language (and therefore thought and language that seem figurative) involves analyzing its interacting complex adaptive systems. The network model is only a modest gesture in this direction. In it, existing conceptual and formal elements and their pairings are inputs to integration, which is selective and which results in emergent structure. Outputs of integration can become inputs to integration. The result is pathwise development of a system in which elements stand in relation to other elements. What can arise in the system at any moment in its evolution depends on what has already arisen that survives. The system is dynamic; it never stands still. Conceptual integration exploits accidents as a fundamental part of its functioning; indeed, basic (''literal'') structure in the system can arise from the exploitation of remarkable accidents. Products of integration that seem at one time figurative may seem at other times literal. Formal blending to create new forms may be guided by pressure from conceptual blending. These operations are not deterministic or algorithmic, but instead are guided by optimality principles and by degree of success in the moment of operation. In my view, the cognitive operations involved in the evolution of the conceptual and formal patterns we see in figurative examples such as ''land yacht'' or ''jail bait'' are identical to those we see in literal examples such as ''fire station'' or ''brown cow.''

Our last traditional inquiry into figurative language and thought was: *What is the appropriate relation of an abstract theory of figures to a rich theory of individual figurative events?*

Actual figures occur only in dynamic, on-line construction of complete meanings. The study of figure typically does not focus on this condition. The central products of the study of figure are typically lists of abstract elements— ''figures''—with examples: here is antithesis and here are examples; here is metonymy and here are examples; here is the basic metaphor LIFE IS A JOURNEY and here are examples.

In this style of analysis, the examples are adduced to refine the elements of the theory rather than as objects of case study. To define metonymy and provide an example does not supply an analysis of the specific example, or at least the construction of meaning prompted by that specific example. Historically, the study of figure has taken on the job of proposing abstract elements—figures— and giving examples but has not taken on the job of explaining the dynamism

FIGURE **81**

and completeness of individual examples. Typically, the study of figure attempts to isolate and exemplify partial structures that get used in the construction of meaning but not to give a theory of that actual use.

Traditional grammar follows the same pattern: here is a partial structure we call "noun" and here are some examples of nouns; here is a partial structure we call "verb" and here are some examples of verbs; here is a partial structure we call the "passive construction" and here are some examples of passive constructions.

Modern grammar specializes in this kind of analysis of partial instruments: here is verb argument structure, with examples; here is ergativity, with examples; here is inflectional morphology, with examples. None of these abstract partial structures could itself be a full meaning; they are all partial instruments whose utility derives from their availability to be recruited in actual linguistic and conceptual events. The dynamism of the actual full meanings is not modeled. Most models of grammar assume that there exists an abstract object of study—called the "language"—that transcends the full and dynamic particular linguistic events in individual brains, just as principles of physics transcend actual physical events.

The impulse to construct a theory that consists of abstract elements is strong and understandable, given the success of the mathematical model of theoretical knowledge. Models of mind and language that follow the mathematical tradition look for elemental structures that serve as partial instruments. Theories of semantic primitives, innate concepts, language bioprograms, and symbolic artificial intelligence (such as conceptual dependency diagrams) follow this tradition.

This tradition is not exclusively formal, and it is not exclusively objectivist, either. The theory of basic metaphor (with which I have been associated) attempts to isolate a quite small number of elemental basic metaphors (maybe 600) that we all know, and to provide examples of each, with the examples meant as evidence for the existence of the abstract elements of the theory.

The central danger for such partial models of conceptual construction is that they might not "scale up" appropriately. The well-known failure of attempts to scale up from partial artificial intelligence models to full models is worth remembering in this respect. An analogy from the neurosciences makes the danger clearer: we have a folk theory that assumes we assign color to a spot in the visual field according to the kind of light reflected from that spot in the visual field, but what happens is much more complicated. (Hubel, 1995; Zeki, 1993). There are three kinds of cones in the retina, each sensitive to one of three wavebands of light called (inaccurately) red, blue, and green. Suppose we have three projectors, each of which shines one of the wavebands of light with an intensity we can set on a dial. Suppose we turn on the projectors, at certain settings, to illuminate a painting that consists of rectangles of color. Suppose, finally, we pick out a red rectangle and measure for each of those wavebands the intensity of light reflected from the red rectangle. Now we look at a green rectangle and adjust the intensity of light coming from each projector until our measuring device shows that, for each of the wavebands, the identical intensity of light is now being reflected from the second rectangle as was coming from the first when it looked red. *We will still find that the second rectangle looks green and the first rectangle looks red.* The brain is able to compute, for each waveband, a record of differential reflectance of light across the visual field and then to perform a differential computation across the three differential records, to produce an assignment of constant color under remarkably different conditions of illumination. In this way, we are able to "discount the illuminant" as we attempt to find constancy in the environment. The point of this analogy is that a partial model of color vision does not scale up to a successful model of actual color vision, because what is happening in assigning features to any part of the visual field depends upon the overall activity of vision. We need a model of the operation of the whole in order to account for any part of color vision. Partial models of partial instruments of color vision do not scale up to the kind of global model of computation over global records that is needed to account for color constancy.

The observational data we wish to account for in the case of thought and language all consist of on-line, dynamic construction of full meanings and full expressions. Catalogs of partial instruments that may underlie that data are useful to the extent that they actually help us to account for the data, but it cannot be assumed in principle that the data will be accounted for as linear compositions of individual partial resources. In 1956, George Miller complained that scientific journals had become catalogs of parts for machines that scientists never build.[12] Cognitive scientists, linguists, and rhetoricians are vulnerable to the analogous observation. The network model is a modest attempt to take a step in the direction of modeling the on-line, dynamic construction of full meanings that arise through conceptual integration. The operation of conceptual integration can recruit from many domains, and it can develop elaborate mappings and projections. It is not algorithmic or deterministic, but it is guided by optimality principles sensitive to purpose and situation.

From the view of the network model, the contrast of literal versus figurative appears to be unproductive as a theoretical principle for distinguishing cognitive operations. The original view of figure, which Quintilian set aside, in which a figure is any pairing of a formal pattern with a conceptual pattern and in which figures stand in relational networks, is by contrast basic and indispensable.

Language offers sets of prompts for cognitive operations such as conceptual integration. We conduct those cognitive operations on conceptual structures available to us. A theory of figure that embraces this characterization faces great challenges as it attempts to develop a model of cognitive operations, a model of the relational network of form-meaning pairs that prompt us to perform these

FIGURE   **83**

cognitive operations, a model of gradients of distinction in the products of those cognitive operations, a model of the ways in which form-meaning pairs arise and evolve, and a model of the ways in which these cognitive operations and figures perform in actual, on-line, dynamic creations of meaning and expression.

The study of figure has been sidetracked from these issues since the classical rhetoricians, with the surprising and humbling result that the study of figure, one of the oldest bodies of knowledge in the human sciences, remains in our age still in its infancy.

ACKNOWLEDGMENTS

This study was conducted while I was Agnes Gund Member of the School of Social Science, Institute for Advanced Study, Princeton, in 1996 and 1997. I am grateful for support provided by the Institute, the School, and Agnes Gund.

NOTES

1. "figuras quae σχήματα Graece vocantur," Quintilian, book 9, chap. 1, section 1 [Loeb edition, vol. 3, p. 348]

2. Book 21, chaps. 7–15 [1457b]. The Greek word I have translated as "expression" means "name" or "noun" as opposed to "verb," but it also means "expression," which must be Aristotle's meaning, since his first example is a verb and his second is a modifier.

3. President George Bush preferred when speaking of himself as agent to omit the subject: "Moved to Texas. Invested in oil. Raised a family." Television journalists noted that this form is associated with an ethos of humility, and that other politicans had begun to employ it to the same effect. Pragmatic effects of this sort are often part of a grammatical construction. Analysts of figure are attuned to such constructions and even to constructions that border on ungrammaticality, such as *anthimeria*, which Arthur Quinn illustrates in *Figures of Speech* with many Shakespearean expressions: "The thunder would not peace at my bidding" (*King Lear*), "Lord Angelo dukes it well" (*Measure for Measure*), "The fair, the chaste, and unexpressive she" (*As You Like It*), "The mutable, rank-scented many" (*Troilus and Cressida*) (Quinn, pp. 50–51).

4. "The figure [σχῆμα] that is most characteristic of Purity is the use of a straightforward construction with the [subject-]noun in the nominative case. . . ." (Hermogenes, 1987, p. 10), a translation of "Σχῆμα δεκαφαρότητος ἡ ὀρφότης" (Hermogenes, 1913, p. 229). "I can prove that the use of [the σχῆμα of] straightforward sentences with the subject[-noun] in the nominative case is most characteristic of Purity" (Hermogenes, 1987, p. 10), a translation of "ἡ οὖν ὀρφότης τὸ σχῆμα. ὅσον ἐφ' ἑαυτῷ. καφαρόν. τεκμήριον δέ" (Hermogenes, 1913, p. 230). Also quoted in Fahnestock (in press).

5. Tzvetan Todorov (1982) observes that "one important consequence of" the definition of figure as a pairing of form and meaning "is that, if it is taken literally, all discourse is figurative" (p. 66). In chap. 3, "The End of Rhetoric," pp. 84–110, Todorov offers an insightful history of the theory of figure.

6. The following disussion of image schemas in expression is based on Francis-Noël Thomas and Mark Turner, *Clear and Simple as the Truth: Writing Classic Prose,* pp. 67–71. "Image schema" is Mark Johnson's term. See Johnson, 1987, p. xiv. For an introduction to research on image schemas, see Mark Turner, *The Literary Mind,* chap. 2, "Human Meaning," and Appendix, "Further Reading on Image Schemas."

7. See "The Body of Our Thought and the Thought of Our Body," chap. 4 of Mark Turner, *Reading Minds: The Study of English in the Age of Cognitive Science.*

8. For the original work on the XYZ construction, see Mark Turner, *Reading Minds,* chap. 9, "The Poetry of Connections, III," and Gilles Fauconnier and Mark Turner, 1994, "Conceptual Projection and Middle Spaces."

9. Charles Fillmore maintains a website dedicated to construction grammar. It includes lecture notes, a bibliography, and a "constructicon." It is available as a link from my website, http://www.wam.umd.edu/~mturn.

10. The website for conceptual integration has the URL address: http://www.wam.umd/edu/~mturn/WWW/blending.html.

11. "Great America II," 1993, 190, p. 100.

12. As quoted in George A. Cowan, "Conference Opening Remarks," in George A. Cowan, David Pines, and David Meltzer (1994), p. 2.

REFERENCES

Aristotle. *Poetics.* (1995). Ed. and trans. S. Halliwell. In *Aristotle,* vol. 23. Cambridge, MA: Harvard University Press [Loeb].

Aristotle. (1991). *On rhetoric: a theory of civic discourse.* Trans. G. A. Kennedy. New York: Oxford University Press.

Burke, K.. (1969 [1945]). *A grammar of motives.* Berkeley: University of California Press.

Burke, K. (1969 [1950]). *A Rhetoric of Motives.* Berkeley: University of California Press.

[Cicero]. (1954). *Rhetorica ad Herennium.* Trans. H. Caplan. Cambridge, MA: Harvard University Press [Loeb].

Coulson, S. (1995). Analogic and metaphoric mapping in blended spaces. *Center for Research in Language Newsletter, 9:*1, 2–12.

Coulson, S. (1997). "Semantic leaps: The role of frame-shifting and conceptual blending in meaning construction." Doctoral dissertation, University of California, San Diego.

Cowan, G. A., Pines, D., & Meltzer, D., (Eds.). (1994). *Complexity: Metaphors, models, and reality* [Santa Fe Institute Studies in the Sciences of Complexity, Proceedings, vol. 19]. Reading, MA: Addison Wesley.

Demetrius. *On style.* (1995 [1932]). Ed. and trans. D. C. Innes; based on the translation by W. R. Roberts. In *Aristotle,* vol. 23. Cambridge, MA: Harvard University Press [Loeb].

Fahnestock, J. (In press). *Figures of argument: Studies in the rhetoric of science.* New York: Oxford University Press.

Fauconnier, G. (1997). *Mappings in thought and language.* Cambridge: Cambridge University Press.

FIGURE 85

Fauconnier, G., & Turner, M. (1994). "Conceptual projection and middle spaces," UCSD Cognitive Science Technical Report 9401. San Diego. [Available from http://cogsci.ucsd.edu and from http://www.wam.umd.edu/˜mturn]

Fauconnier, G., & Turner, M. (1996). "Blending as a central process of grammar." In A. Goldberg (Ed.), *Conceptual structure, discourse, and language.* Stanford: Center for the Study of Language and Information.

Fauconnier, G., & Turner, M. (In press a). "Principles of conceptual integration." In J.-P. Koenig (in press).

Fauconnier, G., & Turner, M. (In press b). "Conceptual integration networks." *Cognitive Science.*

Fauconnier, G., & Turner, M. (In preparation). *Making sense.*

Fillmore, C., Kay, P. & O'Connor, C. (1988). "Regularity and idiomaticity in grammatical constructions: The case of *let alone." Language, 64,* 501–38.

Freeman, M. (1997). "Grounded spaces: Deictic-self anaphors in the poetry of Emily Dickinson." *Language and Literature, 6:*1, 7–28.

Gagné, C. L., & Murphy, G. L. (1996). "Influence of discourse context on feature availability in conceptual combination." *Discourse Processes, 22,* 79–101.

Geertz, C. (1973). *The interpretation of cultures.* New York: Basic.

Goldberg, A. (1995). *Constructions: A construction grammar approach to argument structure.* Chicago: University of Chicago Press.

Goldberg, A. (1996) "Construction grammar." In Brown & Miller, (Eds.), *Concise encyclopedia of syntactic theories.* Oxford: Elsevier Science Limited.

Grush, R. & Mandelblit, N. (In press). "Blending in language, conceptual structure, and the cerebral cortex." In Koenig (in press)

Hermogenes. (1913). Περὶ ἰδεῆν. In H. Rabe (Ed.), *Hermogenis Opera.* Leipzig: Teubner.

Hermogenes. (1987). *On types of style.* Trans. C. W. Wooten. Chapel Hill: University of North Carolina Press.

Hubel, D. H. (1995). *Eye, brain, and vision.* New York: Scientific American Library.

Israel, M. (1996). "The *Way* Constructions Grow." In A. Goldberg (Ed.), *Conceptual structure, discourse, and language.* Stanford: Center for the Study of Language and Information.

Johnson, Mark. (1987). *The body in the mind.* Chicago: University of Chicago Press.

Kay, Paul. (1995). "Construction grammar." In J. Verschueren, J.-O. Ostman, & J. Blommaert (Eds.), *Handbook of pragmatics.* Amsterdam: J. Benjamins.

Kay, Paul., & Fillmore, C. (1995). "Grammatical constructions and linguistic generalizations: the *What's X doing Y?* construction." Unpublished manuscript, Department of Linguistics, University of California, Berkeley.

Kennedy, G., ed., commentator, trans. (1991). Aristotle. *On rhetoric: A theory of civic discourse.* New York: Oxford University Press.

Koenig, J.-P., ed. (In press). *Conceptual structure, discourse, and language,* vol. 2. Stanford: Center for the Study of Language and Information.

Lakoff, G. (1987). *Women, fire, and dangerous things: What categories reveal about the mind.* Chicago: University of Chicago Press.

Lakoff, G., & Johnson, M. (1980). *Metaphors we live by.* Chicago: University of Chicago Press.

Lewis, C. S. (1936). *The allegory of love.* Oxford: Oxford University Press.

Longinus. (1995 [1932]). *On the sublime.* Trans. W. H. Fyfe and rev. D. Russell. In *Aristotle,* vol. 23. Cambridge, MA: Harvard University Press [Loeb].

Mandelblit, N. (1995). "Beyond lexical semantics: Mapping and blending of conceptual and linguistic structures in machine translation." In *Proceedings of the Fourth International Conference on the Cognitive Science of Natural Language Processing,* Dublin.

Mandelblit, N. (1997). "Grammatical blending: Creative and schematic aspects in sentence processing and translation." Doctoral dissertation, University of California, San Diego.

Oakley, T. (1995). "Presence: the conceptual basis of rhetorical effect." Doctoral dissertation, University of Maryland.

Quinn, A. (1982). *Figures of speech: Sixty ways to turn a phrase.* Salt Lake City: Gibbs M. Smith, Inc.

Quintilian. (1921). *Institutio oratoria.* Four volumes. Trans. H. E. Butler. Cambridge, MA: Harvard University Press [Loeb].

Ramey, Martin. (1997). "Eschatology and ethics." In *The problem of the body: The conflict between soteriology and ethics in Paul.* Doctoral dissertation, Chicago Theological Seminary.

Richards, I. A. (1936). *The philosophy of rhetoric.* New York: Oxford University Press.

Robert, A. (In press). "Blending in the interpretation of mathematical proofs." In Koenig (in press).

Sun, D. (1994). "Thurber's Fables for our time: A case study in satirical use of the great chain metaphor." *Studies in American Humor, 3(1),* 51–61.

Sweetser, E. (1990). *From etymology to pragmatics: metaphorical and cultural aspects of semantic structure.* Cambridge: Cambridge University Press.

Thomas , F.-N., & Turner, M. (1994). *Clear and simple as the truth: Writing classic prose.* Princeton: Princeton University Press, 1994.

Todorov, T. (1982). *Theories of the symbol.* Trans. C. Porter. Ithaca: Cornell University Press.

Traugott, E. (In press). "Subjectification in grammaticalization." In D. Stein & S. Wright (Eds.), *Subjectivity and subjectification in language.* Cambridge: Cambridge University Press.

Traugott, E. (1996). "On the role of constructions in grammaticalization." In B. Joseph & R. Janda (Eds.), *Handbook of historical linguistics.* Oxford: Blackwell.

Turner, M. (1987). *Death is the mother of beauty: Mind, metaphor, criticism.* Chicago: University of Chicago Press.

Turner, M. (1989). "Categories and analogies." In D. Helman (Ed.), *Analogical reasoning: Perspectives of artificial intelligence, cognitive science, and philosophy.* Dordrecht: Kluwer.

Turner, M. (1991). *Reading minds: The study of English in the age of cognitive science.* Princeton: Princeton University Press.

Turner, Mark. (1996a). "Conceptual blending and counterfactual argument in the social

FIGURE 87

and behavioral sciences,'' In P. Tetlock & A. Belkin (Eds.), *Counterfactual thought experiments in world politics*. Princeton: Princeton University Press.

Turner, M. (1996b). *The literary mind*. New York: Oxford University Press.

Turner, M. & Fauconnier, G. (1995). ''Conceptual integration and formal expression.'' *Metaphor and Symbolic Activity, 10*:3, 183–203.

Turner, M. & Fauconnier, G. (in press). ''Conceptual integration in counterfactuals.'' In Koenig (in press).

Veale, T. (1996). ''Pastiche: A metaphor-centered computational model of conceptual blending, with special reference to cinematic borrowing.'' Manuscript. [Available from the Conceptual Integration Web Page: http://www.wam.umd.edu/~mturn/WWW/blending.html]

Vickers, B. (1988). *In defence of rhetoric*. Oxford: Clarendon Press.

Zbikowski, L. (1996) ''Conceptual blending and song.'' Unpublished manuscript, Department of Music, University of Chicago.

Zeki, S. (1993). *A vision of the brain*. Oxford: Blackwell.

CHAPTER 3

The Fight Over Metaphor in Thought and Language

Raymond W. Gibbs, Jr.

The scholarly study of figurative thought and language has exploded in recent years. It seems impossible to study how people think, act, speak, and interact without having to address some aspect of figurative thought and language. When I was busy working on my book *The Poetics of Mind* in the late 1980s and early 1990s, I used to conduct an experiment with myself in which I would go to my university's main library (primarily for the humanities and social sciences) and visit the current periodical room. I would randomly choose a shelf, close my eyes, and pick up a journal. My hypothesis was that at least 50% of the time the journal selected would contain an article that related to some aspect of figurative language. Not surprisingly, to me anyway, after several years of doing this, I found that my hypothesis was quite close to being true.

This small personal experiment always amused me and still does as I continue to conduct it, but a closer look at the scholarly work reveals many heated controversies over how best to study and describe all things figurative. My book on figurative thought, language, and understanding (Gibbs, 1994), noted above, attempted to address some of the traditional concerns of linguists, philosophers, anthropologists, and literary theorists from the perspective of a cognitive psychologist/psycholinguist who had conducted numerous experimental investigations on how people learn, make sense of, and interpret different kinds of figurative language (e.g., metaphor, idioms, proverbs, irony, oxymora, indirect speech acts, and so on). My work, then as now, adhered to what I dub the *cognitive wager,* which commits me to the idea that the conceptual and experiential basis of linguistic categories and constructs is of primary importance. Language structure and behavior should not be studied as if they were autonomous from ordinary thought, but as reflections of general conceptual organization, categorization principles, and processing mechanisms (Lakoff, 1990).

This research strategy has provided a considerable body of evidence showing that many aspects of language use and structure are intimately connected to people's everyday conceptual systems and that much of our ordinary cognition is constituted by metaphor, metonymy, and other figurative modes of thinking (Gibbs, 1994; Johnson, 1987; Lakoff, 1987; Turner, 1991). My empirical work has sought to explore the possibility that how we speak about our experiences is closely tied to how we figuratively conceptualize our lives. This approach differs from that adopted by many scholars studying figurative language use and has led to several interesting arguments between me (as well as several cognitive linguists) and other members of the psychological community.

I do not wish to repeat much of what I discussed in my book, but rather to address in this chapter some of the controversies that have recently arisen in cognitive science specifically on questions regarding the relationship between metaphoric thought and language (also see Katz, 1996). To what extent does the ubiquity of metaphoric language reflect metaphoric thought? How can we best understand the relationship between metaphoric thought and language use? Should we distinguish between processing metaphor and metaphor processing? Finally, what motivates metaphoric thought and language?

As readers of *The Poetics of Mind* will no doubt realize, an important aim of my book was to show how metaphor was one of a number of tropes that structure different aspects of how people think and use language. I would like to address other aspects of figurative thought and language in this chapter but, because of space limitations, will focus primarily on the topic of metaphor. However, I maintain my earlier commitment to explore the diversity of ways people think, speak, and understand others via a variety of figurative schemes.

My main message in this chapter is that scholars must explicitly acknowledge some of the methodological and theoretical differences in metaphor seen both between and within various academic disciplines. As I argue, metaphor scholars make many claims that seem inappropriate given the limits of their methodological commitments (e.g., the cognitive wager), their methodological paradigms, and the ultimate aims of their theories.

PAST AND RECENT BATTLES

Perhaps the most controversial claim about metaphor in the last 20 years is that this trope is not merely a figure of speech but a specific mental mapping that significantly influences how people think, reason, and imagine in everyday life (Gibbs, 1994; Johnson, 1987, 1993; Kovecses, 1986, 1990; Lakoff, 1987; Lakoff & Johnson, 1980; Lakoff & Turner, 1989; Sweetser, 1990; Turner, 1991). The im, advocated by cognitive linguists, philosophers, and some psycholinguists, suggests that verbal metaphors are not mere ornamental, communicative devices to describe topics inherently difficult to describe in literal terms. Instead, verbal metaphors, including conventional expressions based on metaphor, reflect underlying conceptual mappings in which people metaphorically conceptualize vague, abstract domains of knowledge (e.g., time, causation, spatial orientation, ideas, emotions, concepts of understanding) in terms of more specific, familiar, and concrete knowledge (e.g., embodied experiences) (see Croft, 1993, for a discussion of metaphor and cross-domain highlighting). These sources to target domain mappings tend to be asymmetrical (but see Turner & Fauconnier, 1995) in that completely different inferences result when the direction of the mappings is reversed (e.g., TIME IS MONEY is quite different from the, perhaps, anomalous idea that MONEY IS TIME).

Evidence in favor of conceptual metaphors is found in a variety of sources, including the systematicity of conventional expressions, novel extensions of conventional language, polysemy, and psycholinguistic findings (see Gibbs, 1994; Johnson, 1987; Kovecses, 1986; Lakoff, 1987; Sweetser, 1990; Turner, 1991). Moreover, a significant amount of psychological research has shown the influence of verbal metaphors in categorization, problem solving, decision making, learning, and memory (Gibbs, 1994). These empirical studies illustrate, at the very least, that providing someone with a particular way of metaphorically construing an idea or situation clearly affects many aspects of how people learn, remember, solve problems, and make decisions.

Yet many cognitive psychologists, in particular, are critical of the claim that systematic patterns of conventional language, novel extensions, or polysemy actually reveal that people ordinarily *think* about many concepts in terms of metaphor (Glucksberg & Keysar, 1990; Honeck & Temple, 1994; Keysar & Bly, 1995; McGlone, 1996; Murphy, 1996; Ortony, 1988; Stock, Slack, & Ortony, 1993). These scholars question, among other things, whether metaphorical talk necessarily reflects metaphorical thinking. They suggest various reasons for why people might speak metaphorically without having to think metaphorically, at least in the sense that the ubiquity of metaphor in language does not reflect the persuasiveness of metaphor in structuring human concepts. As an analogy, some psychologists suggest that we should not assume that metaphoric language indicates metaphoric thought in the same way that we should not assume that, because people have 22 linguistic terms for a concept like snow, they actually conceptualize snow in 22 different ways (Murphy, 1996).

It makes good sense, in my view, to adopt a skeptical attitude toward any claim that scholars can directly infer properties of human thought from the analysis of linguistic structure and behavior. After all, plentiful potential motivations may explain why people speak about objects, events, other people, and their own lives in particular ways. Furthermore, many aspects of language are conventional or arbitrarily determined, such as the fact that I am sitting on something English speakers call a "chair," an object that could have easily been called a "table." Thus, for one possible alternative, English speakers might talk about their lives in terms of journeys or talk about their emotional experiences in terms of containers and heat simply as matters of convention without recognizing, even tacitly, anything about the putative connection between different verbal expressions and systematic patterns of metaphorical thought (i.e., conceptual metaphors).

Beyond the claim that people might employ metaphor about certain topics for arbitrary reasons, cognitive psychologists have raised several other objections about the idea that metaphor is conceptual. First, they argue that the linguistic data per se does not prove that metaphorical mappings get computed automatically and effortlessly during metaphor understanding (Glucksberg, Brown, & McGlone, 1993; Honeck & Temple, 1994). After all, cognitive linguistics does not provide any evidence on whether metaphorical thought plays a role in how people learn verbal metaphors or immediately produce and comprehend them in everyday discourse. This is not surprising given that cognitive linguists do not conduct experiments with the appropriate methodologies to tap into very fast, mostly unconscious, mental processes that operate when verbal metaphors are comprehended.

Psychologists have argued with me, in both public and private, that there is some circularity in how cognitive linguists argue for the psychological reality of conceptual metaphor. Thus, trying to infer aspects of conceptual knowledge from an analysis of systematic patterns of linguistic structure results in theories that seem post hoc. For instance, the claim that the systematicity in expressions such as "He's wasting our time," "I save an hour doing my paper on the computer," and "I can no longer invest that much energy into my marriage" is due to the presence of an independent, preexisting conceptual metaphor (TIME IS MONEY) provides only a *motivated* explanation for linguistic behavior. Cognitive psychologists and psycholinguists wish to *predict* behavior in advance according to the hypothetico-deductive method of scientific inference. What they seek is empirical, objective evidence that people's conceptual knowledge somehow *predicts* the existence of different linguistic behavior, not that people's linguistic behavior can be explained post hoc by positing theoretical conceptual metaphors.

I do not entirely agree with this characterization of how cognitive linguistics does its work, nor do I look negatively on *motivated* explanations of human behavior (see Casad, 1988, and Wierzbicka, 1985, for two good examples of motivated explanations of data that have hitherto been considered arbitrary or unpredictable). Yet I recognize the need to provide empirical demonstrations for many of the ideas about human conceptual knowledge that have been proposed in cognitive linguistics (e.g., for notions such as conceptual metaphor, image schema, radial structures, mental spaces, and so on).

Another difficulty in assessing whether metaphor exists as part of people's mental representations of concepts and is employed in ordinary language understanding is that linguists and psychologists interpret terms such as *mental representation, language understanding,* and *automaticity* differently. In fact, psychologists themselves are also divided as to the meanings of these same concepts. For example, the issue of automatic metaphorical mappings usage in metaphor understanding is complex because automaticity may relate to various aspects of how metaphors are understood. Thus, metaphorical thought may play no role in immediate metaphor comprehension, but people may still employ metaphorical schemes quite automatically in many other aspects of everyday thought. Cognitive linguistic analyses suggest that several systematic metaphorical mappings motivate the meanings and that use of many verbal metaphors constitutes only one kind of evidence in favor of the automatic, pervasive use of metaphor in human cognition. This does not mean, once again, that these metaphorical schema are ordinarily accessed each and every time a metaphor is read or heard. But it does mean that metaphor has *some* role in explaining some aspects of how many linguistic expressions are created and understood.

At the same time, psychologists and linguists clearly have different theoretical goals in studying metaphor. Much of the work in cognitive linguistics is unique because it attempts to infer something about conceptual knowledge based on the analysis of systematic patterns of linguistic structure. These analyses of systematic patterns in language suggest a variety of conceptual and preconceptual structures, including idealized cognitive models, images schema, metaphoric and metonymic mappings, mental spaces, radial structures, and so on. This emphasis on the contents of what people know and the bodily experiences that give rise to such knowledge is quite different from the major focus in cognitive science on the general architectural form of human thought and language. Thus most cognitive psychologists focus on the architecture of mind and on the mental computations that operate within this representational system. They do not worry, as cognitive linguists do, about uncovering the specific beliefs and concepts people have or how people come to know what they do about themselves and the world. Cognitive linguists (and their allies in philosophy, anthropology, and psychology) view knowledge as arising out of people's bodily interactions with the world. Under this view, knowledge is perceived not as static, propositional, and sentential, but as grounded in patterns of bodily experience.

As is the case with all scientific methods, there are limitations to the strategy of trying to infer something about conceptual structure from a systematic analysis of linguistic structure and behavior. The primary limitation is one shared by most linguistic research, namely, the problem of making conclusions about phenomena based on the individual analyst's own intuitions. Distrust of the practice of relying on private, unverifiable intuitions as a source of data is an important reason for the growing interest in functionalist approaches to linguistics (Hopper, 1991). Cognitive psychologists simply do not accept hypotheses about human conceptual knowledge, or anything for that matter, that are based on a theorist's intuitive speculations, even when such speculations are based on a systematic analysis of linguistic structure and behavior. To many, the idea, for example, that conceptual metaphors underlie our everyday experience or motivate our use and understanding of different linguistic expressions cannot be accepted as "psychologically real" because such a theory is based on intuitive explanation. They seek "objective" evidence elicited from experimental participants who have no preconceived notion about the phenomenon of interest. Although cognitive psychologists have in recent years begun to study people's introspections in several domains (e.g., reading, problem solving, decision making), a strong belief remains that linguistic analyses of human mental activities are unreliable because they rely on theorists' introspective judgments.

THE INTERACTION OF METAPHOR IN THOUGHT AND LANGUAGE

What role does metaphoric thought play in how people use and understand language? I argue that at least four psychological hypotheses address this question (Gibbs, 1994). These hypotheses are not mutually exclusive but reflect a hierarchy of possibilities about the interaction between metaphoric patterns of thought and different aspects of language use and understanding. Let us consider each of these hypotheses, paying close attention to the appropriate methodologies needed to assess validity.

Hypothesis 1: *Metaphoric thought plays some role in the historical evolution of what words and expressions mean.* This claim is clearly within the domain of expertise for cognitive linguistics. For instance, Sweetser (1990) has shown in detail that many polysemous words in Indo-European languages acquired their nonphysical meanings via metaphorical extensions from earlier acquired, concrete, physical meanings. To take just one example, metaphorical mapping between the idea of visually seeing things to intellectually understanding things defines a pathway for semantic change. Conceptual metaphors such as UNDERSTANDING IS SEEING explain not only how words change their meanings historically (i.e., why the physical sense of *see* regularly extends via metaphor toward a nonphysical meaning), but also why polysemous words have their specific meanings (e.g., why it just makes sense to us to talk about understanding ideas using expressions such as "clearly see the point you're making in this essay"). With few exceptions, words in Indo-European languages meaning "see" reg-

ularly acquire the meaning "know" at widely scattered times and places. Although several linguists and psychologists argue against the relevance of Sweetser's data to theories of how people interpret polysemous words in context (Groefsema, 1996; Murphy, 1996; Ruhl, 1989), there does appear to be linguistic evidence in support of hypothesis 1.

Hypothesis 2: *Metaphoric thought motivates the linguistic meanings that have currency within linguistic communities, or may have some role in speakers'/hearers' presumed understanding of language.* Several kinds of linguistic evidence support the claim that metaphor motivates the meanings of linguistic expressions for contemporary speakers/hearers. The first is the systematicity of literal expressions. Consider the following fairly mundane utterances often used to talk about love and relationships: "Look how far we've come." "It's been a long, bumpy road." "We're at a crossroads." "We may have to go our separate ways." "Our marriage is on the rocks." "We're spinning our wheels."

Why are each of these expressions acceptable ways of talking about, and understanding, love relationships? All of these (and other) conventional expressions cluster together under one basic metaphorical system of understanding: LOVE IS A JOURNEY (Lakoff & Johnson, 1980). This conceptual metaphor involves understanding one domain of experience, love, in terms of a very different, more concrete domain of experience, journeys. There is a tight mapping according to which entities in the domain of love (e.g., the lovers, their common goals, the love relationship, etc.) correspond systematically to entities in the domain of a journey (e.g., the traveler, the vehicle, destinations, etc.). In a similar way, a different metaphorical conceptualization of love, LOVE IS A NUTRIENT, motivates many other conventional expressions such as "I was given new strength by her love," "I thrive on love," "He's sustained by love," and "I'm starved for your affection."

Most theories of linguistic metaphor provide no reason why literal expressions like those presented above cluster as they do (Gibbs, 1993). In general, metaphor theorists view these literal expressions as having little to do with metaphor, although they sometimes see such statements as reflecting different "dead" metaphors. But it is not just arbitrary or an accident that we use, for example, "thrive," "sustained," and "starved" when speaking of love. We do so because a great deal of our conceptual understanding of love is metaphorically structured (e.g., LOVE IS FIRE, LOVE IS MAGIC, LOVE IS A PHYSICAL FORCE, and so on). The hypothesis that some concepts may be metaphorically structured makes it possible to explain what until now has been seen as unrelated conventional expressions.

A second, related source of evidence for the metaphorical motivation for contemporary linguistic expressions appears in the elaboration of conventional metaphors in poetry and literature (Deane, 1995; Freeman, 1995; Lakoff & Turner, 1989; Turner, 1987, 1991, 1996). One analysis of Shakespeare's play

Macbeth provides several interesting examples of CONTAINER metaphors, which map the CONTAINER image-schema (more on this later) onto different target domains (Freeman, 1995). These target domains are referred to by various individual words, phrases, complete expressions, as well as in overall themes, characters, and physical and psychological settings in the play. Thus, the king of Norway, Sweno, is described as "that spring whence . . . Discomfort swells" (1.2.27–28). Before her murder, Lady Macduff discovers herself contained "in this earthy world, where to do harm / Is often laudable, to do good sometime / Accounted dangerous folly" (4.2.74–76). Duncan's murdered body is viewed as a container: "Yet who would have thought the old man to have had so much blood in him?" Finally, throughout the play, Lady Macbeth talks of herself and her husband as containers. She says of her husband "Yet I do fear they nature / It is too full o' th' milk of human kindness / To catch the nearest way" (1.5.14–16). But she wishes for him to be empty of "human kindness" and to be filled with the liquid of her own spirits: "Hie thee hither / That I may pour my spirits in thine ear / And chastise with the valor of my tongue / All that impedes thee from the golden round" (1.4.23–26).

These examples highlight just a few of the many ways that we use our ideas about containers to conceptualize many aspects of human traits. Each of them makes sense to us, both as ordinary readers and experienced critics, because of our own embodied understanding of containment experiences, which give rise to a whole host of conventional metaphors seen in everyday language (e.g., "I fell in love with him, but was dumped two months later," in which we think of love, as we do many emotions, as a container that we are either in or out of). Cognitive linguists, unlike virtually all other metaphor theorists, have explicitly acknowledged the metaphorical links between conventional words and expressions and more creative, poetic language. An expanding body of research is exploring the connections between the body, conventional metaphors, and poetic language, all of which is consistent with the claim in hypothesis 2.

Another source of evidence on the metaphorical nature of thought related to hypothesis 2 comes from recent studies on polysemy, words that have multiple meanings that are systematically related. For example, the preposition "over" has more than 100 usages (Brugman & Lakoff, 1988). Some refer to specific physical schema such as the "above" meaning in "The bird flew over the house" and "The painting hangs over the fireplace" or the "cover" meaning in "The board is over the hole" and "The city clouded over." Other senses of "over" are figurative and exhibit the metaphorical projection of knowledge from a physical domain to a nonphysical or more abstract domain. For instance, "She has strange power over me" extends the "above" sense via the very common conceptual metaphor CONTROL IS UP; LACK OF CONTROL IS DOWN. Two different metaphors apply to "Sam was passed over for promotion." The first, CONTROL IS UP, LACK OF CONTROL IS DOWN implies that the person who passed over Sam was in control of Sam's status. The second common metaphor that applies here is CHOOSING IS TOUCHING, which implies that, because there was no physical contact between the person in control and Sam, Sam was not chosen. Both of these independently existing conceptual metaphors motivate why we can easily use "over" to refer to nonphysical domains of experience.

One might argue that the different meanings of polysemous words are really arbitrarily defined or just based on metaphors that are no longer part of our everyday thinking. Consider the following simple expressions: "I see what you mean." "That's a very clear argument." "What's your outlook on this project?" "The argument looks different from my point of view." "Let me point out something to you in her argument." "Tell me no more, I've got the whole picture."

Conventional examples such as these are often seen as classic cases of dead metaphors, although, again, the historical evidence suggests that conceptual metaphors might facilitate the extension of physical senses to nonphysical ones for words like "see" (Sweetser, 1990). This does not mean that polysemous words are necessarily motivated by conceptual metaphors in contemporary speakers' minds. Nonetheless, very few ordinary speakers would disagree with the idea that we conceptualize and talk about intellectual activities in terms of vision (i.e., UNDERSTANDING IS SEEING). Conceptual metaphors thus partially motivate why we talk about understanding or knowing in terms of "seeing" things. This metaphorical mapping of our knowledge about human vision onto the domain of understanding or knowing is not temporary but is very much a part of our everyday conceptual system.

My discussion of just some of the linguistic evidence in favor of hypothesis 2 is based on the idea that linguistic analyses, such as these described here, reflect something about speakers'/hearers' presumed cognition. What is meant by "presumed" is that some hypothetical speakers/listeners employ conceptual metaphors in thinking of different, abstract concepts. It is less clear whether ordinary speakers actually structure their concepts this way or access metaphorical knowledge automatically in reasoning and ordinary language use. The best way to draw this inference is to propose a slightly different hypothesis, presented next, on the interaction of metaphor in thought and language.

Hypothesis 3: *Metaphoric thought motivates real-life, contemporary speakers' use and understanding of why various words and expressions mean what they do.* Getting evidence in support of this hypothesis requires experimental methods that employ hypothetical-deductive research strategies (especially in regard to explicitly falsifying hypotheses).

In fact, various psycholinguistic evidence supports the idea that metaphors such as ANGER IS HEATED FLUID IN A CONTAINER are really conceptual and part of how ordinary people think of many concepts and not, more simply, just generalizations of linguistic meaning. These include studies that have examined people's mental imagery for idioms (Gibbs & O'Brien, 1990), proverbs (Gibbs, Strom, & Spivey-Knowlton, 1997), context-sensitive use of idioms (Nayak & Gibbs, 1990; Gibbs & Nayak, 1991) and euphemistic phrases (Pfaff, Gibbs, & Johnson, 1997), folk understanding of how the source domains in conceptual metaphors constrain what idioms and proverbs mean (Gibbs, 1992; Gibbs & Beitel, 1985), use of conceptual metaphors in organizing information in text processing (Allbritton, McKoon, & Gerrig, 1995), and use of conceptual metaphors in drawing inferences when reading poetic metaphors (Gibbs & Nascimento, 1996).

Each of these psycholinguistic studies employs different experimental methods to assess whether (a) people conceptualize of certain topics via metaphor, and (b) whether conceptual metaphors assist people in making sense of why verbal expressions, particularly idioms and metaphors, mean what they do. It is important to note that not every methodology available to contemporary psychologists is amenable to studying the psychological validity of hypothesis 3. For instance, in various unpublished research I have attempted to ask people to verbally paraphrase poetic metaphors in several experiments without finding much evidence that people consistently refer to conceptual metaphors in doing this task (see McGlone, 1996, also discussed later). Moreover, it is also important to recognize that methods used to study certain aspects of metaphor in thought and language do not apply to all aspects of how concepts are understood or how all aspects of language are understood. For example, using mental imagery to examine the possible constraining influence of metaphor in motivating aspects of idioms' or proverbs' meanings (see Gibbs & O'Brien, 1990; Gibbs, Bogdonovich, Sykes, & Barr, 1997) does not imply that people ordinarily create mental images when they read or hear idioms, proverbs, or verbal metaphors in conversation. Similarly, the fact that people can, when asked, make judgments about the similarity of meaning between idioms and their putative underlying conceptual metaphors (Nayak & Gibbs, 1990) does not imply that people always instantiate conceptual metaphors when processing idioms. Not every method is useful for assessing metaphor in thought and language.

I will not go into detail about the positive evidence just cited on conceptual metaphor in figurative language use (see Gibbs, 1994, and more recent articles). I do wish to talk about some of the criticism offered by cognitive psychologists about various aspects of this psycholinguistic work. Murphy (1996) raises several critical points in a recently published article. He dismisses many of the psycholinguistic studies as irrelevant to how people conceptualize the concepts to which various linguistic expressions refer. After all, these studies address only the metaphorical nature of how specific linguistic expressions are understood and represented. These studies specifically do not, in Murphy's view, examine people's nonlinguistic understanding of particular concepts. Thus, one should not conclude from these empirical studies that people necessarily non-linguistically conceptualize certain concepts (e.g., anger) in terms of metaphor. All the data suggest, if anything, is how people's talk about certain topics is influenced by metaphor. The underlying mental representation for abstract concepts may have little to do with metaphor (Murphy, 1996).

In my reply to Murphy, I acknowledged the need for nonlinguistic data on metaphorical concepts and argued that some of my work demonstrates a convincing link between nonlinguistic understanding of certain concepts and linguistic understanding of conventional phrases used to talk about these concepts (Gibbs, 1996). For example, in one set of studies I specifically examined whether complex idiomatic meanings can be partly predicted based on the independent assessment of people's nonlinguistic, and in part, embodied, understanding of particular source domains (Gibbs, 1992). I noted that cognitive linguistic work suggests that people make sense of idioms such as ''blow your stack,'' ''flip your lid,'' and ''hit the ceiling'' because, so it is argued, they metaphorically conceptualize anger in terms of heated fluid in a container (i.e., ANGER IS HEATED FLUID IN A CONTAINER) (Kovecses, 1986; Lakoff, 1987). Even though the existence of this conceptual metaphor does not predict that certain idioms or conventional expressions *must* appear in the language, its presence provides a partial motivation for why specific phrases (e.g., ''blow your stack,'' ''get pissed off'') are used to refer to particular events (e.g., getting very angry).

My experimental strategy to see if this might be true was to make specific predictions about what various idioms, say those motivated by ANGER IS HEATED FLUID IN A CONTAINER, actually mean by looking at the inferences that arise from the mapping of people's nonlinguistic knowledge of heated fluid in a container onto the idea of anger. To do this, I asked participants about their understanding of events corresponding to particular source domains in various conceptual metaphors (e.g., the source domain of heated fluid in a container for ANGER IS HEATED FLUID IN A CONTAINER). For instance, participants were asked to imagine the embodied experience of a sealed container filled with fluid, and then they were asked something about causation (e.g., What would cause the container to explode?), intentionality (e.g., Does the container explode on purpose or does it explode through no volition of its own?), and manner (e.g., Does the explosion of the container occur in a gentle or a violent manner?).

Participants gave highly consistent responses to these questions, noting that the cause of a sealed container exploding its contents out is the internal pressure caused by the increase in the heat of the fluid inside the container, that this explosion is unintentional because containers and fluid have no intentional agency, and that the explosion occurs in a violent manner. My claim is that these responses provide a rough, nonlinguistic profile of people's understanding of a particular source domain concept. These profiles are rough approximations of what cognitive linguists and others refer to as the *image-schematic structures* of the source domains (Gibbs & Colston, 1995; Lakoff, 1990; Turner, 1991,

1996). In this study, by the way, nothing was said to the participants about idioms or any other kind of language. These individuals provided only their intuitions about different nonlinguistic experience.

With these different nonlinguistic profiles about certain abstract concepts, I then tried to predict something about people's understanding of idioms. My idea was that people's intuitions about various source domains map onto their conceptualizations of different target domains in very predictable ways. Not surprisingly, when people understand anger idioms, such as "blow your stack," "flip your lid," or "hit the ceiling," they infer that the cause of anger is internal pressure, that the expression of anger is unintentional, and that it is done is an abrupt, violent manner. People do not draw the same inferences about causation, intentionality, and manner when comprehending literal paraphrases of idioms, such as "get very angry." Additional experiments showed that people find idioms to be more appropriate and easier to understand when they are seen in discourse contexts consistent with the various entailments of these phrases, which, again, were predicted in advance from the nonlinguistic analysis of the source domain concepts.

Several important conclusions can be drawn from these psycholinguistic studies on the interaction of metaphor in thought and language. First, these psycholinguistic studies are significant for hypothesis 3 because they provide independent, nonlinguistic ways of predicting something about the specific metaphorical meanings of some linguistic expressions. In this sense, psycholinguistic evidence is available to suggest that people tacitly conceptualize certain concepts in metaphorical ways and this enables them to make sense of various conventional phrases' meanings (see Gibbs & Nascimento, 1996, for evidence relating to people's motivated understanding of creative, poetic metaphors).

Another important conclusion is that the data described here generally provide experimental evidence in support of the idea that the mapping of source-to-target domain information in conceptual metaphors preserves the image-schematic structure, or cognitive topology, of the source domains (Lakoff, 1990; Turner, 1991). One of the major concerns with metaphoric thought is to describe exactly how source domain information is mapped into target domain knowledge in metaphor (whether it be conceptual metaphors or linguistic metaphors). A significant amount of empirical research is devoted to this topic, and several major alternative accounts explain how these mappings are accomplished (Katz, 1992). I will not attempt in this chapter to survey the different alternative accounts (see Gibbs, 1994). Nonetheless, the idea that image-schematic structure is preserved in metaphorical mappings is an interesting concept that has important implications for the question of where metaphor comes from and how various concepts are metaphorically structured in human cognition. I shall address both of these topics in two of the following sections.

Finally, these psychological findings are hard to reconcile with the view that the figurative meanings of idioms are determined only on the basis of their individual lexical items or for arbitrary, or historically opaque reasons (cf. Keysar & Bly, 1995; Murphy, 1996; Stock et al., 1993). Contemporary speakers appear to have tacit intuitions about their metaphorical understanding of certain abstract concepts that leads them to talk about these concepts in particular metaphoric ways. No other theory of idiomaticity comes close to being able to describe exactly why idioms have very specific meanings for contemporary speakers or why people appear to quickly draw specific inferences about what idioms mean.

I think that at least some of my psycholinguistic evidence is germane to the question of whether links exist between metaphorical thought and language. Nonetheless, various other criticisms have very recently been raised about other aspects of the psycholinguistic studies described here. One criticism is that asking people about their intuitions about why idioms mean what they do is an unreliable way of examining the conceptual foundations for figurative meaning. Much of what a person believes about why idioms, and other conventional expressions, mean what they do, depends on their knowledge of the stipulated (i.e., historically given) figurative meaning of the phrase and does not depend on recognizing something about the possible conceptual metaphors that give rise to idioms and conventional expressions in the first place. This view acknowledges that metaphors might play a role in the historical evolution of idiomatic meaning (hypothesis 1), but ordinary speakers primarily understand why the parts of idioms mean what they do because they *first* learn the individual meaning for entire idiom phrases and only *then* infer something about what the parts might mean (Keysar & Bly, 1994; Nunberg, Sag, & Wasow, 1994; Stock et al., 1993), all of which presumably gives rise to idioms with specific figurative meanings.

One recently published set of experiments tested this general idea by first having people learn either the original or opposite meanings of unfamiliar idioms (e.g., for the idiom "The goose hangs high" meaning either "things look good," its original meaning, or "things look bad") (Keysar & Bly, 1995). Later on, when participants were asked to rate whether an idiom's meaning made sense, the learned meanings were generally perceived as being more transparent than the nonlearned meanings. Significantly, this result was obtained whether the original meaning of the idiom was stipulated or not. In other words, if people were told that the meaning of "The goose hangs high" is "things look bad," when in fact its original meaning was "things look good," they believed that the meaning presented to them originally made more sense as best capturing the idiom's meaning. Keysar and Bly (1995) interpreted these findings to suggest that methodologies that assess people's intuitions about why idioms mean what they do should not be trusted. This includes data from Gibbs (1992) and other studies showing that people's intuitions about the meanings of idioms appear to be explained, to some extent, by their knowledge of conceptual metaphors.

Part of the difficulty I have in assessing the importance of Keysar and Bly's (1995) findings is that the vast majority of the idioms they studied are based on metonymy, not metaphor. Thus, the phrase "The goose hangs high" means "things look good" because the act of hanging a dead goose up for all to see metonymically stands for an entire sequence of events leading up to the successful slaughter of the goose for food. Contemporary speakers often have great difficulty explaining why metonymically based idioms mean what they do, even for widely used expressions. For example, consider the classic idiom "kick the bucket." If you ask contemporary speakers about why this phrase means "to die," few speakers report that it refers to the method of slaughtering hogs where the animal was strung up on a wooden frame and its throat cut. "Bucket" is thought by historical linguists to be an English corruption of "buquet," a French word for the wooden frame that the hog kicked in its death struggle. Thus, the hog's act of kicking the "buquet," which turned into kick the "bucket," metonymically stands for the entire series of events in capturing and slaughtering hogs.

My claim is that Keysar and Bly's (1995) data have no bearing on the issue of contemporary speakers' tacit understanding of metaphoric thought and language because they have not examined people's potential use of conceptual metaphors in making sense of idioms. We still must pay attention to the psychological evidence, obtained using a variety of tasks, that appears consistent with the idea that people make sense of idioms precisely because of their metaphorical knowledge of various concepts.

A different study that raises questions for some of the earlier data on idioms examined Italian speakers' mental images for Italian idioms (Cacciari & Glucksberg, 1995). Using a procedure similar to that used by Gibbs and O'Brien (1990), Cacciari and Glucksberg presented participants with different idioms and asked them to describe their mental images for these expressions. Participants overwhelmingly produced images based on the idioms' concrete literal meaning. Cacciari and Glucksberg suggest that these concrete literal images do not directly reflect anything about idiomatic meanings or the conceptual metaphors that might underlie many idioms. Thus, it is premature to assume, as do Gibbs and O'Brien (1990), that an analysis of people's mental images for idioms uncovers the constraining influence of metaphorical thought.

But Gibbs and O'Brien (1990) did not claim that ordinary speakers' mental images for idioms were simply based on what idioms figuratively mean or even the conceptual metaphors underlying idiomatic phrases. In fact, they found, similar to Cacciari and Glucksberg (1995), that people primarily form very concrete, literal images for American idioms (e.g., "blow your stack"). What's more interesting, though, is that people's mental images across different idioms (e.g., "blow your stack," "flip your lid," or "hit the ceiling") are highly consistent (e.g., some force acts to release the internal pressure of a container in a violent manner). We showed that this consistency is not due to these phrases having similar figurative meanings, but can be explained in terms of the idea that each idiom is motivated by a similar conceptual metaphor (e.g., ANGER IS HEATED FLUID IN A CONTAINER). These conceptual metaphors form part of the link between idiomatic phrases and their overall figurative meanings. In this way, the data from mental imagery tasks appear relevant to hypothesis 3. Of course, people do not ordinarily form mental images when processing familiar idioms in discourse. Yet the mental imagery task can be employed to demonstrate the constraining influence of conceptual metaphors in motivating speakers' intuitions about why particular idiomatic phrases have their specific figurative meanings.

A third set of studies whose results were interpreted as contrary to hypothesis 3 is reported by McGlone (1996). Participants in a first experiment paraphrased verbal metaphors, such as "The lecture was a three-course meal." Only 24% of these paraphrases contained any references consistent with underlying conceptual metaphors, such as IDEAS ARE FOOD. Even when participants were asked to give figurative paraphrases of the verbal metaphors, they still most frequently produced paraphrases inconsistent with related conceptual metaphors. Thus, when given the verbal metaphor "Dr. Moreland's lecture was a three-course meal for the mind," only a third of the paraphrases mentioned source domain terms (e.g., "food") related to the conceptual metaphor IDEAS ARE FOOD. Nonetheless, almost all of the metaphorical paraphrases reflected some recognition of the stereotypical properties of three-course meals that might be attributed to lectures, such as "large quantity," and "variety." A third study asked participants to rate the similarity between different metaphorical expressions. The data showed that people do not perceive expressions motivated by conceptual metaphor to be any more similar in meaning than they did expressions motivated by different conceptual metaphors. Thus, "Dr. Moreland's lecture was steak for the mind" was not seen as more similar to "Dr. Moreland's lecture was a three-course meal for the mind" than was "Dr. Moreland's lecture was a full tank of gas for the mind." A final study showed that conceptual metaphors consistent with a verbal metaphor were not better recall cues than were unrelated cues for participants trying to remember the verbal metaphors. Overall, the findings from these studies were taken to imply that people's interpretations of verbal metaphors are not necessarily related to their putative, underlying conceptual metaphors.

McGlone rightly acknowledges that his studies do not present verbal metaphors in a context in which these conceptual metaphors might become more apparent, nor did the studies employ on-line measures of linguistic processing.

In this regard, similar to the studies that support hypothesis 3, McGlone's data have no specific bearing on whether metaphor plays a role in the immediate comprehension of verbal metaphors (see hypothesis 4).

I think McGlone's data are interesting in many respects, although they are not especially surprising. First, it is not clear that having people verbally paraphrase a metaphor is the best method for tapping into different types of possibly metaphorical knowledge that might be used when people interpret, or make sense of, verbal metaphors. After all, other empirical methods have shown some influence of conceptual metaphors on comprehension of, at least, idiomatic and proverbial phrases. One should not imply that the failure to find effects using one task invalidates the positive evidence in favor of hypothesis 3 using different tasks unless some principled reasons are given for preferring one task over another. Paraphrase tasks are notoriously insensitive as measures of people's, especially children's, ability to understand metaphors (see Gibbs, 1994, chap. 9 for a review of the data on this).

It could also very well be the case that people are less able to access, or simply do not access, conceptual metaphors when interpreting novel linguistic metaphors (e.g., ''Prof. Moreland's lecture was a three-course meal for the mind''), whereas conceptual metaphors are used in making sense of the specific figurative meanings of highly familiar idioms, such as ''John blew his stack.'' Other evidence, nevertheless, demonstrates that people refer quite regularly to conceptual metaphors when interpreting poetry (Gibbs & Nascimento, 1996).

I question, then, whether McGlone's failure to find positive evidence in support of the conceptual metaphor view implies that all the other evidence in support of hypothesis 3 should be dismissed. At the very least, though, we need more work like McGlone's for the simple reason that psychologists too often are critical of the conceptual metaphor view without actually conducting studies to assess whether specific metaphorical mappings (e.g., LOVE IS A JOURNEY, IDEAS ARE FOOD) have a role in linguistic understanding.

In general, a significant amount of experimental research has been conducted to examine whether conceptual metaphors play some role in how people make sense of many verbal expressions or consciously interpret these phrases. Several recent studies take issue with the claim of hypothesis 3, but I think it fair to say that a preponderance of the evidence supports this hypothesis.

Hypothesis 4: *Metaphoric thought functions in people's immediate on-line use and understanding of linguistic meaning.* Although preexisting conceptual metaphors appear to influence many aspects of how people make sense of idiomatic meaning, some scholars have criticized the conceptual metaphor approach as a theory of immediate metaphor, proverb, and idiom comprehension (Glucksberg & Keysar, 1990; Glucksberg, Keysar, & McGlone, 1992; Glucksberg et al., 1993; Honeck & Temple, 1994; Kreuz & Graesser, 1991). These researchers argue that even though prestored metaphorical mappings may be available, such knowledge may not always be accessible and ordinarily used in any given context. One recent set of studies, for example, showed that conceptual metaphors influence people's judgments of the appropriateness of idioms in different contexts, but do not appear to be accessed during immediate idiom comprehension, at least as measured by global reading times for idioms in different metaphoric contexts (Glucksberg et al., 1993; but see Pfaff et al., 1997, for positive evidence on the role of conceptual metaphor in processing euphemistic statements).

Hypothesis 4 is of greatest interest to psychologists because of their desire to provide detailed theories of the moment-by-moment processes that operate when language is immediately comprehended. Explaining how on-line language processing operates is, indeed, one of the most important theoretical goals in cognitive science. But let me note here that characterizing on-line processing provides only one aspect of what it means to understand language. As suggested by hypothesis 3, the ability to make sense of *why* some word or phrase means what it does is a different, but still critical, part of how people use language. Psycholinguists mostly ignore this and other aspects of language understanding and consequently fail to explore significant links between thought and language.

In any event, let us consider some of the possible ways that people may use conceptual metaphors in understanding various kinds of metaphorical language. First, imagine that one hears the idiomatic expression ''John blew his stack'' in a conversation in which it is clear that the speaker's intended meaning is roughly ''John got very angry.'' As noted earlier, the figurative meaning of ''blew his stack'' is partly motivated by the conceptual metaphor ANGER IS HEATED FLUID IN A CONTAINER. The question here is to what extent do people compute or access some conceptual representation for ANGER IS HEATED FLUID IN A CONTAINER when they immediately process the figurative meaning of ''John blew his stack.''

One series of recently completed experiments demonstrates that people appear to compute or access metaphorical representations during their immediate understanding of idioms like blew his stack (Gibbs, Bogdonovich, et al., 1997). In these studies, participants read stories ending with idioms and then quickly gave lexical decision responses to visually presented letter-strings that reflected either something about the conceptual metaphors underlying these idioms (e.g., ''heat'' for ANGER IS HEATED FLUID IN A CONTAINER, having just read ''John blew his stack'') or letter-strings that were unrelated to these conceptual metaphors (e.g., ''lead''). There were two important findings. First, people were faster to make these lexical decision responses to the related metaphor targets (i.e., ''heat'') having just read idioms than they were to either literal paraphrases of idioms (e.g., ''John got very angry'') or control phrases (e.g., phrases still appropriate to the context such as ''John saw many dents''). Second, people having read idioms were faster in recognizing related metaphorical targets than

unrelated ones, but not literal paraphrases or control p
results suggests that people are immediately computin
something related to the conceptual metaphor ANGER IS F
TAINER when they read idioms. In another experiment,
to make lexical decision responses to metaphor targe
read an idiom motivated by a similar conceptual metapl
stack'') than an idiom with roughly the same figurativ
by a different conceptual metaphor (e.g., "John bit her head off," which is
motivated by the conceptual metaphor ANGER IS ANIMAL BEHAVIOR). And people
were faster to respond to related targets having read idioms motivated by similar
conceptual metaphors than when they read idioms motivated by different conceptual metaphors. Again, it appears that people compute or access the relevant
conceptual metaphor for an idiom during some aspect of their processing of
these phrases.

My interpretation of the Gibbs, Bogdonovich, et al. (1997) idiom studies has
been appropriately conservative. First, because participants made their lexical
decision responses after reading and understanding the idiom phrases, their faster
reaction times to the targets, having read idioms, as opposed to literal or control
phrases, do not directly imply that people actually compute or access conceptual
metaphors precisely when they are actively processing the meanings of idioms
in real-time. Many psycholinguists argue that the best method for determining
immediate comprehension processes is to use on-line tasks, such as a cross-
modal priming paradigm in which participants make lexical decisions to visually
presented targets while they are still listening to, or just finished listening to,
words or phrases of interest (see Simpson, 1994, and Tabossi & Zardon, 1995,
for reviews of these studies). But our decision in Gibbs, Bogdonovich, et al.
(1997) to initially look at idiom processing using an all-visual paradigm was
prompted by our desire to make sure that people had actually understood the
idioms they were reading (indicated by their pushing a comprehension button)
before assessing whether some conceptual metaphor had been activated. After
all, one would not wish to conclude that conceptual metaphors were not immediately computed or accessed during idiom understanding if participants had
not completed their comprehension of these figurative phrases. Our idiom results
should be interpreted only to suggest that conceptual metaphors seem to be
activated either during or soon after idioms are understood.

A second point about the Gibbs, Bogdonovich, et al. (1997) findings is that
they do not tell us whether people must compute or access an idiom's underlying
conceptual metaphor in order to interpret what that idiom figuratively means.
Thus, it is not clear that people must compute or access the conceptual metaphor
ANGER IS HEATED FLUID IN A CONTAINER to comprehend the figurative meaning
of idioms such as "blew his stack" or "hit the ceiling." Although the psycholinguistic evidence from earlier studies clearly implies that people often make

idioms precisely because of their knowledge of conceptual metaphors s, 1992; Gibbs & O'Brien, 1990; Nayak & Gibbs, 1990), there is no dence, including the data from Gibbs, Bogdonovich et al. (1997), to specifically conclude that conceptual metaphors must be activated to figure out an idiom during on-line language processing. This conservative conclusion makes good sense given that people often are familiar with many idioms, conventional expressions, and certain poetic phrases and thus need not struggle to create meanings for these phrases each and every time they encounter them in discourse.

A third aspect of the Gibbs, Bogdonovich et al. (1997) data to keep in mind is that even if people compute or access conceptual metaphors quickly during idiom processing, this does not imply that all of the entailments one might draw because of the source (HEATED FLUID IN A CONTAINER) to target (ANGER) mapping are also accessed. The reaction-time findings merely show that some aspects of the underlying conceptual metaphor ANGER IS HEATED FLUID IN A CONTAINER is present soon after people understand idioms like "blew his stack." It is unclear at what point people begin to draw some of the complex entailments associated with a conceptual metaphor (e.g., inferences having to do with causation, intentionality, consequences, and so forth) when they hear or read idioms. I say this even though other evidence shows that people appear to draw at least some of these complex inferences when reading idioms (Gibbs, 1992).

The final caveat about the Gibbs, Bogdonovich, et al. (1997) findings is that they do not tell us whether people actively compute metaphoric representations or merely access in an associative manner preexisting conceptual metaphors. When people read an idiomatic expression like "John blew his stack," they may very well quickly access the conceptual metaphor ANGER IS HEATED FLUID IN A CONTAINER given that this metaphor is so closely tied to the idiom, even if one does not need the metaphor to actually understand what the idiom means in discourse. People may not actually compute from scratch a source (HEATED FLUID IN A CONTAINER) to target (ANGER) domain mapping, and draw all the complex set of inferences associated with the conceptual metaphor, during ordinary idiom understanding.

There are several other possibilities about the role of metaphoric representations in language understanding that must be considered. I mentioned that people may not need to compute or access conceptual metaphors to understand what idioms mean, given their familiarity with the meanings of these phrases. But it is quite possible that people must compute or access conceptual metaphors precisely to make immediate sense of more creative, innovative, metaphorical language. This may occur via the computational re-creation of the conceptual metaphor (i.e., mapping source domain information onto target domain knowledge) or from the activation of the preexisting conceptual metaphors.

Of course, people may access conceptual metaphors more quickly when understanding idioms than when they read novel linguistic metaphors because of the highly conventionalized, tight link between idioms and conceptual metaphors. This might be especially true given that most conceptual metaphors give rise to several different idiomatic or conventional expressions. For example, the conceptual metaphor ANGER IS HEATED FLUID IN A CONTAINER gives rise to many idiomatic and conventional expressions, including, but not limited to, "blew his stack," "hit the ceiling," "flip your lid," "get hot under the collar," "blow off steam," and so forth. The frequency with which idioms are used and recognized as being motivated by conceptual metaphors might make these conceptual metaphors more salient and more accessible when idioms are heard or read.

People may also infer an underlying conceptual metaphor for a poetic metaphor sometime after some initial interpretation for this linguistic expression has been understood. In this situation, a reader, for instance, may comprehend the meaning of a verbal metaphor and then recognize how it links with preexisting conceptual metaphors. Recognizing that a particular verbal metaphor relates to a specific conceptual metaphor could enable readers to create a richer set of meanings for the verbal expression once the entailments of the conceptual metaphor are applied to the initial meanings of the poetic metaphor.

Additional psycholinguistic experiments must be conducted before more definitive answers can be given to these other possibilities on how conceptual metaphors are used during immediate linguistic understanding (hypothesis 4). My honest impression is that it might be difficult to design appropriate on-line studies needed to settle some of these theoretical issues. Most of the existing on-line methodologies were originally created to look at lexical processes in sentence comprehension (see Simpson, 1994, for a good review). The time needed for participants to make judgments for most words and phrases reflecting more complex inferences possible during ordinary and literary language processing might be too slow and thus involve more conscious, strategic processes rather than tap into more immediate cognitive and linguistic processes. At the very least, it is fair to say that the kinds of methods available to linguists and philosophers are not appropriate for assessing on-line cognitive processes in figurative language understanding. We should be cautious, then, in interpreting the cognitive linguistic analyses when evaluating claims about immediate, or automatic, linguistic processing.

THE REPRESENTATION OF METAPHORICAL CONCEPTS

Part of the fight over whether metaphors exist in thought and not just language focuses on the possible mental representation of metaphorical concepts. As noted earlier, cognitive linguists often argue that metaphor is best understood as a mental mapping that helps structure vague, abstract concepts in terms of familiar, concrete knowledge domains. Cognitive psychologists often take issue with these general claims. Murphy (1996), for example, attempted to evaluate the psychological validity of metaphoric representations. He identifies two possible hypotheses about the role of metaphor in conceptual representation. The *strong view* proposes that many concepts are not understood via their own representations but by metaphorical connections to knowledge in different domains. For instance, people have not an independent, nonmetaphorical concept for love, but one closely connected via metaphorical links to other, truly independent concepts such as journeys. The *weak view* proposes that people have well-developed, independent concepts, but these are often metaphorically linked to other concepts with similar structure. Thus, people have a distinct, nonmetaphorical concept for love, but this concept has well-established connections to distinct concepts from different domains of experience, like journeys, which are structured similarly in that both source and target domain concepts share similar underlying attributes or relations.

Murphy raises several problems with the strong view and generally favors some version of the weak view. For instance, Murphy finds it problematic that many abstract concepts have several metaphors presumably structuring their mental representations. According to cognitive linguistics analyses, the concept of love, for example, can be understood through several different metaphors (e.g., LOVE IS A JOURNEY, LOVE IS INSANITY, LOVE IS AN OPPONENT, LOVE IS A VALUABLE COMMODITY). The entailments of these different metaphors vary in certain respects. Thus, LOVE IS A JOURNEY refers to the structure of a love relationship over time, whereas LOVE IS AN OPPONENT personifies love as an opponent against whom we often struggle. These different metaphors appear to be inconsistent with one another at times, and it is unclear, in Murphy's view, how one resolves such inconsistencies in the mental representation for our concept of love. Murphy warns that the multiple metaphors structuring our concept of love leave no room for all of them to co-exist. He notes that different metaphors may highlight different aspects of a concept, but rejects this possibility because there are too many conflicts between different metaphors for each of them to structure the same concept.

This criticism of multiple metaphors assumes an objectivist view of mental representations in which the attributes of each concept must fit together like pieces of a jigsaw puzzle. But there is no special reason why human conceptual systems must be like jigsaw puzzles. And there is no justification for assuming that concepts must be monolithic entities. Why cannot people possess alternative ways of construing the same experience, such as being in love? A good deal of linguistic, psychological, and anthropological evidence shows that each of us may make sense of certain experiences in different metaphorical ways at different times. This seems to be especially true for experiences or ideas that do not come with a clearly delineated structure of their own (Lakoff, 1987). The fact that people possess alternative, metaphorical models of many experiences and abstract ideas is not at all a problem because two different conceptualizations are often needed to solve different types of real-world problems (see Gentner & Gentner, 1983, for an example of how different metaphors for electricity are needed to solve different electricity problems).

The so-called problem of multiple metaphors for concepts can be easily handled if we view concepts not as fixed, static structures but as temporary, dynamic, and context-dependent representations. Under this view, concepts are not stable structures stored in long-term memory but are temporary constructions in working memory created on the spot from generic and episodic information in long-term memory. Because temporary conceptualizations are doing the traditional work of concepts in controlling categorization behavior, it is important to refer to these as *concepts,* and to use *knowledge* in referring to the body of information in long-term memory from which concepts are constructed (Barsalou, 1993). The results of several lines of research on relatively concrete items indicate that substantial flexibility exists in how people conceptualize the same category on different occasions (Barsalou, 1987, 1993). Different people store highly similar information for a category in long-term memory, and this information remains quite stable within individuals over time. Yet the significant flexibility shown in many experiments on defining categories arises not from differences in knowledge but from differences in the retrieval of this knowledge from long-term memory. On different occasions, different individuals retrieve different subsets of features from their extensive knowledge of a category. In the same way, an individual may retrieve different aspects of his or her knowledge of a category on different occasions.

If we view concepts as dynamic, temporary representations, then we can easily understand how different metaphorical mappings might operate to help people make sense of their experiences and solve different problems in their everyday lives. The LOVE IS A JOURNEY metaphor might be used to create a particular conceptualization of love in certain situations, while LOVE IS AN OPPONENT might be more appropriate to use in forming a concept in other situations. One anthropological study of how Americans view their marriages over time revealed significant conceptual flexibility in that some metaphors for marriage seem best at some times during the relationship but not others (Quinn, 1991). These alternative ways of thinking about human concepts allow, even encourage, the use of multiple metaphors to access different aspects of our rich knowledge about love or marriage to differentially conceptualize these experiences at various moments of our experience. Each metaphoric construal of a concept in some context results in an independent, yet still metaphorical concept.

Although metaphorical concepts may be temporary representations, conceptual metaphors may still be represented as part of knowledge in long-term memory. The frequent instantiation of conventional metaphorical mappings (e.g., LIFE

IS A JOURNEY) in creating concepts might result in encoding of these mappings as part of our permanent knowledge. These permanent conceptual metaphors might be represented in a relatively complex manner so that all of the typical entailments of these metaphorical mappings are explicitly encoded. This idea seems especially reasonable given that the source domains for many conceptual metaphors arise from recurring patterns of embodied experiences (see the later section on embodied meaning), information that would also likely be part of the repository of thoughts, impressions, experiences, and factual knowledge that makes up our long-term memory. We clearly need detailed studies of specific concepts to see which aspects of concepts are metaphoric and which are not. I believe that the methodologies of cognitive psychology, linguistics, and anthropology can each make a own unique contribution to this effort.

DISTINGUISH METAPHOR PROCESSING FROM PROCESSING METAPHOR

I want to mention another topic about metaphor in thought and language that deserves special consideration. For the most part, metaphor scholars have been interested in defining metaphor and exploring how people interpret metaphorical language. Yet we should pay attention not only to how people process metaphorical language but to how people use *metaphor processing* as a general mode of understanding that can be applied to any kind of situation or language. For instance, in many cases, especially in reading allegorical literature, a specific metaphoric processing is given to a particular text. When readers adopt such strategies, the processing that occurs is metaphoric even though there is no special linguistic or textual material that might be viewed as metaphorical. Many poems and classic texts, such as Dante's *Divine Comedy* or Melville's *Moby Dick,* are best understood and appreciated as strongly allegorical once they are interpreted metaphorically. Many children's fairy tales can clearly be metaphorically analyzed as referring to domains of experience quite outside the local characters and situations in these stories. Children hearing stories such as ''Snow White,'' ''The Three little Pigs,'' ''Hansel and Gretel,'' and ''Rapunzel'' appear to make allegorical connections between the characters and events in these tales and their own lives.

Consider the story of ''Pinocchio.'' In this classic story, the moral problems the central character faces are conveyed in a physical dimension. The story is dominated by three central themes: ''if you tell a fib your nose will grow,'' ''listen to your conscience,'' and ''be a good boy.'' Each theme reflects an underlying conceptual metaphor of progressively more abstract terms: the nose as measure of truth, the conscience as audible agent, and goodness as humanity. Each metaphor in the fantasy is reified. Pinocchio's nose grows. His conscience is personified as an invisible, but audible creature (i.e., Jiminy Cricket in the Walt Disney movie). Finally, having become good, Pinocchio turns into a real boy; his humanity reifies his morality. This reification gives the story its poignancy and its enduring quality as a classic tale.

Literary critics have often noted that the best allegories were written in times of spiritual speculation (e.g., Dante in the Middle Ages, Bunyan in the Puritan period, Hawthorne and Melville during nineteenth-century American transcendentalism, and Kafka in the twentieth century). In the second half of the twentieth century, many Southern novelists and playwrights (e.g., Faulkner, McCullers, O'Connor, Williams) created allegorical literature with strong ties to biblical themes, mostly attempting to deal with the metaphysical issues of humanity's search for God and some understanding of our own struggles in life. These stories reveal our strong need to conceptualize our lives in terms of metaphor, as shown in the writings of great authors, and in our ability as novice readers and experienced critics to engage in metaphorical processing (see Turner, 1996, for an extended argument on the importance of parables in human cognition).

To give another example, a significant part of how we interpret poetry must be explained in terms of metaphor processing (and not just processing metaphor). Consider these two stanzas from a poem by Adrienne Rich titled "Diving into the Wreck" (Rich, 1973).

First having read the book of myths,
and loaded the camera,
and checked the edge of the knife-blade,
I put on
the body-armour of black rubber
the absurd flippers
the grave and awkward mask.
I am having to do this
not like Cousteau with his
assiduous team
aboard the sun-flooded schooner
but here alone.

I came to explore the wreck.
The words are purposes.
The words are maps.
I came to see the damage that was done
and the treasures that prevail.
I stroke the beam of my lamp
slowly along the flank
of something more permanent
than fish or weed

This poem allegorically presents a modern hero. Rich adopts as her motif the actions of a fully equipped scuba diver, who goes alone into the sea to explore a sunken ship for any precious cargo. The diver's careful preparation for the dive emphasizes the solitariness of her actions, and the diving into the depths illustrates the archetypal motif of the male hero on a valiant journey, such as Beowulf's undersea journey to seek vengeance on Grendel's mother. Like Beowulf, the diver in Rich's poem goes down into the water and experiences the power that comes with the heroic venture. But unlike the story of Beowulf, and other traditional stories of male heroes, this story has no battle. Instead, there is a slow ease to the exploration of the diver. Rich is, in effect, creating a new myth, not predicated on a male's power over a woman, but entering into a new feminine world, as if one is entering the womb of a mother, sister, or lover.

Later in the poem, Rich defines a new character, a merging of the masculine and feminine:

> There is the place.
> And I am here, this mermaid whose dark hair
> streams black, the merman in his armored body
> We circle silently about the wreck
> we dive into the hold.
> I am she: I am he

The diver now appears androgynous, and Rich asks us to consider the two sides' harmonious behavior as we, in our own solitude, undertake our own journeys.

Much of our understanding and appreciation of literature and poetry, as illustrated in this brief analysis of ''Pinocchio'' and Rich's poem ''Diving into the Wreck,'' requires that we draw metaphorical connections between concrete source domains (e.g., the description of diving to explore a wreck) to unmentioned, but inferred, target domains (e.g., the joys and perils of taking risks in our own life's journeys). Some literary theorists have noted how it is possible to produce a poetic reading of a poem or text precisely because of a reader's explicitly literary way of interpreting it (Lodge, 1977; Steen, 1994; Wellek & Warren, 1949). Metaphoric processing, as opposed to processing metaphoric language, may be distinguished as an intentionally selected strategy of reading (Sateen, 1994). In this way, metaphor may legitimately be viewed as one type of literary strategy that colors people's imaginative understanding of texts and real-world situations.

Of course, it is quite possible that people, at least in some situations, might immediately, and nonstrategically, begin to metaphorically process a text or situation. What triggers this type of processing in the absence of explicit verbal metaphors is somewhat unclear. Yet just as people might quickly conceptualize some real-world experience (e.g., falling in love) in metaphorical ways to better understand that experience, people might employ metaphor processing as an indispensable part of how they make sense of many ordinary events in their lives. Thus, metaphor processing might not be just a special literary strategy employed only by certain readers when interpreting texts.

THE EMBODIED MOTIVATION FOR METAPHORICAL CONCEPTS

Finally, where does the ability to think metaphorically come from? Why is it that certain conceptual metaphors, but not others, are used by people in speaking about abstract concepts? The traditional view of metaphor is that people employ metaphor for strictly communicative purposes (e.g., compactness, vividness) (Ortony, 1975). Many scholars now recognize that metaphor is essential for how we communicate about abstract ideas that are difficult to verbalize and about aspects of our ordinary experience. In this way, metaphor is indeed necessary and not just nice or ornamental (Ortony, 1975).

One of the important claims of cognitive semantics is that much of our knowledge is not static, propositional, and sentential, but is grounded in and structured by various patterns of our perceptual interactions, bodily actions, and manipulations of objects (Gibbs & Colston, 1995; Johnson, 1987; Lakoff, 1987, 1990; Turner, 1991, 1996). These patterns are experiential gestalts, called *image schema,* that emerge throughout sensorimotor activity as we manipulate objects, orient ourselves spatially and temporally, and direct our perceptual focus for various purposes. Image schema cover a wide range of experiential structures that are pervasive in experience, have internal structure, and can be metaphorically elaborated to provide for our understanding of more abstract domains.

For example, central to our understanding of the conceptual metaphor ANGER IS HEATED FLUID IN A CONTAINER is the embodied experience of containment. We have strong kinesthetic experiences of bodily containment ranging from situations in which our bodies are in and out of containers (e.g., bathtubs, beds, rooms, houses) to experiences of our bodies as containers in which substances enter and exit. A big part of bodily containment is the experience of our bodies being filled with liquids, including stomach fluids and blood and sweat, that get excreted through the skin. Under stress, we experience the feeling of our bodily fluid becoming heated. These various, recurring bodily experiences give rise to the development of the image schema for CONTAINMENT.

One of the interesting things about image schema is that they motivate aspects of how we think, reason, and imagine. The same image schema can be instantiated in many domains because the internal structure of a single schema can be metaphorically understood. Our CONTAINMENT schema, to continue with this example, is metaphorically elaborated in a large number of abstract domains of experiences (e.g., concepts about emotions, the mind, linguistic meaning, moral obligations, social institutions). Moreover, this single schema helps motivate some of the complex ways we structure single abstract concepts. For instance, the conceptual metaphor ANGER IS HEATED FLUID IN A CONTAINER takes the image schema for CONTAINMENT as part of its source domain and maps this image-schematic structure onto anger, which gives rise to a number of interesting entailments. Thus, when the intensity of anger increases, the fluid in the container rises (e.g., "His pent-up anger welled up inside of him"). We also know that intense heat produces steam and creates pressure on the container (e.g., "Bill is getting hot under the collar" and "Jim's just blowing off steam"). Intense anger produces pressure on the container (e.g., "He was bursting with anger"). Finally, when the pressure of the container becomes too high, the container explodes (e.g., "She blew up at me"). Each of these metaphorical entailments is a direct result of the conceptual mapping of heated fluid in the container, a direct bodily experience, onto the concept of anger. It is difficult to explain the richness of these metaphorical inferences without appealing to people's embodied experiences for heated fluid in containers that are then metaphorically projected to help individuals make sense of their anger experiences. Some of my work on idioms' meanings (Gibbs, 1992, reviewed earlier) shows, in part, how aspects of people's intuitions about idiomatic meaning can be predicted from an independent analysis of different embodied experience (e.g., heated fluid in the body). Gibbs, Beitel, Harrington, and Sanders (1995) provide experimental evidence on the embodied motivation for metaphoric uses of the polysemous word "stand."

The embodied motivation for metaphor provides a natural, nonarbitrary reason for why people regularly construct asymmetrical metaphorical mappings to better understand many abstract concepts. I am not arguing that people learn metaphorical representation only from their embodied experiences, because their experience with the language itself will help people to tacitly infer via generalization many metaphorical concepts. But it is clear that there are important links between people's recurring bodily experiences, their metaphorical projections of these image schema to better structure many abstract concepts, and the language used to talk about these concepts.

CONCLUSIONS

The fight over metaphor in thought and language is at a critical point in the cognitive sciences. There is enough evidence from both linguistics and psychology on the possibility that people construe many concepts in terms of metaphor that it is time for psychologists to actually conduct additional experimental studies to see if, when, and in what way certain concepts are metaphorically represented. Simply arguing against metaphoric representations without actually testing for the presence of metaphor in many concepts is no longer sufficient. Psychologists must also explain the linguistic evidence about why people talk about concepts in particular metaphorical ways. The challenge for those who argue against metaphor in thought is to account for the precise inference patterns of meaning that people employ in talk about concepts without employing metaphorical cognition.

I firmly believe that linguistic evidence is entirely appropriate for making several specific claims about metaphor's role in the interaction of thought and language. Linguistic analyses seem directly germane to establishing the reality of metaphor in language change, grammatical structure, word meaning, and in capturing important element of speakers'/listeners' presumed knowledge about systematic and novel patterns of language use. Furthermore, linguistic analyses are also essential for discovering cultural models of thought, language, and behavior (a topic I have not touched on here). I challenge cognitive psychologists, and others, to embrace the findings from related disciplines and all metaphor scholars to recognize the limitations of their methods in making claims about metaphor's essential role in human experience. My most significant claim is that adopting the cognitive wager should prompt more scholars to see intimate connections between metaphor in thought and language.

REFERENCES

Allbritton, D., McKoon, G., & Gerrig, R. (1995). Metaphor-based schema and text comprehension: Making connections through conceptual metaphors. *Journal of Experimental Psychology: Learning, Memory, and Cognition, 21,* 612–625.

Barsalou, L. (1987). The instability of graded structure in concepts. In U. Neisser (Ed.), *Concepts and conceptual development: Ecological and intellectual factors in categorization* (pp. 101–140). New York: Cambridge University Press.

Barsalou, L. (1993). Flexibility, structure, and linguistic vagary in concepts: Manifestations of a compositional system of perceptual symbols. In A. Collins, S. Gathercole, M. Conway, & P. Morris (Eds.), *Theories of memory* (pp. 22–101). Hillsdale, NJ: Erlbaum.

Brugman, C., & Lakoff, G. (1988). Cognitive topology and lexical networks. In S. Small, G. Cotrell, & M. Tannenhaus (Eds.), *Lexical ambiguity resolution* (pp. 477–508). Palo Alto: Morgan Kaufman.

Cacciari, C., & Glucksberg, S. (1995). Imaging idiomatic expressions: Literal or figurative meanings? In M. Everaert, E-J. van der Linden, A. Schenk, & R. Schreuder (Eds.), *Idioms: Structural and psychological perspectives* (pp. 43–56). Hillsdale, NJ: Erlbaum.

Casad, G. (1988). Conventionalization of Cora locationals. In B. Rudzka-Ostyn (Ed.), *Topics in cognitive linguistics* (pp. 121–164). Amsterdam: John Benjamins.

Croft, W. (1993). The role of domains in the interpretation of metaphors and metonymies. *Cognitive Linguistics, 4,* 335–370.

Deane, P. (1995). Metaphors of center and periphery in Yeat's "The Second Coming." *Journal of Pragmatics, 24,* 627–642.

Freeman, D. (1995). "Catch(ing) the nearest way": *Macbeth* and cognitive metaphor. *Journal of Pragmatics, 24,* 689–708.

Gentner, D. & Gentner, D. R. (1983). Flowing waters or teeming crowds: Mental models of electricity. In D. Gentner & A. Stevens (Eds.), *Mental models* (pp. 99–129). Hillsdale, NJ: Erlbaum.

Gibbs, R. (1992). What do idioms really mean? *Journal of Memory and Language, 31,* 485–506.

Gibbs, R. (1993). Why idioms are not dead metaphors. In C. Cacciari & P. Tabossi (Eds.), *Idioms: Processing, structure, and interpretation* (pp. 57–78). Hillsdale, NJ: Erlbaum.

Gibbs, R. (1994). *The poetics of mind: Figurative thought, language, and understanding.* New York: Cambridge University Press.

Gibbs, R. (1996). Why many concepts are metaphorical. *Cognition, 61,* 309–319.

Gibbs, R., & Beitel, D. (1995). What proverb understanding reveals about how people think. *Psychological Bulletin, 118,* 133–154.

Gibbs, R., Beitel, D., Harrington, M., & Sanders, D. (1994). Taking a stand on the meanings of *stand*: Bodily experience as motivation for polysemy. *Journal of Semantics, 11,* 231–251.

Gibbs, R., Bogdonovich, J., Sykes, J., & Barr, D. (1997). Metaphor in idiom comprehension. *Journal of Memory and Language, 37,* 141–154.

Gibbs, R., & Colston, H. (1995). The cognitive psychological reality of image schema and their transformations. *Cognitive Linguistics, 6,* 347–378.

Gibbs, R., & Nascimento, S. (1996). How we talk when we talk about love: Metaphorical concepts and understanding love poetry. In R. Kreuz & M. MacNealy (Eds.), *Empirical and aesthetic approaches to literature* (pp. 291–308). Norwood, NJ: Ablex.

Gibbs, R., & Nayak, N. (1991). Why idioms mean what they do. *Journal of Experimental Psychology: General, 120,* 93–95.

Gibbs, R., & O'Brien, J. (1990). Idioms and mental imagery: The metaphorical motivation for idiomatic meaning. *Cognition, 36,* 35–68.

Gibbs, R., Strom, L., & Spivey-Knowlton, M. (1997). Conceptual metaphors in mental imagery for proverbs. *Journal of Mental Imagery, 21,* 83–110.

Glucksberg, S., Brown, M., & McGlone, M. (1993). Conceptual metaphors are not automatically accessed during idiom comprehension. *Memory & Cognition, 21,* 711–719.

Glucksberg, S., & Keysar, B. (1990). Understanding metaphorical comparisons: Beyond similarity. *Psychological Review, 97,* 3–18.

Glucksberg, S., Keysar, B., & McGlone, M. (1992). Metaphor understanding and accessing conceptual schema: Reply to Gibbs (1992). *Psychological Review, 99,* 578–581.

Groefsema, M. (1995). Can, may, must, and should: A relevance theoretic account. *Journal of Linguistics, 31,* 53–79.

Honeck, R., & Temple, J. (1994). Proverbs: The extended conceptual base and the great chain metaphor theories. *Metaphor and Symbolic Activity, 9,* 85–112.

Hopper, M. (1991). Functional explanation in linguistics and the origins of language. *Language & Communication, 11,* 3–28.

Jackendoff, R. (1990). *Semantic structures.* Cambridge, MA: MIT Press.

Johnson, M. (1987). *The body in the mind.* Chicago: University of Chicago Press.

Katz, A. (1992). Psychological studies on metaphor processing: Extensions to the placement of terms in semantic space. *Poetics Today, 13,* 607–632.

Katz, A. (1996). Experimental psycholinguistics and figurative language: Circa 1995. *Metaphor and Symbolic Activity, 11,* 17–37.

Keysar, B., & Bly, B. (1995). Intuitions of the transparency of idioms: Can you keep a secret by spilling the beans? *Journal of Memory and Language, 34,* 89–109.

Kovecses, Z. (1986). *Metaphors of anger, pride, and love.* Amsterdam: John Benjamins.

Kovecses, Z. (1990). *Emotion concepts.* New York: Springer.

Kreuz, R., & Graesser, A. (1991). Aspects of idiom comprehension: Comment on Nayak and Gibbs. *Journal of Experimental Psychology: General, 120,* 90–92.

Lakoff, G. (1987). *Women, fire, and dangerous things.* Chicago: University of Chicago Press.

Lakoff, G. (1990). The invariance hypothesis: Is abstract reason based on image-schema? *Cognitive Linguistics, 1,* 39–74.

Lakoff, G., & Johnson, M. (1980). *Metaphors we live by.* Chicago: University of Chicago Press.

Lakoff, G., & Turner, M. (1989). *More than cool reason: A field guide to poetic metaphor.* Chicago: University of Chicago Press.

Lodge, D. (1977). *The modes of modern writing.* London: Arnold.

McGlone, M. (1996). Conceptual metaphors and figurative language interpretation: Food for thought? *Journal of Memory and Language, 35,* 544–565.

Murphy, G. (1996). On metaphoric representation. *Cognition, 60,* 173–204.

Nayak, N., & Gibbs, R. (1990). Conceptual knowledge in the interpretation of idioms. *Journal of Experimental Psychology: General, 119,* 315–330.

Nunberg, G., Sag, I., & Wasow, T. (1994). Idioms. *Language, 70,* 491–538.

Ortony, A. (1975). Why metaphors are necessary and not just nice. *Educational Theory, 25,* 45–53.

Ortony, A. (1988). Are emotion metaphors conceptual or lexical? *Cognition and Emotion, 2,* 95–103.

Pfaff, K., Gibbs, R., & Johnson, M. (1997). Metaphor in using and understanding euphemisms and dysphemisms. *Applied Psycholinguistics, 18,* 59–83.

Quinn, N. (1991). The cultural basis of metaphor. In J. Fernandez (Ed.), *Beyond metaphor: The theory of tropes in anthropology* (pp. 56–93). Stanford, CA: Stanford University Press.

Ruhl, C. (1989). *Monosemy: A study in linguistic semantics.* Albany: State University of New York Press.

Simpson, G. (1994). Context and the processing of words. In M. A. Gernsbacher (Ed.), *Handbook of psycholinguistics* (pp. 359–374). San Diego: Academic Press.

Steen, G. (1994). *Understanding metaphor in literature.* London: Longman.

Stock, O., Slack, J., & Ortony, A. (1993). Building castles in the air: Some computational and theoretical issues in idiom comprehension. In C. Cacciari & P. Tabossi (Eds.), *Idioms: Processing, structure, and interpretation* (pp. 229–247). Hillsdale, NJ: Erlbaum.

Sweetser, E. (1990). *From etymology to pragmatics: The mind-body metaphor in semantic structure and semantic change.* Cambridge: Cambridge University Press.

Tabossi, P., & Zardon, F. (1993). The activation of idiomatic meaning in spoken language comprehension. In C. Cacciari & P. Tabossi (Eds.), *Idioms: Processing, structure and interpretation* (pp. 145–162). Hillsdale, NJ: Erlbaum.

Turner, M. (1987). *Death is the mother of beauty: Mind, metaphor, criticism.* Chicago: University of Chicago Press.

Turner, M. (1991). *Reading minds: The study of English in the age of cognitive science.* Princeton: Princeton University Press.

Turner, M. (1996). The literary mind. New York: Oxford University Press.

Turner, M., & Fauconnier, G. (1995). Conceptual integration and formal expression. *Metaphor and Symbolic Activity, 10,* 183–204.

Wellek, R., & Warren, A. (1949). *Theory of Literature.* Harmondsworth: Penguin Books.

Wierzbicka, A. (1985). *Lexicography and conceptual analysis.* Ann Arbor, MI: Karoma.

CHAPTER 4

Why Do We Speak Metaphorically?

Reflections on the Functions of Metaphor in Discourse and Reasoning

Cristina Cacciari

> Anna Pavlova, walking about her drawing room, went up to any circle that was pausing or too loud in conversation, and by a single word or change of position set the conversational machine going again in its regular, decorous way.
>
> LEO TOLSTOY, *War and Peace*

INTRODUCTION

What is the role of figurative language in the "conversational machine" so elegantly described in *War and Peace?* When planning the production of a sentence, a speaker faces several choices, one of which concerns the ways in which each chunk of what that speaker intends to convey will be "shaped": literally, ironically, metaphorically, and so forth.

Such a choice is of course anything but neutral, involving semantic as well as pragmatic relevance and effects. Nevertheless, very little is known about the motivations underlying the decisions of speakers as to which kind of communicative register to adopt, given a specific discourse context, knowledge of the addressee, awareness of the extent of common ground shared, and so forth. Such a lack of knowledge in a field—the psycholinguistic studies on language production—in which some hundreds of pages of references already exist suggests the persistence of the traditional view, according to which metaphor mainly concerns style, and not sentence planning processes, let alone reasoning and conceptualization.[1] In this chapter, I argue that:

1. Verbal metaphors[2] are used for conceptualizing and making expressible relevant parts of our inner life and everyday cognitive activity;
2. Metaphors do so in at least two ways: (a) by creating new conceptual entities that extend preexisting categories, and (b) by using the expressive properties of objects and events as a perceptual basis;
3. Metaphors represent a way to deal with the relative inability of language to account for, or directly express, the complexity of our perceptual experiences.

STYLE OR REASONING?

It has been widely demonstrated by scholars working on figurative language that metaphor—the trope *par excellence*—is not simply a stylistic device for embellishing discourse. Metaphor plays a central role in everyday discourse and in shaping the ways we think (Gibbs, 1994; Glucksberg & Keysar, 1990, 1993; Lakoff, 1987; Turner, 1991, 1996). Still, most of the current theories of language ignore the contribution of figurative language to discourse comprehension and production. Current models on lemma selection in language production (cf. Bierwisch & Schreuder, 1992; Levelt, 1991), as I noted, are virtually silent as to why a speaker would select a figurative expression (e.g., a metaphor, an idiomatic expression, or a proverb) instead of a "corresponding" literal expression. Similarly, standard semantic theories still assign a peripheral and theoretically uninteresting role to figurative language (with the important exception of cognitive linguistics, but see Chierchia & McConnel-Ginet, 1990; Cruse, 1986).

Two long-standing assumptions (highly disputed, of course, cf. Gibbs, 1994; Glucksberg & Keysar, 1990; Katz, chap. 1; Lakoff, 1987; Lakoff & Turner, 1989; MacCormac, 1985; Ortony, 1993; Sperber & Wilson, 1986; Tannen, 1989) contribute to this silence. Such assumptions can be summarized as follows: (a) a figurative expression can, without loss, always be paraphrased literally; (b) literality is the realm of clear and intersubjectively shared meanings, whereas figurative language introduces obscurity and arbitrariness because it is based on subjectivity and on the "connotative penumbra" (Levinson, 1983) of word meanings.

The view I am endorsing in this chapter strongly questions both these assumptions. A speaker's choice of a metaphorical over a literal expression cannot be simply interpreted as a matter of idiosyncratic preference: metaphor (my main concern in this chapter, but a similar line of reasoning can be generalized to other tropes as well) is not a fancy way to say something that could have been equally well said literally (cf. Black, 1962, 1979).

THE FUNCTIONS OF METAPHOR

Traditional accounts of figurative language insist that metaphors are often used to describe something new by reference to something familiar, but the scope of metaphorical expressions extends well beyond this general function. As a first step toward uncovering some of the reasons why a speaker would speak metaphorically instead of literally, let us examine what we know about some of the functions played by metaphor in everyday discourse and reasoning.[3]

Bridging from Abstract Domains to Perceptual Experiences

> Double sound, cold tension of the straight lines, warm tension of the curved lines, the rigid to the infinity, the flexible to the compact.
>
> VASILY KANDINSKY

People use metaphors for conceptualizing abstract concepts in terms of the apprehendable, as when spatial concepts and terms are extended to refer to temporal concepts and terms (Clark, 1973). Metaphors are often used to express ideas that are inexpressible by literal language (Ortony, 1980). For instance, the vocabulary available in English for describing sensory experience such as auditory timbre is quite impoverished: by using terms metaphorically, as in such expressions as "a warm, richly textured organ chord," we can express the (literally) inexpressible (cf. Beck, 1978, 1987; Marks, 1982; Marks & Bornstein, 1987).

As Beck (1987) pointed out, "[M]etaphors force the mind to construct a high-order linkage between the entities referred to. Metaphors are like bridges" (p. 11). This bridging function is accomplished insofar as metaphors are used to connect:

1. Abstract entities (e.g., "God is Love");
2. Abstract concepts to sensory-perceptual experiences. As an example, consider the way in which a young Italian composer, Piovani, describes his ideative activity: "I do not write musical scores but sonorous ideas";
3. Perceptual experiences belonging to different sensory modalities. In synesthetic metaphors, for instance, words that pertain to one sensory modality (e.g., perception) are extended to express another sensory modality (e.g., audition). The title of a drawing of the Russian painter Kandinsky, where perceptual-geometrical entities such as lines are described by using adjectives coming from the domain of sounds, provides us with a very clear example: "Double sound, cold tension of the straight lines, warm tension of the curved lines, the rigid to the infinity, the flexible to the compact."

In the next two sections, I confine myself to considering the roles played by metaphors when they are used to "translate" some form of prelinguistic perception into an expressible content; namely I examine the relationship between expressive properties and metaphorical language (point 2), and the problem of synesthetic metaphors (point 3).

Metaphorical extensions or expressive properties?

> I am clouded and bruised with the prints of minds and faces and things so subtle that they have smell, color, texture, substance, but no name.
>
> VIRGINIA WOOLF, *The Waves*

> Things spill light on things.
>
> LUCRETIUS, *On the Nature of Things*

According to Beck (1978, p. 85), many metaphors take advantage of a "process whereby images and sensory associations that develop at a level where a network of sensory associations prevails are transferred to a level where thoughts are ordered according to a logic of verbal categories. Metaphors cross over such categorical divides as animate/inanimate, cosmic/biological, human/animal by recourse to associative and sensory logic." This is certainly so for most literary and poetic metaphors. However, this form of mediation between nonverbal and verbal thinking, between cross-modal sensory experiences and semantic system, can be found even in mundane metaphors, if it is true, as Fernandez claimed (1991), that metaphors bridge gaps.

It should be noted that the relationships of linguistic metaphor to sensory-perceptual properties have not yet been theoretically spelled out. Are metaphors really perceptually based, are they rooted in cultural models of our everyday experience, or are they based on abstract-amodal representations of our perceptual experience? We are far from having clear-cut answers, but we can try to elucidate the problem. Let us start by considering the problem of polysemy (i.e., the existence of multiple senses in a single lexical item).

It is widely posited that a large part of polysemy is due to metaphorical usage.[4] The problem is not strictly linguistic at least for those like Sweetser (1991), for instance, who claim that linguistic categorization does not depend just on our naming of distinctions that exist in the world, but "also on our metaphorical and metonymic structure of our perception of the world" (1991, p. 9).

Quite frequently, color words[5] are used to express something other than a perceptual dimension. Take the word "white." To Sweetser, "if we use a word meaning 'white' to mean 'honest', 'candid' rather than using our word for 'purple', it is not just a fact about the language. It is a fact about (at least) the cultural community that sees whiteness as metaphorically standing for honesty or moral purity'' (p. 8). The connection between the word meaning ''white'' and truth, honesty, and so forth, far from being explained in ''a truth-conditional manner as the sharing of objective features'' (Turner, personal communication) is experientially motivated by metaphoric connections like those described in conceptual metaphors such as KNOWING IS SEEING.

Hence, to pursue Sweetser's line of thought, polysemous senses of this kind are not perceptually but *metaphorically* motivated because there is no systematic objective correlation in the world that might explain the acquisition of such secondary senses of, say, ''white,'' except correlations that are cognitively rooted. In a footnote (no. 9, pp. 149–50), Sweetser admits that ''one important *partial* correlation which presumably underlies these metaphors is that of daylight with visibility, warmth, and relative safety.'' No place other than a ''partial correlation'' is left for the possibility that also the perceptual characteristics of ''white'' might account for the fact that in our culture it has acquired its connotative meaning.

Although I certainly agree with Sweetser that metaphor cannot be accounted for by a truth-conditional semantics, the point I want to make about the relationship between sensory experience and language goes in a different direction. The motivation underlying our usage of ''white'' to mean ''true'' (and so forth) is not at all metaphorical, and is instead to be found in the subjective resonance that ''white'' as a color produced on human beings.[6] My claim is that the origin, the rationale whereby we use ''white,'' ''candid,'' and so forth to mean something more than a perceptual quality lies in the sensory properties of colors, or of objects, that interact with the ways in which we perceive and experience the world.

The feelings we experience when looking at a snow field stand as a reminder of the existence of this radically alternative way for explaining the relationship between the semantic system and the perceptual facts, and hence for explaining the use of the meaning of ''white'' to denote moral values (to take only one of a much broader class of examples[7]). Such an alternative viewpoint strongly questions that it is by metaphorical extension that ''white'' has acquired such secondary senses or connotations.

The color-temperature association is another interesting case. To Marks and Bornstein (1987, p. 59) it reflects a range of universal experiences: ''[W]ith fire and flames, with the warmth of the sun, the cool lakes and rivers and so forth. Throughout the world, the sun appears yellow, whereas large bodies of water appear blue and green, and these associations transcend specific cultures.''

My line of reasoning is aimed at showing that the ways in which we categorize our perceptual experiences are rooted at the same time in *the perceptual world, in its properties and in our experience of it*. This is not to deny a role for the conceptualization of such experience, of course. For instance, consider the different relevance and reliability that we attribute to the knowledge obtained from the sense organs (cf. Leon, 1988; Nelkin, 1990). It is out of the question that in our culture sight has a privileged status. As noted by Napolitano Valditara (1994) in a fascinating essay on the relationship between vision metaphors and the forms or the rationality in the ancient Greek culture, this privilege comes to us from the ancient Greek culture, from Aristotle to Plato, from Parmenides to Senofonte: "[T]he Greek philosophical language borrowed from ordinary language terms and expressions connected with the act of vision and adapted them, technically, for describing acts of knowledge and the original permeation between being and knowing" (p. 8). Aristotle put seeing among the "perfect actions," establishing in this way a bridge between sight and knowledge and the excellence of vision over the other sensory activities.

The view according to which perceptual objects possess internal characteristics or properties that produce emotional resonances belongs to a long-standing tradition: a number of philosophers (e.g., Descartes, Locke, Galilei, Brentano, to name a few), then Gestalt psychologists (Koffka, 1935; Metzger, 1941), and, more recently, experimental phenomenologists (Bozzi, 1989, 1990) claimed it. To this viewpoint, the perceptual "white," and not the connotation of the linguistic concept of "white," is responsible for the feeling of pureness, cleanness, and so forth and, as a consequence, is reflected in the linguistic use of this color (so to speak) to express a set of moral values. As Koehler (1947, pp. 134–35) pointed out, "[W]hen subjective experiences are given names which also apply to perceptual facts, this does not happen in a random fashion."

The same is true of course for other color words. Consider for instance "black" and "red," as Bozzi recently pointed out: "Black is lugubrious and red is alive. . . . [T]hese characteristics (being black or being red) magnetize precisely those adjectives; these characteristics are not purely verbal or associative, but are *perceptual ingredients that are present inside the objects themselves*" (Bozzi, 1990, p. 100, italics added).

But what kind of percept properties can contribute to explain these subjective resonances or "names correspondence," as Koehler put it? According to Gestalt psychologists,[8] objects possess three different kinds of property:

1. *Primary properties* such as form or extension (those described by natural sciences);
2. *Secondary properties* such as color or sound (perceptually tied to an observer's activity);
3. *Tertiary (or expressive) properties* that still belong to the perceiver's observation of an object but, unlike secondary properties, pertain to the object in that they belong to it (and are not mere associations). These properties are "rooted in the more internal resonance rooms of the subject but are topologically placed in the external things" (Bozzi, 1990, p. 100). As Wertheimer

claimed (quoted in Bozzi, 1990, p. 90), the color "black" "is lugubrious (mournful) yet before being black."

That the color "black" possesses such expressive properties is of course well-known to artists, as the following two quotations from *The Waves*[9] of Virginia Woolf (1931) suggest: "I sink down on the black plumes of sleep; its thick wings are pressed to my eyes" (p. 27); "The heat is going—said Bernard—from the Jungle. The leaves flap black wings over us" (p. 23).

Expressive properties do not characterize only colors. As Koffka (1935, p. 7) wrote: "Each thing says what it is.... [A] fruit says 'Eat me'; water says 'Drink me'; thunder says 'Fear me.' " Koffka, according to Gibson's interpretation (1977, p. 77), did not believe that "a meaning of this sort could be explained as a pale context of memory images or an unconscious set of response tendencies. The postbox 'invites' the mailing of a letter, the handle 'wants to be grasped' and things 'tell us what to do with them.' "[10] Objects had hence what Koffka called a "demand character."

These characteristics emerge from the objects and events that surround us and impose their "affordances"[11] on us (Gibson, 1979). Affordances, to Gibson, are not emotional projections or experienced associations; they are in the object and pertain to the object as it is for shape, color, movement or sound. Their direction is from the object to the perceiver. Gibson's radical proposal goes to the point of saying that affordances are contained in the optical information[12] reaching the eye of the perceiver.

To return to Sweetser's example of whiteness to mean pureness, one should consider the possibility that, instead of being due to an arbitrary (or purely associative) metaphorical extension, the color "white" might itself contain (in our culture) the tertiary properties or affordances of cleanness and pureness. As Gibson maintained: "[A]ffordances are in a sense objective, real and physical, unlike values and meanings, which are often supposed to be subjective, phenomenal and mental" (1979, p. 129). This might be the basis for our use of the word meaning "white" to also mean good, nonharmful (as in the opposition between white versus black magic).

To conclude on this point, what these metaphors do, at least assuming some version of the viewpoint of the Gestalt tradition, is something more subtle than simply enriching meanings via extensions. Many metaphors (not dissimilarly from caricatures, see Bozzi, 1990; Gibson, 1979; Gombrich, 1982) use the expressive properties of events and things that surround us for giving names to mental contents otherwise difficult to shape linguistically.

To further clarify this point, I present two literary examples that differ in terms of conceptual complexity: Virginia Woolf's lapidary description of the lifestyle of one of her characters and Robert Musil's metaphorical description of the mathematical concept of infinity (in the novel *Young Torless*[13]).

Let us start with Virginia Woolf. I have already cited the novel *The Waves* as a wonderful repertoire of metaphors rooting their meaning in the expressive properties of colors. In the following example, I am concerned with the purposeless life of a protagonist that is succinctly defined using everyday objects and acts. The metaphor (quoted in Gentner, Falkenhainer, & Skorstad, 1987[14]) is: "She allowed life to waste like a tap left running." As Gentner et ل. (1987) pointed out, "[T]he reader starts off with some notion of water flowing through a tap into a drain, and with the idea that waste occurs if an agent allows such a flow to occur with no purpose" (p. 177). It is easy to imagine a tap left running and almost hear the noise of the water flowing. It is at the same time a compelling (at least for me) feeling that such waste cannot be stopped, even though it should. This is precisely what the metaphor wants us to feel: the "tension" between the need for an action in contrast with the (metaphorical) absence of it in the protagonist.

To use Ricoeur's term, this metaphor has a "thickness": in order to interpret it, one has to consider the richness of "metaphoric details" (Jackendoff & Aaron, 1991, p. 336) on which this metaphorical description of the life of the protagonist is built. An analysis based on a structured set of mappings from the source domains to the target domains leaves unanswered a basic question concerning many good literary metaphors, that is, where does their aesthetic effect come from (Jackendoff & Aaron, 1991). The communicative force and literary elegance of this metaphoric "conceptual blend" (Turner, chap. 2) capitalizes on the richness of conceptual, perceptual, and affective components that even a very mundane and common action (leaving a tap opened) can trigger. This action acquires an emotional salience precisely because of the metaphoric topic with which it is paired: the protagonist's life. The waste of tap water hence becomes a compelling exemplar of all the possible wastes of *maîtrise* on one own's life.

Let us turn now to a long and complex cluster of metaphors that, for sake of argument, I consider as a single complex metaphorical statement. In *Young Torless,* Musil (1906) describes the young protagonist's encounter with an abstract concept such as infinity. What follows is the description of Torless's perception of what infinity might look like[15]:

It was a shock. Straight above him, shining between the clouds, was a small blue hole, fathomlessly deep. He felt it must be possible, if only one had a long, long ladder, to climb up and into it. But the farther he penetrated raising himself on his gaze, the further the blue, shining depth receded. And still it was as though some time it must be reached, as though by sheer gazing one must be able to stop it and hold it. . . . It was as if, straining to the utmost, his power of vision were shooting glances like arrows between the clouds; and yet, the further and further it aimed, still they always fell just a little short. . . . There in the sky, it [the concept of infinity] was standing over him, alive and threatening and sneering'' (Robert Musil, *Young Torless,* pp. 71–72).

Where does the aesthetic quality and conceptual complexity of this metaphor come from? Even at a first glance, it is clear that the building blocks used by Musil to construct the metaphor are rooted in vision (in the glance of the protagonist) and in the expressive qualities of the perceptual objects that characterize the metaphor: the sky, the small blue hole, the point that moves farther on whenever the observer moves. The writer asks us to visualize ourselves climbing an endless ladder and trying to catch an abstract notion as if it were a concrete object. And the closer one gets to this unreachable point in the sky, the farther the point moves. Even if glance was as thin, pointy, and quick as an arrow, such a point would be unreachable.

This metaphor is based on a network of sensory-perceptual association: Musil wants to direct the reader's interpretation toward a perceptual experience. It asks the reader to imagine, if not to perceive, the endless movement of Torless, the transformation of a glance into an arrow lanced through the clouds, and the progressive escaping of this luminous and unreachable point in the sky.

For shifting from infinity as a mathematical notion to infinity as a perceptual experience, Musil, who was—as were many of his contemporaries—well aware of the limit of language,[16] used a complex cluster of metaphors, hence attributing to tropes a cognitive force only recently recognized by researchers. This kind of metaphor, by making appeal to the expressive properties of objects and events, allows the expression of subjective feelings as well as of abstract concepts. Metaphor, so to speak, moves the border of what is linguistically tractable or expressible by addressing our attention toward sensory, cross-modal perceptions. As Beck noted, metaphors are verbal devices based on a ''sensory logic at the semantic level'' and this ''entails a movement from abstract to concrete. It also involves the introduction of affect and the notion of perceptual qualities'' (Beck, 1987, p. 85).

Metaphor, to pursue Musil's words, provides a speaker with a means for making the connection, the bridge that young Torless is looking for: ''he felt the urge to search for some bridges, some connection, some means of comparison between himself and the wordless things confronting his spirit'' (*Young Torless,* p. 73).

The limits of language and rationality were keenly experienced by many writers and artists living in Vienna at the turn of the century. As Gargani (1983) noted in a volume on the links between literature and science in the Austrian culture, ''By experimenting with a stylistic device based on metaphors and similes, Musil looked for the answer human beings should give in the age of the *Civilization* [Zivilisation]'' (Gargani, 1983, p. 49).

To Musil, we can no longer describe the world around us (even our inner life) "with straight words" that belong to a "unilateral intelligence," because, as he wrote, "the word is not at all the support of a concept . . . but is only a seal put over an unstable bundle of representations" (quoted in Sonino, 1983, p. 87). As Wittgenstein wrote, "words are like a pellicle over deep waters" (quoted in Sonino, 1983, p. 90). Metaphor, with its capacity to introduce a "sensory logic at the semantic level" (Beck, 1987, p. 85), is a way to fill this gap, for overcoming the rigidity of plain—straight—literal language since metaphors allude to a more complex scenario of interrelated meanings and experiences of the world.[17]

To conclude on this point, I would certainly endorse Beck's view that "if forced to delimit the concept of metaphor, I would insist on the experiential, body-linked, physical core of metaphoric reasoning abilities" (Beck, 1987, p. 11). Both Woolf's lapidary description of her character and Torless's need to understand an abstract concept such as infinity exploit what has been considered the most distinctive feature of metaphor, namely that it entails a movement from abstract to concrete. I suggest that this is accomplished by making use not only of linguistic means but also of the perceptual qualities of everyday objects and events.

Synesthetic metaphors: crossing the senses.

> La Nature est un temple où de vivant piliers
> Laissent parfois sortir de confuse paroles;
> L'homme y passe ê travers des forets
> de symboles qui l'observent avec des
> regards familiers.
> CHARLES BAUDELAIRE, *Correspondances*

In linguistic terms, a synesthetic description is a description of something one experiences by a definite sense organ by using adjectives whose referent is another (e.g., saying that a color is "warm," a noise "sharp," a vision "painful"). Sensory experiences are by their very nature cross-modal: as Beck put it, "[H]ow can one separate the experience of something smelled (say) from the experience of something tasted, touched, seen or heard?" (1978, p. 84). This brings us full circle to the problem of *synesthetic metaphors*.

On general grounds, the traditional approach to synesthetic language has considered this type of language a peculiar case of the more general phenomenon of cross-modal associations due to a connotative meaning shared by two (or more) modalities (the *semantic mediation* hypothesis). The semantic differential proposed by Osgood, Suci, and Tannenbaum (1957; cf. Osgood, 1980) has been the main instrument for measuring aspects of connotative meaning and phonetic symbolism of this sort.

According to Williams (1976), "[O]ne of the most common types of meta-

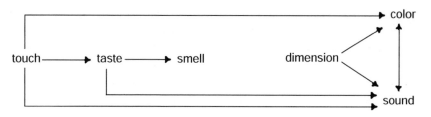

FIGURE 4.1. Model of the metaphorical transfers among sensory modalities (after Williams, 1976).

phoric transfer in all languages is synaesthesia'' (p. 463). Williams investigated the semantic change over time of more than 100 English synesthetic adjectives. He proposed a model according to which there is a systematic sequence in the application of sensory terms from one modality to another (cf. Derrig, 1978; Ullmann, 1945, 1962). William's model of cross-modal sense development (summarized in fig. 4.1) postulates the existence of a hierarchy among the physical senses in the order in which they give or get a meaning from other modalities, with touch at one extreme as the more common ''donor'' and color and sound as more common ''recipients.'' Smell does not seem to contribute to other modalities; taste only to smell and sound, and dimension only to color and sound.

The main ''first-order''[18] types of metaphorical transfer from one sensory modality to another, schematized in figure 4.1, can be summarized as follows:

1. *Touch words*: generally transfer to taste (''sharp taste''), to color (''dull color'') or to sound (''soft sounds''). Quite rare are shifts to vision or smell.
2. *Taste words*: transfer to smell (''sour smell'') and sound (''sweet music''), but they do not transfer back to tactile experience or forward to dimension or color.
3. *Olfactory words*: do not transfer to other senses.[19]
4. *Dimension words*: transfer to color (''flat gray'') or to sound ''(deep sound'').
5. *Color words*: shift only to sounds (''bright sound'').
6. *Sound words*: transfer only to color ''(''quiet green'').

Williams claims that sensory words in English have systematically shifted ''from the physiologically least differentiating, most evolutionary primitive sensory modalities to the most differentiating, most advanced, but not vice versa'' (1976, pp. 464–65). But Williams does not propose any intrinsic reason why this order should be observed.

Tracing back the origin of synesthetic adjectives can prove historically relevant. However, Miller and Johnson-Laird (1976) raise a more general problem questioning the very idea that we still perceive these words as shifts, or borrowings: "Perhaps it is a mistake to think that the concept expressed by a word like 'sharp', which can describe touch, taste, sound, intelligence, terrain, strictness, eagerness, and objects is legitimately applicable only to touch and must be generalized for other applications" (p. 360). As Asch (1958) argued, such adjectives express general concepts of "functional properties or mode of interaction" (1958, p. 93). Therefore, Miller and Johnson-Laird conclude that "a sharp mind may be as good an instance of SHARP as a sharp pain; a warm person may be as good an instance of WARM as a warm tactual experience" (p. 360).

The problem of directionality in synesthetic language had already been raised in the seminal work conducted by Ullmann (1945) on poetry. The distinctiveness scale proposed by Ullmann went from the most distinct modality (sight) to the least distinct one (touch). He examined over 2,000 synesthetic metaphors from English, French, and Hungarian poems, observing a systematic directionality of mapping where the metaphor's topic represents a term belonging to the highest point in the distinctiveness scale while the metaphor's modifier belongs to the lowest point (e.g., "a cold light" was much more frequent than "a lighted coldness").[20] Shen (1997) investigated this issue in a contemporary Hebrew corpus of poetry. He interpreted this preference for mappings from low values onto high ones on the distinctiveness scale as reflecting a cognitive constraint, that is, a "preference for a more 'natural' or 'basic' structure over its inverse" (p. 50). Generally speaking, "this constraint states that a mapping from more accessible or basic concepts onto less accessible or less basic ones seems more natural and is preferred over the opposite mapping" (p. 51).

Sensory similarities, as those expressed by synesthetic language, come in several kinds. Marks and Bornstein (1987) summarized them as follows: (1) similarities related to different proximal sensations coming from perceiving a stimulus from different perspectives; (2) similarities related to the recognition of a three-dimensional object in a two-dimensional representation, or vice versa; (3) similarities related to the recognition of the same stimulus through two or more modalities; (4) similarities related to a difference in the stimulus producing distinguishable sensations that are perceived or responded to as similar; (5) cross-modal or synesthetic similarity where different stimuli that act via different sensory systems are perceived and treated as similar.

As Marks (1982) elegantly demonstrated, if you ask someone "which is brighter, a cough or a sneeze?" the vast majority of people respond that a sneeze is brighter, higher in pitch than coughs, and that high-pitched sounds are like bright lights. Marks (1978) also showed that many synesthetic metaphors in French and English poetry (Marks & Bornstein, 1987) rest on just a few cross-modal resemblances found in synesthetic perception that are special, in that they are general properties of perceptual responses, essentially universal, and presumably innate.

Nearly everyone can understand sensory metaphors such as "the murmur of the grey twilight" or "the loud light of thunder" that are based on the sensory equivalence of softness and dimness, and of loudness and brightness: "[I]n semantic memory, a 'murmur' is coded as prototypically soft, and 'twilight' is coded as prototypically dim" (Marks & Bornstein, 1987, p. 54). Comprehension is not so effortless when the metaphor is more innovative, as in "the sound of coming darkness" (quoted in Marks & Bornstein, 1987, p. 54), where the softness of the sound has to be computed via its metaphorical equivalence with the softness of the coming darkness.

Whereas the variety of sensory metaphors one can come up with is endless, the norms[21] according to which we interpret perceptual synesthesia are limited. Marks and Bornstein (1987, p. 60) analyzed, as a possible example, Kipling's metaphor from Mandalay: "Dawn comes up like thunder": dawn "does not reach especially high on the scale of brightness. Thunder, on the other hand, is loud" (p. 60). This metaphor takes disparate values of intensity from the visual and auditory domains and merges both, changing them.

So far we have considered synesthesia in linguistic and psychological terms (i.e., as concerning language and perception), but this is of course only one perspective. As Cytowic (1989a, b; cf. also Baron-Cohen & Harrison, 1997; Baron-Cohen, Wyke & Binnie, 1987; Cytowic & Wood, 1982a, b), a neurologist who has been working with synesthetic persons,[22] suggested, "Synaesthesia is not just a more intense form of cross-modal metaphor, although for years psychologists pursued this mistaken path. . . . [B]eing a vivid cross-modal association, synaesthesia is obviously a higher cortical function" (1989a, p. 849). Unlike most people who use cross-modal linguistic associations to describe a set of events or emotions, synesthetes "experience a *real percept*" (Cytowic & Wood, 1982a, p. 23).

The first medical reference to this phenomenon is at the beginning of the eighteenth century, when an English ophthalmologist described a blind patient who perceived sound-induced colored visions (Cytowic, 1989a). Some years earlier (1704), sounds to color mathematical connections were at the core of Newton's work and were the bases of the invention of a "clavecin oculaire" (a clavichord playing sound and light simultaneously).

Although the phenomenon has long been known and has fascinated physicians as well as psychologists (e.g., Galton, 1883; Karwoski, Odbert, & Osgood, 1942; Luria, 1968; Odbert, Karwoski, & Eckerson, 1942) and writers (e.g., Goethe, Verlaine, Baudelaire, Maupassant), a well-defined notion of the bases of synesthesia has only recently been proposed, based on the new conceptualizations brought by cognitive neuroscience (cf. Baron-Cohen & Harrison, 1997). According to Cytowic (1989a), synesthesia is defined by five criteria that distinguish it from "imagery or artistic fancy" (p. 850): (1) it "is involuntary and cannot be suppressed; (2) the sensations appear not in the mind, but are usually perceived externally as real; (3) the synesthetic sensations are discrete (few in number and tend to be categorical or generic in nature); (4) they are highly memorable; (5) they are accompanied by strong emotion and a sense of conviction'' (p. 850).

To Cytowic, ''[S]ynaesthesia represents a pre-object or, in the language of micro-genetics, a preliminary display of a normal cognitive process'' (1989a, p. 850). The identification between senses occurs regularly but never reaches the threshold of consciousness for most of us. Each sense ''samples an event, if only just a little. . . . [I]in synaesthesia some of these sensory samplings become bared to consciousness'' (1989a, p. 850). As to what causes synesthesia, Cytowic proposed that the cause of synesthesia should be traced in the fact that parts of the ''brain get disconnected from one another . . . causing the normal processes of the limbic system to be released, bared to consciousness, and experienced as synaesthesia'' (quoted in Harrison & Baron-Cohen, 1997, p. 113). The assertion that the limbic system is the critical brain locus is, at least according to Harrison and Baron-Cohen, (1997) controversial, as evidence reported in their review of neuropsychological theories suggests. Some alternative explanations exist (cf. Harrison & Baron-Cohen, 1997) that relate synesthesia (particularly colored hearing) to (1) the survival of pathways (usually neurally disconnected after neonatal stage in nonsynesthetes) between auditory and visual areas in the brain such that when words, or sounds, produce activation in the auditory areas the visual cortex is also stimulated; (2) the close anatomic proximity of visual and auditory pathways that might cause ''leaks,'' that is, auditory information leaks into pathways and areas that ordinarily deal with visual information; (3) to learned association; (4) to an inherited genetic trait; (5) to environmentally shaped maturation; (6) to cross-modal matching among the senses; (7) to a breakdown in modularity; (8) to ''a perpetuation of a primitive perceptual experience which in evolution was later differentiated into two separate senses'' (Baron-Cohen, Wyke, & Binnie, 1987, p. 766). The enumeration of these various viewpoints on what might cause synaesthesia makes clear that we are far from having a satisfactory account of the neuropsychological and cognitive architecture of synesthesia.

Expressing the Emotional Experience

> Emotions shouldn't color your thinking. Just your wardrobe.
> AD FOR A LIZ CLAIBORNE COLLECTION.

In his *Essay on the Origin of Languages,* written in the first decades of the eighteenth century, Jean Jacques Rousseau elegantly summarized the motivation for using tropes:

As man's first motives for speaking were the passions, his first expressions were tropes. Figurative language was the first to be born. Proper meaning was discovered last. One calls things by their true name only when one sees them in their true form. At first only poetry was spoken; there was no hint of reasoning until much later. (quoted in Johnson, 1981, p. 15)

The Romantic form of appreciation of imagination and poetry and the denial that tropes are based on reasoning no longer belong to what we are willing to accept. Nevertheless, Rousseau captured an essential point, namely, that we often name our feelings and emotions (the passions) by using metaphors (cf. Ricoeur, 1978).

As Ortony (1980, p. 78) claimed, "[T]here are phenomenological and psychological reasons for supposing that metaphors are more image-evoking and more vivid than even their best literal equivalents (if there is any)." One of the domains where metaphor serves its function (that of giving a detailed picture of our subjective experience) is internal states, in particular for describing the quality of *emotional states* (cf. Besnier, 1990; Davitz & Mattis, 1969; Fussell, 1992; Gibbs, 1994; Kovecses, 1986; Lakoff, 1987; Ortony, 1988; Ortony & Fainsilber, 1987).

That effect or emotion states are an important component of the lexicon and that words evoke attitudes has long been known in psychology. Just to mention some relevant examples, one can think of Ogden and Richards's seminal work on the structure of meaning showing that the implications of metaphor for the cognitive/emotive distinction in language were already taken into consideration in the twenties, Osgood's work on connotation in the late fifties based on the attempt to find universal patterns of affective associations (Besnier, 1990), and Asch's (1958) investigation of dual terms (e.g., "cold" used to denote a temperature as well as a person). It is only recently, though, that the structure of the affective or emotional lexicon has been investigated to test the extent to which figurative language (mostly metaphors and idioms) is indeed used.

For instance, Ortony and Fainsilber (1987) argued that because emotional states have an "elusive, transient quality" (p. 181) difficult to express in literal language (although we label emotions literally), metaphorical language might be well-suited to express the quality and intensity of such states. In their study, they had adult participants either linguistically describe how they *felt* when they experienced certain emotions, or what they *did* when they experienced them. They measured the extent to which people used metaphors or literal language in either one of the two conditions. They found a significantly greater proportion of metaphors in the descriptions of feelings than for actions, and more metaphors for intense than for mild emotions.

Additional evidence on the use of metaphors to describe feelings[23] is provided by Williams-Whitney, Mio, and Whitney (1992), who investigated autobiographical and nonautobiographical writing productions by experienced and novice writers. Overall, experienced writers produced more metaphors when describing actions and feeling than novices. More recently, Cacciari and Levorato (1996; Cacciari, Levorato, & Cicogna, 1997) asked a sample of children (third graders and fifth graders), teenagers, and adults to coin new linguistic expressions for labeling a set of emotion targets (e.g., being happy, ashamed, sad) and actions (e.g., telling a lie, revealing a secret, sleeping too much). We found a high proportion of figurative productions (overall 53.7%) that ranged from transparent to opaque metaphors, from metonymies to idiom variants. No significant difference emerged between the proportion of figurative expressions coined for actions (52%) and emotions (55.4%) across ages. It should be noted, however, that the action targets that we selected were mostly (seven out of nine) of a social nature and this might account, at least partially, for the lack of difference. Where the figurative productions related to emotion and action targets differed was in the mean ratings of comprehensibility, creativity, and goodness that we obtained from a separate set of adult judges: the new figurative expressions coined for emotions were judged significantly more comprehensible, creative, and good than those produced for actions.

While these studies investigated the use of linguistic metaphors for communicating various emotional meanings, a different stance has been taken by authors who investigated the structure and content of the folk models underlying emotion concepts and the conventionalized expressions (mostly idioms) by which they are expressed. This line of research is inspired by the conceptual metaphor view and hence assumes that emotion concepts and states are represented and understood via a complex set of metaphorical mappings belonging to domains other than that of emotions (Gibbs, 1994; Gibbs & O'Brien, 1990; Kovecses, 1986; Lakoff, 1987; but cf. Cacciari & Glucksberg, 1995; Glucksberg, Brown, & McGlone, 1993).

Setting and Changing the Conceptual Perspective

> Mother Sugar, otherwise Mrs Marks . . . as time passed, become a
> name for much more than a person, and indicated a whole way of
> looking at life—traditional, rooted, conservative, in spite of its
> scandalous familiarity with verything amoral.
>
> DORIS LESSING, *The Golden Notebook*

As Quinn (1991), among others, argued, metaphor instantiates the cultural models of the world we live in by being a powerful communicative *and* conceptual tool. This shift in the view of metaphor from a strictly linguistic entity to a more general conceptual structure has opened new directions for the study of metaphor (Gentner & Jeziorski, 1993; Gibbs, 1994; Glucksberg & Keysar, 1990, 1993; Lakoff, 1987; Lakoff & Turner, 1989; Murphy, 1996, 1997a). This new way of theorizing about metaphor assumes, as I already said, that metaphor comprehension and production involve many different parallel processes that

extend from a lexical-semantic level to inferential and c
from the use of previously acquired systems of conceptu?
the dynamic creation of new categories.

Metaphors also shed light and take advantage of th
norms shared in a given time in a given community. As
ingly argued, they "are reintroduced over and over ag¿
isfying instantiations of conventional or culturally shared models, ca⌐¬
tiple elements of that model" (p. 79). In a sense, they are real "windows" on
the world and values we live in (Beck, 1978, 1987; Holland & Quinn, 1987;
Sweetser, 1991).

It is important to acknowledge, however, that the idea that metaphor's relevance extends well beyond language has some important predecessors. Black's,
Reddy's and Schon's chapters in the 1979 edition of *Metaphor and Thought*
were already standard bearers of some version of the contemporary conceptual
view of metaphor, even though this went relatively unnoticed at the time.

Black's interaction view of metaphor in the late sixties already posited that
metaphor should be treated as "an instrument for drawing implications grounded
in perceived analogies of structure between two subjects belonging to different
domains" (Black, 1979, p. 31). Black vigorously insisted that some, not all,
metaphors are cognitive instruments that "enable us to see aspects of reality
that metaphor's production helps us to constitute" (p. 38). In a similar line of
thought, Schon (1979) argued that "the notion of (generative) metaphor has
became an interpretative tool for the critical analysis of social policy" (p. 139)
because metaphors create new frames. For instance, describing slum areas as
either a metaphor of disease or as a metaphor of natural community implies
totally different ways of setting the problems, the remedies, and required social
actions: cure and removal on the one hand, and preservation and restoration on
the other. Reddy (1979) acknowledged the conceptual power of metaphors by
saying that "English has a preferred framework for conceptualizing communication and can bias thought process toward this framework" (p. 165). Such a
framework is constituted by the "conduit metaphor" that underlies most of the
expressions concerning the role of language in transferring thoughts: "Language
functions like a conduit, transferring thought bodily from one person to another"
(p. 170). It is not surprising then that Lakoff (1993, p. 203) explicitly pays his
"Homage to Reddy."

The difference between saying that a slum is like a disease or that a slum is
a disease introduces an important change in perspective that reflects the difference between a *comparison* and a *categorization act*. In the first case (the "like"
form), we call the reader's attention to potential similarities between the subject
and the metaphorical vehicle that are marked as indirect by the linguistic op-
erator "like." In the second case (the "is a" form), we suggest instead that the
two entities (slums and diseases) have in common something more than mere

blances in that they belong to the same category sharing relevant features
d social problems and effects in this example). Such a special category,
aving no conventional name of its own, borrows that of a highly typical exemplar, "disease." Metaphorical vehicles, such as *disease* in this example, "label categories that have no conventional names" (Glucksberg & Keysar, 1993,
p. 423).

According to Glucksberg and Keysar (1990, 1993), using the name of a
prototypical category member to refer to a superordinate category not having a
conventional name of its own is based on a strategy analogous to the one used
by languages that have names for basic-level objects but generally lack superordinate category names. One such language is American Sign Language (ASL).
In ASL, basic-level objects have primary signs, comparable to single-word English names such as "chair," "table," "bed." The superordinate category of
"furniture" has no sign of its own in ASL. Instead, ASL signers use basic
object signs that are prototypical of that category, as in

HOUSE FIRE (+) LOSE ALL CHAIR-TABLE-BED ETC., BUT ONE LEFT, BED

which is interpretable as "I lost all my furniture in the house fire but one thing
was left: the bed" (Newport & Bellugi, 1978, p. 62).

At the end of the fifties, a predecessor of the current conceptual views of
metaphor, the psychologist Roger Brown, distinguished between different conceptual levels in a metaphor structure. He claimed that "when someone invents
a new machine, or forms a concept, or buys a dog, or manufactures a soap
powder, his first thought is to name it. These names are almost never arbitrary
creations produced by juggling the sounds of the language into a novel sequence.
. . . The usual method for creating a new name is to use words or morphemes
already in the language, either by expanding the semantic range of some word
or by recombining morphemes" (1958, p. 139). In "the foot of the mountain,"
the word "foot" refers to two categories, a subordinate and superordinate category: "[W]ithin this superordinate category, which we might name, *the foundations or lower parts of things,* are two subordinate categories, the man's foot
and the mountain's base. . . . Metaphor differs from other superordinate-
subordinate relations in that the superordinate is not given a name of its own.
Instead, the name of one subordinate is extended to the other" (p. 140; emphasis
added).

The use of exemplars (e.g., "disease" or "foot") accomplishes the same
attributive goal whether it refers to preexisting categories or when a new attributive category is created. A very common way for creating new categories is to
use the name of a highly salient person or event to refer to an entire class of
persons or events that bear some resemblance with the original. Such procedure
is exemplified in Doris Lessing's *The Golden Notebook* (1962), where she de-

scribes the psychoanalyst who is treating the novel's major protagonist as "Mother Sugar, otherwise Mrs Marks . . . as time passed, become a name for much more than a person, and indicated a whole way of looking at life, traditional, rooted, conservative, in spite of its scandalous familiarity with everything amoral" (p. 26, quoted in Cacciari and Glucksberg, 1994, p. 463). A complex concept having no name borrows the name of what is an ideal exemplar in the small world represented by the characters of the novel, Mother Sugar.

Political commentaries in newspapers often use a "dual reference"[24] mechanism in which the name of a prototypical category instance is used as the name for the category itself (Glucksberg & Keysar, 1993; Glucksberg & Manfredi, 1995; Glucksberg, Manfredi, & McGlone, 1997). As an example, consider the following quotation: "Cambodia had become Vietnam's Vietnam" (in Glucksberg, Manfredi, & McGlone, 1997). The dual function of the word "Vietnam" is explicit: its first mention refers to the country itself, but the second refers, as Glucksberg, Manfredi, and McGlone argued, to "the category of disastrous military interventions that the Vietnam war has come to epitomize."[25] Another interesting example of a reversed, in this case, double reference comes from the following quotation (Turner (1991, p. 198): "Because of its many canals, Venice is sometimes called the Venice of Italy" (James McCauley). Here, the Italian Venice stands as the most known exemplar of the many places full of canals (e.g., Bruges, Amsterdam); it is then nominated again as "the Venice of Italy" to allude, at least to my understanding, to the American habit of naming American towns after European ones (e.g., Paris, Attica, and so forth).

People also use metaphor for describing a referent that has no conventional name. As showed by studies on referential communication, (cf. Krauss & Glucksberg, 1977, for instance), if you ask people to describe irregularly shaped geometrical forms (see fig. 4.2), they do not start from analytical, prolix literal descriptions such as "two triangles, the superior one is inverted, has two descending arcs, one on each side," but instead use a nonliteral strategy of description ("an hourglass with legs on each side"). After repeated references, the group of subjects involved in the referential task names the object metaphorically: the object's name is "the hourglass." For those involved in the communicative interchange, the reference is unequivocal, being the output of a negotiated reference-fixing process (Krauss & Glucksberg, 1977).

When we use a naming strategy in which we name a class of people using a highly salient person (as in Doris Lessing's description of the psychoanalyst of *The Golden Notebook*), we can say that "X is a Y" or that "X is like Y." Do they mean the same? Apparently not. As Glucksberg and Keysar (1990, cf. also Black, 1979) pointed out, we use the "is a" form "to alert a listener that a specific relation is intended, not simply a general assertion of similarity" (Glucksberg & Keysar, 1990, p. 15). If someone says "That actor is a real Bela Lugosi,"[26] he or she intends to include the actor in the category of those best

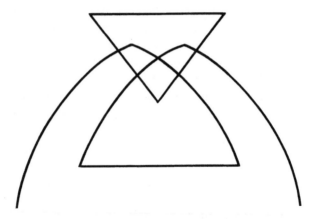

FIGURE 4.2. Object to be named in a referential task (after Krauss & Glucksberg, 1977).

exemplified by Bela Lugosi, so he "takes on all the properties of the *type of actor,* not of the actor Bela Lugosi himself" (Glucksberg & Keysar, 1990, p. 16, italics added). Saying that someone is merely "like" Bela Lugosi can, for instance, signal that the actor tries his best to imitate Bela Lugosi's style (cf. Cacciari, 1995), which leaves unspecified exactly what properties are intended in the comparison. The choice between the "is a" and the "is like" forms produces an enhancement of some properties and, presumably, a suppression of others.[27] As Turner (1991) pointed out, if someone says "She is a witch," we understand that she behaves in a witchy way, not that she looks like a witch: "[T]o indicate that someone looks like a witch, one must say explicitly 'she looks like a witch' (Turner, 1991, p. 185).

Good metaphors do something more than simply calling our attention toward some already existing similarities: they force us to see things in a different perspective and to reconceptualize them accordingly. Such change of knowledge not only occurs at the level of the representation of single entities but involves the domains or semantic fields to which they belong (cf. Lehrer, 1978; Steinhart & Kittay, 1994; Tourangeau & Sternberg, 1981, 1982). This is true also for conventional metaphors that activate much more than a single extended meaning definition in the reader. They provide access to an "encyclopedic schema" made up of different levels of implications. This is the reason why even these meta-phors cannot be concisely paraphrased without losing aspects of their sense (cf. Sperber & Wilson's discussion of "This room is a pigsty," 1986, pp. 235–36).

Despite the agreement about the perspective-changing power of metaphor,[28] there is, as Gentner and Wolff (ms., p. 2) recently noted, "little consensus on *how* such change might occur: that is, on what processes might bring about knowledge change'' (emphasis added). Gentner and Wolff therefore proposed four specific mechanisms by which metaphor (and analogy) can produce a change of knowledge: ''[M]etaphors can highlight, project, re-represent, and restructure'' (p. 35). Let us examine these mechanisms in more detail:

1. *Highlighting* is a rather frequent mechanism in everyday cognition: ''[M]etaphors have the ability to select a certain part of a representation'' (p. 7). The outcome of the mental change induced by metaphor can be either a dismissal of irrelevant information or the attribution of saliency to sections of knowledge that were out of focus. When knowledge selection involves isolating low-salient properties, ''the process can be referred to as *highlighting*'' (Gentner and Wolff, p. 7; emphasis added).

2. *Projection* is a mechanism typical of scientific analogies (and of everyday metaphors as well). It consists of a process whereby candidate inferences are transferred from one domain to another. This ''carry-over'' of information involves a mapping of such inferences ''across parts of the relational structure of the base that are connected to the base's matching structure, but for which there is not yet corresponding structure in the target'' (p. 11). Once the candidate inferences are identified, they are carried over from the base to the target structure.

3. *Predicate re-representation* consists of a decomposition of predicates into subpredicate structures that are then matched to discover potential similarities. As an example, Gentner and Wolff cited the metaphor ''the hotter the anger the sooner quenched,'' where the predicates of two nonidentical entities—anger and temperature—must be put in some form of correspondence.[29]

4. *Knowledge restructuring* occurs when not only individual concepts but systems of knowledge are involved.[30] Again, the history of scientific discoveries provides plenty of examples: the conceptualization of electrons in the atom as distributed around some central force—the solar system—like planets, proposed by Rutherford in the first decade of this century, is a well-known example of knowledge restructuring via a new explanatory metaphor that licensed a number of predications concerning the structure of the hydrogen atom in itself.

A domain in which growing interest has emerged for the conceptual perspective selected by speakers when they use a metaphor is that of legal reasoning (Gibbs, 1994; Winter, 1989). According to Winter, in the domain of legal analysis there is a tradition that considers metaphor as ''transcendental nonsense'': ''This is the realistic attack on metaphor as a formalist or rhetorical trope that distorts legal thinking'' (p. 1160). For much legal thought, Winter argues, figurative language distorts reality and ''propositions'' and ''rigorous logic'' that are the proper bases of legal reasoning. As Justice Benjamin Cardozo stated in

'd in Winter, 1989, p. 1162), "[M]etaphors in law are to be narrowly
though they started as devices for liberating thought, they end often

What Winter shows by examining several legal texts and acts is that most of
the architecture of legal reasoning is based on metaphors.[31] This use of metaphorical templates extends well beyond some sporadic example and touches on
basic parts of the American legal system. Even the first amendment to the Constitution can be read as an extended metaphor: "[O]ur modern understanding
of the first amendment is dependent upon the use of the market metaphor. The
metaphor carries over from the source domain of economic experience certain
normative, cultural assumptions about the usefulness and value of autonomy and
free trade and applies them to target domain of free speech" (Winter, 1989, p.
1190). Also, basic concepts such as those of "rights" and "law" can be interpreted on nonliteral grounds. According to Winter, the "idealized cognitive
model" (Lakoff, 1987) that underlies the metaphorical bases of the concept of
"rights" in the Anglo-Saxon tradition can be summarized as follows: "Law is
person; actions are motions; constraint on actions are constraints on motions;
control is up; rights (and other legal rules) are paths; rational argument is war;
rights are possessions "(p. 1222).

To Winter, this kind of analysis represents a fundamental step toward uncovering the implicit construction of social reality: "[T]o understand the cognitive structure of LAW is to understand what law 'really is'; it is to understand
law's *social* meaning" (p. 1222) and ground legal meaning and practice in a
democratic way.

Saving Face: Metaphor and Indirectness

> It's too bad that you didn't try to learn about wise words before.
> When I was young, old people around here used to make them up
> all the time. Only a few people did it and they were the best talk-
> ers of all. . . . Those old people were smart. One of them would
> make a new one and right away other people would start to use it.
> . . . Only the good talkers can make them up like that. They are the
> ones who *really* speak Apache. They are the ones who make up
> 'wise words' and don't have to use someone else's.
>
> A WESTERN APACHE CONSULTANT SPEAKING TO THE
> ANTHROPOLOGIST KEITH BASSO

In some cultures, metaphors are systematically used to describe persons. For the
Western Apache, for example, nominal metaphors are a distinct speech genre
associated with "wise" adult men and women (Basso, 1976). The interpretation
of these "wise words" relies upon the following characteristics: metaphors specify only one or more "behavioral attributes" that are "indicative of undesirable

qualities possessed by the referents of the metaphor's constituents'' (p. 104). Wise words invariably refer to negative attributes of people.

Perhaps in our culture wise words can also be used in order to maintain standards of politeness (Brown & Levinson, 1978). Literal language can be far too explicit and more ''face-threatening'' than metaphorical language, which can always provide the speaker with an out (''You didn't understand me''). Wise words, unlike explicit attributions, can in fact be ignored or misunderstood (cf. also Drew & Holt, 1988; Fussell, 1992; Katz, chap. 1; Leech, 1983; Levinson, 1978). The figurative structure of many insults or euphemisms exemplifies such preference for indirectness when negative comments are involved. We can use creative figurative language to avoid committing ourselves personally in such a way that, as Gerrig and Gibbs observed (1988, p. 12), ''a speaker can thus voice his or her own opinion without being strictly accountable for it.''

More than a matter of indirectness (a frozen metaphor can in fact be as direct as a literal expression), metaphor's use in interpersonal relationships seems to reflect two other factors: the first is the creation of a sense of in-groupness; that is, metaphor can create a sense of belonging. Second, it communicates a complex set of attributes, often in a rather ambiguous fashion.

As Cohen (1979) pointed out, intimacy within a group can be reached by using a certain communicative style. Metaphor can thus serve this ''achievement of intimacy'' (p. 6): ''[A]ll literal use of language is accessible to all whose language it is. But a figurative use can be accessible to all but those who share information about one another's knowledge, beliefs, intentions, and attitudes'' (p. 7). Like lines of poetry, creative metaphors can create an ''affective mutuality'' in that they create ''common impressions rather than common knowledge. Utterances with poetic effects can be used precisely to create this sense of apparently affective rather than cognitive mutuality'' (Sperber & Wilson, 1986, p. 224).

Much like irony, metaphor can be used to create the community of those who understand it and can figure out the point of the expression. Metaphor invites the addressee to an active reception of the intended content, to a creative ''uptake'' (Richards, 1936). But as Gerrig and Gibbs (1988, p. 8) noted, creativity has ''a dark side: The intimacy it creates can serve as an agent of exclusion.'' Intimacy in fact can have negative consequences for the addressee if he or she does not share the necessary common ground with the speaker and can create two audiences: ''an inner circle in the known and an outer circle in the dark'' (Gerrig & Gibbs, 1988, p. 8).

The demanding nature of metaphor interpretation (of course of the innovative ones) has been stressed also by Davidson (1978, p. 29) when he described metaphor as ''the dreamwork of language'': ''[L]ike all dreamwork, its interpretation reflects as much on the interpreter as on the originator. The interpretation of dreams requires collaboration between a dreamer and a weaker, even if they be the same person; and the act of interpretation is itself a work of imagination. So too understanding a metaphor is as much a creative endeavor as making a metaphor, and as little guided by rules.''

What happens when such creative collaboration fails or is impossible? The risk for metaphor to be vague[32] or worse, much too ambiguous, is one, maybe the crucial, argument for a negative appraisal of the use of metaphor (as we already saw in Justice Cardozo's statement). But, as Black observed (1979, p. 29), one should bear in mind that ''ambiguity is a necessary by-product of the metaphor's suggestiveness.''[33]

That metaphors are more polysemous than literal expressions is suggested by recent evidence on the use of metaphor to describe people (Cacciari, 1998). I asked different groups of subjects either to give a paraphrase or to list the properties of a set of metaphorical vehicles (e.g., ''volcano,'' ''snake,'' ''angel'') and of literal terms (e.g., ''thief,'' ''gentleman,'' ''misanthropist'') commonly used to describe persons. Not surprisingly, I found a broader range of paraphrases for metaphors than for nonliteral terms and a lower intersubject agreement in the interpretations assigned to metaphorical terms with respect to literal ones (cf. also Fraser, 1979; Fussell, 1992, for similar results). As pointed out by Fraser (1979; Black, 1979), the wide variation of interpretations that people often generate when asked to interpret metaphors does not imply that they are inconsistent. After all, people do understand each other when they speak metaphorically, and often as much as (if not much more so) than when they speak literally, if such a sharp distinction indeed can be made (see Powell, 1992; Rumelhart, 1979).

Summarizing Bundles of Properties

> Are they really words? I no more know exactly what words, images and ideas are. No, they are things that shine and make us feel their entire strength; calm and beautiful things, recognizable from every part, signs with no mystery, clear drawings, dancing bodies, cries, slow flights of cormorants, sharks darting in the gelid water, snowed peaks in the distance, valleys, bridges, wakes of ships, tracks of jet planes, footprints on the sand. The words of the speaking voice are all this and even many more things.
> JEAN MARIE G. LE CLÉZIO, *Vers les icebergs.*

> ''Even the word ''dog'': you cannot imagine it; it is only an indication, a hint to certain determinate dogs and canine properties.
> ROBERT MUSIL, *A Man Without Quality*

That metaphor's interpretations are often somewhat idiosyncratic depends also on the fact that metaphors provide a compact form of expression for complex ideas (Ortony, 1980).[34] When alternative literal expressions are available in a language, they may be very prolix by comparison. That this is indeed the case has been recently confirmed, for instance, in the study on the use of metaphor for describing people that I mentioned in the previous paragraph (Cacciari, 1998): not only did metaphors—unlike literal terms—require much more than a single word to be paraphrased, but also a significantly higher number of properties was associated with them.

One might wonder whether figurative language, and particularly metaphor, is subject to paraphrase at all (Townsend, 1988). Black (1979, p. 79) stressed that a literal paraphrase "inevitably says too much—and with the wrong emphasis. . . . [T]he loss in such cases is a loss in cognitive content." On the contrary, Townsend (1988, cf. Beardsley, 1958) defended the possibility of (successfully) paraphrasing figurative language (with the exception of poetry), arguing that one important function of paraphrase "is to select from among multiple possibilities of interpretation. . . . Paraphrase is an interpretive enterprise" (p. 50). Hence, if one means that literal paraphrases have less emphasis, are less vivid, less affectively tuned, and possess less variety of possible nuances of interpretation, then Black is certainly correct. This is in fact the cognitive force of metaphors. Paraphrases are, at best, possible substitutes for a small subset of properties. This is presumably at the core of the relative lack of intersubject agreement on metaphor interpretation that I found.

So, generally speaking, metaphors serve to predicate a complex bundle of properties as a whole that often cannot be synthetically specified. When one interprets an expression such as "My job is a jail" he or she means that his or her job is stifling, unrewarding, confining, etc. It is precisely this *etc.* that constitutes both the emotive force and the cognitive power of metaphor. As Sperber and Wilson (1986) pointed out, in fact, sometimes the difference between a truly creative and a more standardized metaphor lies in the amount of predication (what they call "implicatures") that they respectively allow: "[T]he wider the range of potential implicatures and the greater the hearer's responsibility for constructing them, the more poetic the effect, the more creative the metaphor" (p. 236).

But how can we characterize these units of information that are transferred from the vehicle to the topic (to speak it in the words of the classic Aristotelian viewpoint) and that form the ground for the metaphorical interpretation? Traditional accounts of metaphor comprehension are based on the assumption that in metaphors of the form "An X is a Y," the X and Y nouns are represented either as sets of features or by their positions in a geometric semantic space (cf. Johnson & Malgady, 1979; Marschark, Katz, & Paivio, 1983; Tourangeau & Sternberg, 1981). The standard feature matching approach is summarized in the Venn diagram represented in figure 4.3.

Regardless of specific representations assumptions, feature matching models

"A IS B"

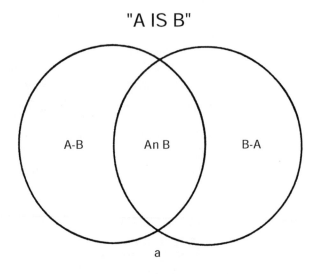

a

"DEW IS A VEIL"

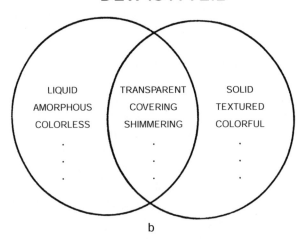

b

FIGURE 4.3. (a) Venn diagram illustration of common and distinctive feature sets for the metaphor ''A is B''; (b) Venn diagram illustration of the partition of open feature sets for the metaphoric example Dew is a veil (after Malgady & Johnson, 1980).

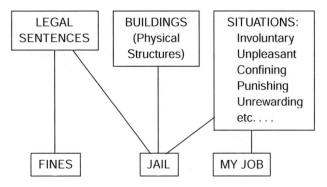

FIGURE 4.4. Cross-classification of jails and jobs: partial illustration (after Glucksberg & Keysar, 1990).

assume that metaphors are first transformed into comparison statements and then the features of the vehicle are compared to, or mapped onto, the features of the topic. These two basic claims—that metaphors are comparisons and that the metaphorical comparison is derived from a sharing of features—have been criticized on several grounds (Cacciari & Glucksberg, 1994; Glucksberg & Keysar, 1990; Johnson, 1996; Katz, chap. 1; Ortony, 1993).

Recently, Glucksberg and Keysar proposed the property attribution model (1990; cf. also Glucksberg, Manfredi, & McGlone, 1997) that suggests a modification of the traditional role assigned to the topic and vehicle functions. In nominal metaphors (such, as for instance, "My job is a jail"), the metaphor topic ("job") and the vehicle ("jail") play distinctive roles in that the topic provides constraints on what is likely to be attributed to it, while the vehicle provides properties to be attributed to the topic. The relevance of a given property to a topic can best be described at the level of dimensions of attribution. As already mentioned, in this model metaphorical vehicles are located at two different levels of category abstraction (as summarized in fig. 4.4, after Glucksberg & Keysar, 1990): the literal concrete level (the subordinate level) where they are members of a class of entities and the more general, superordinate, attributive category level. For example, a metaphor vehicle such as "jail" can refer simultaneously to a concrete physical structure and to the metaphorical category of situations that are involuntary, unpleasant, confining, and so forth. The literal "jail" contains all the properties of the superordinate category "jail" plus the properties that are specific to a jail per se (e.g., having painted walls, being made of concrete, etc.).

One of the problems that traditional matching models are unable to resolve was that of property selection, namely, the difference between "mere sharing" and "pertinent sharing" of features (Glucksberg & Keysar, 1990; Tyler, 1978).

Glucksberg and Keysar's model seems to successfully deal with property selection in that it assumes that (a) different categorical level (''jail'' as a superordinate category and ''jail'' as a member, due to the dual reference function), and (b) matching of attributes of the vehicle that can provide values for attributes of the topic.

Consider the metaphor vehicle ''gold mine'' (Glucksberg, Manfredi, & McGlone, 1997). Such a concept includes concrete properties (containing a precious metal, being a source of wealth, etc.) that are instantiations of a more general concept, that of richness. This general property provides different values to any attribute that can vary along the dimension richness/poorness. If we can reasonably use the concept of richness to predicate something sensible about a specific discourse topic, then the concept is instantiated. So, unlike what is claimed by traditional feature matching models, a metaphor vehicle such as ''gold mine'' does not provide a specific property, but rather a value of an attribute that ranges along the dimension richness/poorness.

Different topics will therefore instantiate different values: ''[L]ibraries that are gold mines contain large and useful collections of books and manuscripts, while inventions that are gold mines will earn a great deal of money'' (Glucksberg, Manfredi, & McGlone,1997). This makes this approach rather flexible in instantiating different attributes depending upon the metaphor topic so that the salience and the values of the attributes are entirely dependent on the concepts highlighted in each metaphor (cf. Murphy, 1996, 1997b).

This mechanism of attribute-value matching proposed by Glucksberg and collaborators bears some interesting resemblances to the framework proposed by Barsalou (1992) for the organization of knowledge in memory. Barsalou claims that, unlike what is posited by feature list models of representation, the characteristics of the knowledge organization of exemplars is dynamic and typically form ''attribute-value sets, with some characteristics (values) being instances of other characteristics (attributes)'' (Barsalou, 1992, p. 25). For instance, ''blue'' and ''green'' are values of ''color,'' ''swim'' and ''fly'' are values of ''locomotion,'' ''round'' and ''squared'' are values of ''shape.'' Attribute-values are interrelated sets of representational components that are not stored independently. These attribute-value sets and relations (together with structural invariants and constraint) will form the basic components of frames.

CONCLUSIONS

Would the ''conversational machine'' described by Tolstoy in the quote with which I opened my chapter function without metaphor? Based on the functions of metaphor discussed in this chapter, my answer is that it certainly would not.

Metaphor in fact "gives word," so to speak, to relev
experience of the world that otherwise would be diffic
to use Koehler's words, metaphors capitalize over the
"facts of the inner life and perceptual facts" may hav
thermore, metaphor enables us to dynamically extend ou
and so is a key mechanism for changing our ways of repre
thought and language. Hence, metaphors are epistemologically an
catively necessary.

As Reider (1972, p. 469) noted, metaphor is "the most economic conden-
sation of understanding of many levels of experience, several fixations, symbolic
connotations, and an aesthetic ambiguity, all in a phrase." To use an analogy,
one can agree with Sticht that just as the tool function of the hammer is "to
extend the strength of the arm and the hardness of the fist, and just as the tool
function of the telescope is to extend the range of the eye" (Sticht, 1993, p.
622), the function of metaphor is to extend human communicative and conceptual capacities. But unlike hammers or telescopes, metaphors also have a life of
their own because they give a linguistic identity to events, persons, and entities
using already existing systems of knowledge. This is one of the reasons why
anthropologists have always been interested in metaphors as part of the symbolic
system adopted by a culture (cf., for instance, Fernandez, 1991). Metaphors in
fact are windows to the systems of knowledge that are relevant and central in
a given culture. If it is true that metaphors are generally used for expressing the
new with the old, then the choice of which parts of our knowledge base will be
used to shape what is to be named or explained is revelative of the systems of
relevance implicitly adopted. That is why metaphor is not only the dreamwork
of language but also the dreamwork of perception and thinking.

NOTES

1. There are very few studies of the processes underlying metaphor production even
by psycholinguists already working on figurative language (e.g., Cacciari & Levorato,
1996; Edwards & Clevenger, 1990; Ortony & Fainsilber, 1987; Fussell, 1992; Katz,
1989; Pitts, Smith, & Pollio, 1982; Williams-Whitney, Mio & Whitney, 1992).

2. I will confine myself to considering verbal metaphors, but this is only one of the
mediums for realizing metaphors. For an analysis of pictorial metaphors, see, for example, Forceville, 1994; Kennedy, 1982.

3. I am here concerned especially with the general characteristics of metaphors in
discourse and reasoning, but metaphors are of course used in specific contexts that impose
a number of constraints that I am not considering here. The role of metaphor is well-
documented in domains such as science (Hesse, 1953; Gentner & Jeziorski, 1993), psychotherapy (Billow et al;, 1987; Reider, 1972; Rothenberg, 1984; Mio & Katz, 1996),

...sign (Dent-Read, Klein, & Eggleston, 1994) organization theories (Grant & ...; 1996; Kensing & Halskov Madsen, 1991).

4. Polysemy belongs to language to court, as many authors argued (e.g., Murphy, 1997b; Nunberg, 1979, 1978).

5. The study of the "affective dimensions of meaning," as Osgood named it, in connection with color has a long history in psychology.

6. As described in the ancient Greek culture with reference to the concept of light or, for instance, by authors such as Lucretius living in the Roman culture.

7. Another among such examples is the association of a drawing and a word first investigated by Koehler (1929, 1947) with respect to two meaningless words such as "takete" and "maluma" (cf. Savardi & Pelamatti, 1996, for a review and some interesting new evidence).

8. The antecedents of the Gestalt theory with respect to this point can be found in the pioneering work on the "figural" or "formal" properties of objects of Von Meinong (1904), and Von Ehrenfels (1890), who in turn was inspired by Mach's notations on feeling a melody.

9. In this novel (written between 1926 and 1929, one of her last) each of the six personages has a color and each feeling has one as well. Virginia Woolf had Neville, one of the characters say, "I am clouded and bruised with the prints of minds and faces and things so subtle that they have smell, color, texture, substance, but no name" (p. 214).

10. Recent development of this idea can be seen in the work by Norman (1988, 1992) on designing objects and work environments.

11. The two notions—tertiary properties and affordances—do not exactly overlap. The first seems to include a broader range of phenomena. For a discussion, see Bozzi, 1990, chap. 3.

12. "The basic properties of the environment that combine to make an affordance are specified in the structure of ambient light and hence the affordance itself is specified in the ambient light" (Gibson, 1977, p. 82).

13. This novel describes the last months spent by the 15-year-old Torless at a military academy located in a remote corner of the Austrian Empire. The Austrian writer Musil (1880–1942) lived in one of the most culturally rich of recent eras—the crisis of the turn of the century. Musil is generally considered by literary critics as a psychological writer of the inner life, but it should be noted that he had a background in experimental psychology as well. In fact, after graduating in engineering with a dissertation on Mach's theories, he got his PhD in Berlin at the Institute of Psychology, directed by Stumpf, where he met both Wertheimer and Koehler and also studied Fechner and von Meinong's works.

14. To Gentner, Falkenhainer, and Skorstad (1987), this is a relational metaphor based on analogical mappings (see their study for a detailed analysis of such mappings).

15. I want to thank Ugo Savardi, who brought this example to my attention. Ugo Savardi has conducted a very interesting analysis of Musil's perceptual metaphors, which is not yet published. Anna Pelamatti, Ugo Savardi, and I are currently engaged in a theoretical project concerning sensory intermodality and metaphor in Musil and Proust.

16. As Musil had Torless say: "It was the failure of language that caused him such anguish, a half awareness that words were merely accidental, mere evasions and never the feeling itself" (*Young Torless*, pp. 72–73).

17. Many literary scholars have identified Musil as one of the more "metaphorical" writers of the age, especially in *A Man Without Quality* (cf. Gargani, 1983).

18. Williams also considers "post–first-order transfers" but they seem to obey the same general constraints.

19. Aristotle in De Anima discussed the five senses in the order sight-hearing-smell-taste-touch and observed the lack of metaphorical olfactory words in Greek, a condition present for Williams (1976) also in other Indo-European languages and in Japanese.

20. Sight and sound for Ullmann are similarly high modalities, so either one is equally likely to be a target or a modifier.

21. To these authors, there is a difference (in the developmental acquisition and neurophysiological functioning) between *synesthetic metaphors* that are based on normative, probably congenital and innate perceptual similarities and *synesthetic metonymies* (e.g., color-temperature associations) that seem to reflect universal experiences. Since the difference between metaphors and metonymies is quite often rather vague, I do not consider it further.

22. Synesthetes (predominantly women, according to Cytowic, 1989) are normal persons (usually having exceptional memory) for which the stimulation of one sense produces an involuntary perception in another sense. One of the more common forms is sight with sound, or "colored hearing."

23. The role of metaphor in the verbal description of psychological states has been widely debated by psychotherapists and psychoanalyists, see Billow et al., 1987, and Gibbs 1994 for a review of the negative and positive aspects of such a role.

24. Dual reference is a mechanism not at all specific to metaphor, as the use of a brand name to denote an entire class of objects shows (e.,g.,"Kleenex" to denote the entire class of paper tissue). What is specific to metaphor is the class-inclusion mechanism proposed.

25. Davidson (1978, p. 32) captured the relevance of the "literal" referent contained in a metaphorical vehicle when he stated that "an adequate account of metaphor must allow that the primary or original meanings of words remain active in their metaphorical setting."

26. Bela Lugosi was the actor who played the vampire in many of the Dracula movies in the 1930s and 1940s; his portrayal came to epitomize the sinister nature of vampires.

27. On the role of suppression and enhancement mechanisms in metaphor interpretation, see Gernsbacher, Keysar, & Robertson (1995) and Newsome & Glucksberg (1996).

28. This peculiar power of metaphor can be interpreted also with reference to Wittgenstein's notion of "seeing as" or "perspectival seeing" (Wittgenstein, 1953; for comments and references see Johnson, 1981).

29. The structural alignment model proposed by Gentner and collaborators treats "metaphor as akin to analogy" (Gentner & Wolff, ms., p. 3): metaphors are basically forms of comparison that are understood via a process of alignment and mapping between the structured representations of the tenor and vehicle (e.g., Gentner, Falkenhainer, & Skorstad, 1988; Gentner & Jeziorsky, 1993).

30. Interesting examples of systems of knowledge mapped metaphorically come from an analysis of the evolution of the mental metaphors used in experimental psychology before the full introduction of computer technology (based on a corpus of articles published in *Psychological Review* from 1894 to 1975) (Gentner & Grudin, 1985; cf. also

Smith, Pollio, & Pitts, 1981, on the metaphors pervading the American intellectual history).

31. The dominant Western iconography of Justice is full of visual metaphors as well. Consider, for instance, "the goddess Justitia, the familiar image of the blind-folded woman who holds aloft the scales of justice in her left hand, also carries a sword in her right" (Winter, 1989, p. 1212).

32. For a rehabilitation of the notion of "vagueness" as a better accommodation of language to the causal structure of the world, see Boyd, 1993.

33. Not all metaphors are of course equal. We are referring to the most felicitous ones. In fact, "metaphors are like jokes; good ones can be very successful, but bad ones can be disastrous" (Ortony, 1980, p. 364).

34. Ortony refers explicitly to metaphors, but idomatic expressions also possess this "summarizing property" (Drew & Holt, 1988, 1992).

REFERENCES

Asch, S. (1958). The metaphor: A psychological inquiry. In R. Tagiuri & L. Petrullo (Eds.), *Person perception and interpersonal behavior* (pp. 86–94). Stanford: Stanford University Press.

Baron-Cohen, S., & Harrison, J. E. (Eds.). (1997). *Synaesthesia. Classic and contemporary readings*. Cambridge, MA: Blackwell.

Baron-Cohen, S., Wyke, M. A., & Binnie, C. (1987). Hearing words and seeing colors: an experimental investigation of a case of synesthesia. *Perception, 16,* 761–767.

Barsalou, L. W. (1992). Frames, concepts, and conceptual fields. In A. Lehrer & E. F. Kittay (Eds.), *Frames, fields and contrasts: New essays in semantic and lexical organization* (pp. 21–74). Hillsdale, NJ: Erlbaum.

Basso, K. H. (1976). "Wise words" of the Western Apache: Metaphor and semantic theory. In K. H. Basso (Ed.), *Meaning in anthropology* (pp. 93–121). Albuquerque: University of New Mexico Press.

Beardsley, M. (1958). *Aesthetics*. New York: Harcourt and Brace.

Beck, B. (1978). The metaphor as a mediator between semantic and analogic modes of thought. *Current Anthropology, 19,* 83–94.

Beck, B. (1987). Metaphor, cognition and Artificial Intelligence. In R. S. Haskell (Ed.), *Cognition and symbolic structure: The psychology of metaphoric transformation* (pp. 9–30). Norwood, NJ: Ablex Publishing.

Besnier, N. (1990). Language and affect. *Annual Review of Anthopology, 19,* 419–451.

Bierwisch, M., & Schreuder, R. (1992). From concepts to lexical items. *Cognition, 42,* 23–60.

Billow, R. M., Rossman, J., Lewis, N., Goldman, D., Kraemer, S., & Ross, P. (1987). Metaphoric communication and miscommunication in schizophrenic and borderline states. In R. S. Haskell (Ed.), *Cognition and symbolic structure: The psychology of metaphoric transformation* (pp. 141–162). Norwood, NJ: Ablex Publishing.

Black, M. (1962). *Models and metaphors*. Ithaca, NY: Cornell University Press.

Black, M. (1979). More about metaphor. In A. Ortony (Ed.), *Metaphor and thought* (pp. 19–43). New York: Cambridge University Press.

Boyd, R. (1993). Metaphor and theory change: What is "metaphor" a metaphor for? In A. Ortony (Ed.), *Metaphor and thought,* 2nd ed. (pp. 481–532). New York: Cambridge University Press.

Bozzi, P. (1989). *Fenomenologia sperimentale.* Bologna: Il Mulino.

Bozzi, P. (1990). *Fisica ingenua.* Milano: Garzanti.

Brown, R. (1958). *Words and things.* New York: Free Press.

Brown, P., & Levinson, S. (1978). Universals in language usages: Politeness phenomena. In E. Goody (Ed.), *Questions and politeness. Strategies of social interaction* (pp. 56–310). London: Cambridge University Press.

Cacciari, C. (Ed.). (1995). Preface. In C. Cacciari (Ed.), *Similarity in language, thought and perception* (pp. 7–13). Turnhout (Bruxelles): Brepols.

Cacciari, C. (1998). Compactness and conceptual complexity of conventionalized and creative metaphors in Italian. In D. Hillert (Ed.), *Syntax and Semantics, vol. 31, A crosslinguistic perspective* (pp. 405-425). New York: Academic Press.

Cacciari, C., & Glucksberg, S. (1994). Understanding figurative language. In M. Gernsbacher (Ed.), *Handbook of psycholinguistics* (pp. 447–477). New York: Academic Press.

Cacciari, C., & Glucksberg, S. (1995). Understanding idioms: Do visual images reflect figurative meanings? *European Journal of Cognitive Psychology, 7*(3), 283–305.

Cacciari, C., & Levorato, M. C. (1996). *Metaphorically speaking: The relationship between language innovation and figurative language.* Poster presented at the 37th Annual Meeting of the Psychonomic Society, Chicago, October 31–November 3.

Cacciari, C., Levorato, M. C., & Cicogna, P. (1997). Imagination at work: Conceptual and linguistic creativity in children. In T. B. Ward, S. M. Smith & J. Vaid (Eds.). *Creative thought: An investigation of conceptual structures and processes* (pp. 145–177). Washington, DC: American Psychological Association.

Chierchia, G., & McConnel-Ginet, S. (1990). *Meaning and grammar: An introduction to semantics.* Cambridge, MA: MIT Press.

Cohen, T. (1979). The cultivation of intimacy. In S. Sacks (Ed.), *On metaphor* (pp. 1–10). Chicago: University of Chicago Press.

Clark, H. H. (1973). Space, time, semantics and the child. In T. E. Moore (Ed.), *Cognitive development and the acquisition of language* (pp. 27–64). New York: Academic Press.

Cruse, D. A. (1986). *Lexical semantics.* Cambridge: Cambridge University Press.

Cytowic, R. E. (1989a). Synesthesia and mapping of subjective sensory dimensions. *Neurology, 39,* 849–850.

Cytowic, R. E. (1989b). *Synesthesia: A union of the senses.* New York: Springer Verlag.

Cytowic, R. E., & F. B. Wood (1982a). Synesthesia: I. A review of major theories and brain basis. *Brain and Cognition, 1,* 23–35.

Cytowic, R. E., & F. B. Wood (1982b). II. Psychophysical relations in the synesthesia of geometrically shaped taste and colored hearing. *Brain and Cognition, 1,* 36–49.

Davidson, D. (1978). What metaphors mean. In S. Sacks (Ed.), *On metaphor* (pp. 29–46). Chicago: University of Chicago Press.

Davitz, J. R., & Mattis, S. (1969). The communication of emotional meaning by metaphor. In J. R. Davitz (Ed.), *The communication of emotional meaning* (pp. 157–176). Westport, CT: Greenwood Press.

Dent-Read, C. H., Klein, G., & Eggleston, R. (1994). Metaphor in visual displays designed to guide action. *Metaphor and Symbolic Activity, 9*(3), 211–232.

Derrig, S. (1978). Metaphor in the color lexicon. In D. Farkas, W. M. Jacobsen, & K. W. Todyris (Eds.), *Papers from the parasession on the lexicon* (pp. 85–96). Chicago: Chicago Linguistic Society.

Drew, P., & Holt, E. (1988). Complainable matters: The use of idiomatic expressions in making complaints. *Social Problems, 35*(4), 98–117.

Drew, P., & Holt, E. (1992). Idiomatic expressions and their role in the organization of topic transition in conversation. In *Proceedings of Idioms. International Conference on Idioms.* Tilburg, the Netherlands, pp. 171–185.

Edwards, R., & Clevenger, T., Jr. (1990). The effects of schematic and affective processes on metaphoric invention. *Journal of Psycholinguistic Research, 19*(2), 91–102.

Fernandez, J. W. (Ed.). (1991). *Beyond metaphor. The theory of tropes in anthropology.* Stanford, CA: Stanford University Press.

Forceville, C. (1994). Pictorial metaphor in advertising. *Metaphor and Symbolic Activity, 9*(1), 1–29.

Fraser, B. (1979). The interpretation of novel metaphors. In A. Ortony (Ed.), *Metaphor and Thought* (pp. 172–185). New York: Cambridge University Press.

Fussell, S. (1992). *Creating and interpreting personality metaphors.* Poster presented at the Annual Meeting of the Eastern Psychological Association, Boston.

Galton, F. (1883). Colour associations. In S. Baron-Cohen & J. E. Harrison (Eds.). (1997). *Synaesthesia. Classic and contemporary readings* (pp. 43–48). Cambridge, MA: Blackwell.

Gargani, A. (1983). Scienza, letteratura e civilizzazione. In R. Morello (a cura di), *Anima ed esattezza. Letteratura e scienza nella cultura austriaca tra Ottocento e Novecento* (pp. 34–52). Casale Monferrato: Marietti.

Gentner, D., Falkenhainer, B., & Skorstad, J. (1987). Metaphor: The good, the bad and the ugly. In *TINLAP-3, Theoretical Issues in natural language processing,* Positions papers, pp. 176–184.

Gentner, D., & Grudin, J. (1985). The evolution of mental metaphors in psychology: A 90-year retrospective. *American Psychologist, 40,* 181–192.

Gentner, D., & Jeziorski. (1993). The shift from metaphor to analogy in Western science. In A. Ortony (Ed.), *Metaphor and thought,* 2nd ed. (pp. 447–480). New York: Cambridge University Press.

Gentner, D., & Wolff, P. Metaphor and knowledge change. Manuscript.

Gernsbacher, M. A., Keysar, B., & Robertson, R. R. W. (1995). *The role of suppression in metaphor interpretation.* Paper presented at the 36th Annual Meeting of the Psychonomic Society, Los Angeles.

Gerrig, R. J., & Gibbs, R. W. (1988). Beyond the lexicon: Creativity in language production. *Metaphor and Symbolic Activity, 3*(1), 1–19.

Gibbs, R. W. (1994). *The poetics of mind. Figurative thought, language and understanding.* New York: Cambridge University Press.

Gibbs, R. W., & O'Brien, J. (1990). Idioms and mental imagery: The metaphorical motivation for idiomatic meaning. *Cognition, 36,* 35–68.

Gibson, J. J. (1977). The theory of affordances. In R. Shaw & B. J. Bransford (Eds.), *Perceiving, acting and knowing* (pp. 67–82). Hillsdale, NJ: Erlbaum.

Gibson, J. J. (1979). *The ecological approach to visual perception*. Boston: Houghton Mifflin Company.

Glucksberg, S., Brown, M., & McGlone, M. (1993). Conceptual metaphors are not automatically accessed during idiom comprehension. *Memory and Cognition, 21,* 711–719.

Glucksberg, S., & Keysar, B. (1990). Understanding metaphorical comparisons: Beyond similarity. *Psychological Review, 97*(1), 3–18.

Glucksberg, S., & Keysar, B. (1993). How metaphor works. In A. Ortony (Ed.), *Metaphor and Thought,* 2nd ed., (pp. 401–424). New York: Cambridge University Press.

Glucksberg, S., & Manfredi, D. (1995). Metaphoric comparisons. In C. Cacciari (Ed.), *Similarity in language, thought and perception* (pp. 67–81). Turnhout (Bruxelles): Brepols.

Glucksberg, S., Manfredi, D., & McGlone, M. (1997). Metaphor comprehension: How metaphors create new categories. In T. B. Ward, S. M. Smith, & J. Vaid (Eds.), *Creative thought: An investigation of conceptual structures and processes* (pp. 327–350). Washington, DC: American Psychological Association.

Glucksberg, S., Manfredi, D. & McGlone, M. (1997). Metaphor comprehension: An interactive property attribution model. *Journal of Memory and Language, 36,* 1, 50–67.

Gombrich, E. H. (1982). *The image and the eye. Further studies in the psychology of pictorial representation*. Oxford: Phaidon Press.

Grant, D., & Oswick, C. (Eds.), (1996). *Metaphor and organizations*. London: Sage Publications.

Harrison, J. E., & Baron-Cohen, S. (1997). Synaesthesia: a review of psychological theories. In S. Baron-Cohen & J. E. Harrison (Eds.), *Synaesthesia. Classic and contemporary readings* (pp. 109–122). Cambridge, MA: Blackwell.

Hesse, M. B. (1953). *Models and analogies in science*. Notre Dame: University of Notre Dame Press.

Holland, D., & Quinn, N. (Eds.). (1987). *Cultural models in language and thought*. Cambridge: Cambridge University Press.

Halskov Madsen, K. (1989). Breakthrough by breakdown: Metaphor and structured domains. In H. Klein & K. Kumar (Eds.), *Information system development for human progress in organizations* (pp. 41–55). Amsterdam: North Holland.

Jackendoff, R., & Aaron, D. (1991). Review article of *More Than Cool Reason* by G. Lakoff and G. Turner. *Language, 67,* 320–338.

Johnson, A. T. (1996). Comprehension of metaphors and similes: A reaction time study. *Metaphor and Symbolic Activity, 11,* 145–160.

Johnson, M. (1981). *Philosophical perspectives on metaphor*. Minneapolis: University of Minnesota Press.

Johnson, M., & Malgady, R. G. (1979). Some cognitive aspects of figurative language: Association and metaphor. *Journal of Psycholinguistic Research, 8,* 249–265.

Karwoski, T. F., Odbert, H. S., & Osgood, C. E. (1942). Studies in synaesthetic thinking II: The role of form in visual responses to music. *Journal of General Psychology, 26,* 199–222.

Katz, A. N. (1989). On choosing the vehicles of metaphors: Referential concreteness, semantic distance and individual differences. *Journal of Memory and Language, 28,* 486–499.

Kennedy, J. (1982). Metaphor in pictures. *Perception, 11,* 589–605.

Kensing F., & Halskov Madsen, K. (1991). Generating visions: Future workshops and metaphorical design. In J. Greenbaum & M. Kyng (Eds.), *Design at work: Cooperative design of computer systems* (pp. 155–168). Hillsdale, NJ: Erlbaum.

Koehler, W. (1929). *Gestalt psychology.* New York: Liveright Publishing Company.

Koehler, W. (1947). *Gestalt psychology,* 6th ed., New York: Mentor Book.

Koffka, K. (1935). *Principles of Gestalt psychology.* New York: Harcourt, Brace & World.

Koveises, Z. (1986). Metaphysics of anger, pride, and love.Amsterdam: John Benjamins Publishing.

Krauss, R. & Glucksberg, S. (1977). Social and nonsocial speech. *Scientific American,* 236, 100–105.

Lakoff, G. (1987). *Women, fire and dangerous things.* Chicago: University of Chicago Press.

Lakoff, G. (1993). The contemporary theory of metaphor. In A. Ortony (Ed.), *Metaphor and thought,* 2nd ed., (pp. 202–251). New York: Cambridge University Press.

Lakoff, G., & Turner, M. (1989). *More than cool reason. A field guide to poetic metaphor.* Chicago: University of Chicago Press.

Leech, G. (1983). *Principle of pragmatics.* London: Longman.

Lehrer, A. (1978). Structures of the lexicon and transfer of meaning. *Lingua, 45,* 95–123.

Leon, M. (1988). Characterizing the senses. *Mind and Language, 3*(4), 243–270.

Lessing, D. (1962). *The golden notebook.* London: Paladin Griffin.

Levelt, W. J. M. (1991). *Lexical access in speech production.* Cambridge, MA: Blackwell.

Levinson, S. C. (1978). Commentary on B. Beck, The metaphor as a mediator between semantic and analogic modes of thought. *Current Anthropology, 19,* 92.

Levinson, S. C. (1983). *Pragmatics.* Cambridge: Cambridge University Press.

Luria, A. (1968). Synaesthesia. In S. Baron-Cohen & J. E. Harrison (Eds). (1997). *Synaesthesia. Classic and contemporary readings* (pp. 101–105). Cambridge, MA: Blackwell.

MacCormac, E. R. (1985). *A cognitive theory of metaphor.* Cambridge, MA: MIT Press.

Malgady, R. G., & Johnson, M. G. (1980). Measurement of figurative language: Semantic features model of comprehension and affiliation. In R. P. Honeck and R. R. Hoffman (Eds.), *Cognition and Figurative Language* (pp. 239–258). Hillsdale, NJ: Erlbaum.

Marks, L. E. (1978). *The unity of senses.* New York: Academic Press.

Marks, L. E. (1982). Bright sneezes and dark coughs, loud sunlight and soft moonlight. *Journal of Experimental Psychology: Human Perception and Performance, 8*(2), 177–193.

Marks, L. E., & Bornstein, M. H. (1987). Sensory similarities: classes, characteristics and cognitive consequences. In R. S. Haskell (Ed.), *Cognition and symbolic structure: The psychology of metaphoric transformation,* (pp. 49–65). Norwood, NJ: Ablex.

Marschark, M., Katz, A., & Paivio, A. (1983). Dimensions of metaphor. *Journal of Psycholinguistic Research, 12,* 17–40.

Metzger, W. (1941). *Psychologie.* Fondamenti di Psicologia della Gestalt. Florence: Giunti.

Miller, G., & Johnson-Laird, P. (1976). *Language and perception.* Cambridge: Cambridge University Press.

Mio J. S., & Katz, A. N. (Eds.). (1996). *Metaphor: implications and applications.* Hillsdale, NJ: Erlbaum.

Murphy, G. L. (1996). On metaphoric representation. *Cognition, 60,* 173–204.

Murphy, G. L. (1997a). Reasons to doubt the present evidence for metaphoric representation. *Cognition, 62,* 99–108.

Murphy, G. L. (1997b). Polysemy and the creation of new word meanings. In T. B. Ward, S. M. Smith, & J. Vaid (Eds.), *Creative thought: An investigation of conceptual structures and processes* (pp. 235–266). Washington, DC: American Psychological Association.

Musil, R. (1906). *Young Torless.* In *Selected writings.* New York: Continuum.

Napolitano Valditara, L. (1994). *Lo sguardo nel buio. Metafore visive e forme grecoantiche della razionalitê.* Bari: Laterza.

Nelkin, N. (1990). Categorizing senses, *Mind and Language, 5*(2), 149–165.

Newport, E. L., & Bellugi, U. (1978). Linguistic expressions of category levels in a visual-gesture language. In E. Rosch & B. B. Lloyd (Eds.), *Cognition and categorization* (pp. 49–71). Hillsdale, NJ: Erlbaum.

Newsome, M. R., & Glucksberg, S. (1996). *Do young and older adults suppress metaphor-irrelevant properties during metaphor comprehension?* Poster presented at the 37th Annual Meeting of the Psychonomic Society, Chicago.

Norman, D. (1988). *The design of everyday things.* New York: Basic Books.

Norman, D. (1992). *Turn signals are the facial expressions of automobiles.* New York: Norton & Company.

Nunberg, G. (1978). *The pragmatics of reference.* Bloomington, Indiana: Indiana Linguistic Club.

Nunberg, G. (1979). The non-uniqueness of semantic solutions: polysemy. *Linguistics and Philosophy, 3,* 143–184.

Odbert, H. S., Karwoski, T. F., & Eckerson, A. B. (1942). Studies in synaesthetic thinking I: Musical and verbal association of color and mood. *Journal of General Psychology, 26,* 153–173.

Ortony, A. (1980). Some psycholinguistic aspects of metaphor. In R P. Honeck & R. R. Hoffman, (Eds.). *Cognition and figurative language* (pp. 69–83). Hillsdale, NJ: Erlbaum.

Ortony, A. (1988). Are emotion metaphors conceptual or lexical? *Cognition and Emotion, 2*(2), 95–103.

Ortony, A. (1993). Metaphor, language, and thought. In A. Ortony (Ed.), *Metaphor and thought,* 2nd ed., (pp. 1–16). New York: Cambridge University Press.

Ortony, A. & Fainsilber, L. (1987). The role of metaphor in the descriptions of emotions. *TINLAP-3, Theoretical issues in natural language processing,* positions papers, pp. 181–184.

Osgood, C. E. (1980). The cognitive dynamics of synesthesia and metaphor. In R. P. Honeck & R. R. Hoffman, (Eds.), *Cognition and figurative language* (pp. 203–238). Hillsdale, NJ: Erlbaum.

Osgood, C. E., Suci, G. J., & Tannenbaum, P. H. (1957). *The measurement of meaning.* Urbana: University of Illinois Press.

Pitts, M. K., Smith, M. K., & Pollio, H. R. (1982). An evaluation of three different theories of metaphor production through the use of an intentional category mistake production. *Journal of Psycholinguistic Research, 11*(4), 347–368.

Powell, M. J. (1992). Folk theories of meaning and principles of conventionality: Encoding literal attitude via stance adverb. In A. Lehrer & E. F. Kittay (Eds.), *Frames, fields and contrasts: New essays in semantic and lexical organization* (pp. 333–353). Hillsdale, NJ: Erlbaum.

Quinn, N. (1991). The cultural basis of metaphor. In J. W. Fernandez (Ed.), *Beyond metaphor. The theory of tropes in anthropology* (pp. 56–93). Stanford, CA: Stanford University Press.

Reddy, M. J. (1979). The conduit metaphor: A case of frame conflict in our language about language. In A. Ortony (Ed.), *Metaphor and thought* (pp. 164–201). 2nd ed. New York: Cambridge University Press.

Reider, N. (1972). Metaphor as interpretation. *Journal of Psycho-Analysis, 53,* 463–469.

Richards, I. A. (1936). *The philosophy of rhetoric.* Oxford: Oxford University Press.

Ricoeur, P. (1978). The metaphorical process as cognition, imagination, and feeling. In S. Sacks (Ed.), *On metaphor* (pp. 141–157). Chicago: University of Chicago Press.

Rothenberg, A. (1984). Creativity and psychotherapy. *Psychoanalysis and Contemporary Thought, 7,* 233–268.

Rumelhart, D. E. (1979). Some problems with the notion of literal meaning. In A. Ortony (Ed.), *Metaphor and thought* (pp. 78–90). New York: Cambridge University Press.

Savardi, U., & Pelamatti, A. (1996). Inversioni espressive intermodali in Takete e Maluma. *Annali dell'Istituto di Psicologia* (pp. 113–127). Verona: Cierre Edizioni.

Schon, D. A. (1979). Generative metaphors: A perspective on problem-setting in social policy. In A. Ortony (Ed.), *Metaphor and thought* pp. 137–163). 2nd ed. New York: Cambridge University Press.

Shen, Y. (1997). Cognitive constraints on poetic figures. *Cognitive Linguistics, 8*(1), 33–72.

Smith, M. K., Pollio, H. R., & Pitts, M. K. (1981). Metaphor as intellectual history: Conceptual categories underlying figurative usage in American English from 1675–1975. *Linguistics, 19,* 911–935.

Sonino, C. (1983). Musil e il frammento. In R. Morello (a cura di), *Anima ed esattezza. Letteratura e scienza nella cultura austriaca tra Ottocento e Novecento* (pp. 83–95). Casale Monferrato: Marietti.

Sperber, D., & Wilson, D. (1986). *Relevance: Communication and cognition.* Oxford: Basil Blackwell.

Steinhart, E., & Kittay, E. (1994). Generating metaphors from networks: A formal interpretation of the semantic field theory of metaphor. In J. Hintikka (Ed.), *Aspects of metaphor* (pp. 41–94). Amsterdam: Kluver Academic Publishers.

Sticht, T. (1993). Educational uses of metaphor. In A. Ortony (Ed.), *Metaphor and thought,* 2nd ed. (pp. 621–632). New York: Cambridge University Press.

Sweetser, E. (1991). *From etymology to pragmatics. Metaphorical and cultural aspects of semantic structure.* Cambridge: Cambridge University Press.

Tannen, D. (1989). *Talking voices: Repetition, dialogue and imagery in conversational discourse.* Cambridge: Cambridge University Press.

Tourangeau, R., & Sternberg, R. (1981). Aptness in metaphor. *Cognitive Psychology, 13,* 27–55.

Tourangeau, R., & Sternberg, R. (1982). Understanding and appreciating metaphor. *Cognition, 9,* 27–55.

Townsend, D. (1988). The problem of paraphrase. *Metaphor and Symbolic Activity, 3*(1), 37–54.

Turner, M. (1991). *Reading minds. The study of English in the age of cognitive science.* Princeton: Princeton University Press.

Turner, M. (1996). *The literary mind.* Oxford: Oxford University Press.

Tyler, S. A. (1978). *The said and the unsaid.* New York: Academic Press.

Ullmann, S. (1945). Romanticism and synaesthesia. *Publications of the Modern Language Association of America, 60,* 811–827.

Ullmann, S. (1962). *Semantics: An introduction to the study of meaning.* Oxford: Basil Blackwell & Mott.

Williams, J. M. (1976). Synaesthetic adjectives: A possible law of semantic change. *Language, 32*(2), 461–478.

Williams-Whitney, D., Mio J. S., & Whitney, P. (1992). Metaphor production in creative writing. *Journal of Psycholinguistic Research, 21*(6), 497–509.

Winter, S. L. (1989). Transcendental nonsense, metaphoric reasoning, and the cognitive stakes for law. *University of Pennsylvania Law Review, 137,* 1105–1237.

Wittgenstein, L. (1953). *Philosophical Investigations.* Oxford: Blackwell.

Woolf, V. (1931). *The waves.* New York: Harcourt Brace.

CHAPTER 5

Counterpoint Commentary

Albert N. Katz, Mark Turner, Raymond W. Gibbs, Jr.,
and Cristina Cacciari

Although intellectual discussion of nonliteral language has a history that can be traced to the ancient Greek philosophers, systematic and continuing experimental study of metaphor and other forms of nonliteral language started only about 20 years ago. And for most of that period, nonliteral language often was treated as an intellectual orphan, with a home neither in mainline cognitive science nor as a topic in the study of ordinary language. Today, the study of nonliteral language plays an important role in both fields. The important review article by Ortony, Reynolds, and Arter (1978), a succession of books in psychology (especially those edited by Ortony [1979] and by Honeck and Hoffman [1980]), and the establishment, in 1986, of the journal *Metaphor and Symbolic Activity* (now called *Metaphor and Symbol*) all combined to bring the study of metaphor, idioms, indirect requests, irony, and other tropes into experimental psychology. The success of this enterprise is well-documented in Ray Gibbs's book, *The Poetics of Mind* (1994). At about the same time that the initial stirrings were being felt in experimental psychology, linguistic and literary considerations of metaphor were also having their impact on cognitive science, being led by Reddy's chapter in the Ortony volume; the seminal work *Metaphors we Live By* written by Lakoff and Johnson (1980); the extension to poetic writing by Mark Turner (1987), *Death is the Mother of Beauty*; and the development of an active web site for ''blending and conceptual integration'' (http://www.wam.umd.edu/~mturn/WWW/blending.html).

Despite (or, perhaps because of) the active interdisciplinary consideration of metaphor, disagreement on several key issues remains: what, if any, is the role of literal language in the processing of nonliteral language? What occurs on-line and what occurs as a consequence of the initial processes? Is there a conceptual base that underlies our understanding and appreciation of language that is, on the surface, quite distinct? When is metaphor required and when is its use just nice? What processing characteristics are common to different figures of language and which ones are trope-specific?

It is to these types of question that this book is directed. In the initial discussion of this project, we quickly decided that each author would determine which questions he or she wished to emphasize. Each chapter would then be circulated to the other contributors, who would then write a commentary and any follow-up critiques that they wished to make.

The review chapter by Katz was an attempt to place the more recent literature on figurative language within the larger and more traditional experimental literature on language and thought. His emphasis was on recent research that does not support strong modular models of language, even for the most basic of language functions such as word access and syntactic analysis. Thus, multiple sources of knowledge, including knowledge of the world (both physical and social) play an early role in interpreting linguistic input, including so-called nonliteral input. This conclusion is quite compatible to that of Gibbs, taken from another perspective, and in a more general sense with the construction grammarians described in Turner's chapter. On a more negative note, Katz argues that a detailed cognitive model for the on-line processing of nonliteral literal language is lacking, a point echoed in the various commentaries. As Turner put it, finding a full model of on-line processing "will be extraordinarily difficult, requiring the sustained collaborative work of psychologists, neurobiologists, cognitive neuroscientists, rhetoricians, linguists, and others concerned with interpretation and invention."

Turner reviewed the literature from the perspective of cognitive linguistics and, as he noted in a commentary, "the view of metaphor as conceptual has an ancient and continuous history. . . . This tradition of looking at things has merely been suppressed in various schools of thought." In his chapter he briefly reviewed the history of this tradition, of the pairing of expressions with conceptual patterns, from the early Greek philosophers to more modern theoreticians, including construction grammarians, work on mental spaces, integration, blending, and implications that arise from the network model that he has developed with Gilles Fauconnier (Fauconnier and Turner, in press). From this perspective most of the "traditional" questions in figurative language are inappropriate: literality and figurativeness do not suggest different cognitive operations but emerge as a consequence of the nature of the mapping to conceptual structure, such as "the relative status and degree of entrenchment of the relevant mental arrays in the conceptual structures brought to bear on a linguistic expression." In this chapter he expands upon his earlier work to show how the nature of blending affects our feeling that an expression is literal or figurative and how other traditional questions, such as whether figurative language is mirrored in figurative thought, use an inappropriate set of assumptions about the independence of language and thought.

In his chapter, Gibbs directly addresses what Cacciari refers to as the main point of disagreement in the recent empirical literature: ''[A]re we first figurative thinkers and consequently figurative language users or the other way around?'' Gibbs takes the perspective of an experimental scientist in trying to answer this question, though clearly arguing for other empiricists to examine a wider literature and for the need to adopt different techniques of study. He adopts what he calls the ''cognitive wager,'' the position that language structure and behavior should be studied as ''reflections of general conceptual organization, categorization principles, and processing mechanisms.'' He outlines four psychologically testable hypotheses that follow from taking the wager, reviews the growing literature that supports each of the hypotheses, and argues for the psychological reality of a metaphoric level of representation, basing much of his arguments on linguistic evidence and cleverly constructed psychological experiments.

Finally, Cacciari explicitly decided to avoid discussing, to quote from her commentary, ''the controversies that have recently arisen in the (unfortunately still small) community of figurative language researchers regarding the relationship between metaphoric thought and metaphoric language.'' Feeling that the basic points in the controversy have been well aired by now, she argues that it is time for the small community to frame the problems differently and to carry out more experimental work in order to test positions, many of which, as currently framed, appear to be almost unfalsifiable. As she put it: ''[M]y feeling [is] that it is time to move on, or better, it is time to refresh the discussion, trying new pathways for our theoretical and experimental efforts to investigate figurative language.'' In her chapter, Cacciari suggests what some of these pathways could be. She speculated on the relations between sensory experiences, mental representations, and linguistic expression. In her hands, ''to capture the perceptual and experiential complexity of the world we live in, language has to be 'stretched' and hence used metaphorically to increase its descriptive and communicative force.'' She provides a set of cogent examples to challenge our conceptions of the language-thought relation.

The variety of topics chosen for presentation, the differing conceptual frameworks brought to bear, and the methodological appropriateness of different approaches found in the various chapters characterize much of the study of figurative language today. And, not surprisingly, the differences were debated in the commentary that follows.

ON ON-LINE AND OFF-LINE PROCESSING

Several commentators noted that one has to be cautious about inferring the nature of representations and of processes from our conscious (phenomenological) experiences. As Gibbs put it: "It is essential to draw a distinction between the 'products' of understanding (i.e., the feeling we get that some utterance has 'literal' or 'figurative' meaning and the underlying cognitive and linguistic processes that give rise to these products." Turner agrees: "It is dangerous to equate cognitive process with what we seem to be aware of in consciousness." And here Gibbs and Turner speculate about the nature of the on-line processing that occurs.

GIBBS: Consider two examples from Turner's chapter: (1) "President Franklin Delano Roosevelt moved at a quick pace during his first 100 days in office," and (2) "FDR made the dust fly as he sped along during his first 100 days in office." Turner discussed these examples, and many others, to demonstrate how the basic type of conceptual integration needed to understand both these statements is very similar, if not identical, even though we often feel that the first has literal meaning, while the second has a figurative interpretation. Both statements reflect blends that are specifications of the abstract conventional blend "purposive agent as traveler on a path."

Yet consider the exact processes by which people comprehend these statements as they are read. What meanings have been constructed at the very moment, or soon after, when people have read "move at a quick pace" or "made the dust fly"? Part of the task of a detailed psychological theory of figurative language understanding requires that we specify the complex set of cognitive and linguistic processes that occur at each moment in the on-line processing of speakers'/authors' expressions. Although we might conclude that readers ultimately determine that "move at a quick pace" and "made the dust fly" express meanings not necessarily having to do with physical journeys and the ruckus that can occur when one moves quickly through some environment, these meanings come into awareness only after we have read the entire sentence in each case and interpreted its intended meaning in context. But, again, what happens earlier in the on-line processing of each expression? When do readers infer that these statements reflect the idea of "purposive agent as traveler on a path"?

My own view is that difficulties in defining what it means to say that some word or utterance has a "literal" meaning makes it unlikely that normal linguistic processing is literal (Gibbs, 1994). Empirical studies show that how people conceive of the literal meaning for different kinds of figurative language depends entirely on what aspect of the complex concept of "literal" people are working with (Gibbs, Buchalter, Moise, & Farrar, 1993).

In most instances, however, scholars maintain the belief that the literal meanings of many words and sentences tend to be their context-free meanings. Under this view, we assume that people are doing literal analysis of phrases such as "move at a quick pace" and "made the dust fly" in the sense of figuring out their meaning apart from contexts before we construct their meaning figuratively in context. I want to suggest several other ways to think about how people might process figurative expressions on-line that do not require the postulation of context-free literal meanings for either words or entire expressions. The first idea is based on the fact that many words are polysemous in having several related senses. The words "moved" and "made" (along with "dust") are richly polysemous, with each lexical item having several dozen meanings. Although psychologists tend to assume that the meanings of ambiguous words are not related in meaning, there is experimental evidence to suggest that people access a whole chain of senses for polysemous words during immediate processing and even maintain some activation for unrelated meanings for several seconds "downstream" in ordinary sentence processing (Williams, 1992). Under this view of linguistic processing, people may immediately access some figurative meanings that are conventionally part of a polysemous word's meaning. Thus, people might immediately create on-line linguistic representations that are sensitive to possible figurative uses of a word in context (e.g., such as when they infer the meaning of "make" in "make the dust fly").

One reason why the above characterization might have some validity concerns my second, related proposal for how people process different figurative utterances during immediate linguistic processing. As Turner describes in several places in his article, one of the key constraints in building conceptual networks is grammatical constructions. Grammatical constructions reflect conventional form-meaning correspondences that are not "strictly predictable from knowledge of the rest of the grammar" (Goldberg, 1995, p. 2; also see Fillmore, Kay, & O'Connor, 1988). Various linguistic studies have demonstrated that different senses of polysemous words, as well as larger phrasal units, fall out of the interaction between grammatical properties and higher-level conceptual knowledge (often described as knowledge reflected in mental space constructions along the lines proposed by Fauconnier and Turner's network model for conceptual integration) (Brugman, 1996; Goldberg, 1995). For instance, Lee (1996) has identified a number of grammatical constructions that function to limit the possible meanings of the verb "make" in different discourse context. Under this view, the meaning of "make" in any context is not simply due to the post hoc application of contextual information to select the correct sense of the verb after all of its meanings have been initially activated. Instead, grammatical constructions operate to constrain the construction of meaning networks so that the multiple meanings of polysemous words and phrases, such as "make the dust fly" in the second Turner sentence, may not require time-consuming, mostly bottom-up, processes whereby lexical information is first accessed and then reconciled with pragmatics.

In other words, grammatical constructions may place significant constraints on interpretation processes so that people, in some cases anyway, may easily infer the figurative meaning of a particular word or phrase. Although there has been no psycholinguistic empirical work on the influence of grammatical constructions on immediate language processing, this is clearly an interesting, important future direction for work on figurative language understanding.

TURNER: The network model of conceptual integration is offered as a step toward greater attention to the processes of on-line construction of meaning. There are surely other operations involved, as Gibbs rightly remarks, even when the achieved and accepted interpretation is obviously a conceptual integration. For example, the provisional interpretation of "FDR moved at a quick pace" may, and probably does, involve a process of framing FDR as the agent of actual bodily motion, and that provisional interpretation can be quite complicated if there is activation of background knowledge that FDR, a victim of polio, used a wheelchair. To reach a final interpretation of this phrase as referring to FDR's presidential activity, the provisional interpretation of FDR as moving bodily has to be overridden, set aside, dispreferred, or otherwise demoted.

But what is the relationship among these various alternative interpretations that arise during on-line construction of meaning? The hypothesis of serial processing, which Gibbs seems to lean toward, may run into the unsettling facts of neurobiological time constraints: given the speed of understanding and the slowness of synaptic transmission, there appears to be enough time for only on the order of a 100 or so serial activations of neurons during the entire course of the understanding. This is serial poverty. It suggests that we might look at parallel processing rather than serial processing, since there appears to be great parallel capacity. Maybe we understand even a simple phrase by running many quite different possible interpretations in parallel, with one or two winners percolating into consciousness. Perhaps the phenomenon of backtracking is actually not so much the introduction of a new interpretation that overrides an old one serially as a new percolation into consciousness of a partial interpretation that has been running all along in parallel.

From time to time, there have been suggestions that the construction of meaning is massively parallel, provisional, and dependent on some selection process that picks winning constructions out of a mass competition. Claude Rawson (1985, pp. 6–7) writes that Jonathan Swift quoted with approval an Irish prelate who said:

> [T]hat the difference betwixt a mad-man and one in his wits, in what related to speech, consisted in this: That the former spoke out whatever came into his mind, and just

in the confused manner as his imagination presented the ideas. The latter only expressed such thoughts, as his judgment directed him to chuse, leaving the rest to die away in his memory. And that if the wisest man would at any time utter his thoughts, in the crude indigested manner, as they come into his head, he would be looked upon as raving mad.

With moderate violence, we can turn this into a suggestion that we always construct in parallel, multiple, confused, and partial interpretations and that sanity depends on keeping most of them out of consciousness.

ON LITERAL AND NON-LITERAL LANGUAGE

In one way or another each of the chapters grappled with the difference(s) between literal and nonliteral language. There is no question that people "feel" a difference, such as the "feeling" that the concept "lemon" is somehow more literal when used in a sentence such as "My least favorite fruit is a lemon" than when used in a sentence such as "My last car was a lemon." But what does this difference mean? If this question was asked 20 years ago, the most popular answer would be that literal and nonliteral meanings are quite distinct and that the process of comprehending nonliteral meaning is different from that of comprehending literal meaning. The standard model of the day would have literal meaning as the basic form of representation, and the comprehension of nonliteral meaning would involve inferences not found with the comprehension of literal meaning. Moreover, these inferences would occur only when one failed to find an appropriate literal interpretation. The last 20 years of research has in general shown little support for this so-called "standard pragmatic" model (see Gibbs, chap. 3; Katz, 1996, chap. 1): literal meaning analysis does not appear to be an obligatory aspect of comprehending tropes, nor does the failure to find context-appropriate literal meaning in a linguistic expression appear to be a precondition for seeking a nonliteral interpretation.

In his chapter, Katz pointed out that the 20 years of research should not be taken as evidence that literal meaning is not obligatory in some circumstances. In a commentary, Gibbs acknowledges that literal meaning analysis might occur at an early word access level, Katz outlines what he believes might be instances in which literal meaning might be processed for sentence or larger linguistic units, and Cacciari argues that in many situations the literal meaning is semantically related to the figurative meaning.

GIBBS: Although many scholars, including me, have often argued that people are not constructing literal representations for the entire meanings of linguistic statements (Gibbs, 1984, 1994), people must do something with the words they read or hear, and it could very well be that some initial processing of all language involves accessing what words literally mean. In fact, recent studies of idiom processing suggest that people comprehend idiom phrases in a literal manner until readers encounter a "key point" in each phrase that signals it should be interpreted figuratively (Cacciari & Tabossi, 1988; Tabossi & Zardon, 1993). It could be the case that all kinds of figurative language, not just idioms, are understood in this manner.

KATZ: I agree with Gibbs: in constructing meaning from an expression, the individual words in that expression must be processed on-line, and it is likely that this processing activates core properties associated with the word, what some have called context-independent information (Barsalou, 1982) and others the conceptual "core" (Smith, 1988). And it is these core properties that are typically associated with literal meaning. So literal meaning (at least as I have defined it) must play some role in the early phases of comprehension.

A general argument in psycholinguistics is that at the earliest stages of language processing, multiple analyses are being performed, but most of these are relatively quickly abandoned. That is, multiple senses of the words in the utterances, and multiple syntactic possibilities, are rapidly aroused. However, the language parser tends to settle on a preferred interpretation for an utterance long before the utterance is completed. This argument is, of course, completely compatible with the received wisdom that literal meaning is not necessary for the processing of the larger linguistic units usually considered in the study of figurative language. As several of us have noted, literal meaning does not appear to be an obligatory aspect of comprehending tropes, nor does the failure to arouse literal meaning appear to be a precondition for seeking a nonliteral interpretation.

But, one can ask, at what point does the parser abandon the to-be-lost interpretations? If the context is sufficiently ambiguous (or rich in multiple possibilities), will multiple interpretations be kept active for relatively long periods of time? In some instances (e.g., sarcasm) multiple interpretations are almost certainly kept active for fairly long periods. But what about literal interpretations of utterances intended (or that can be taken, accidentally) as being nonliteral? The received wisdom, mentioned before, indicates that the strong version of the standard pragmatic model is incorrect, meaning that literal meaning processing is not obligatory. The research, however, does not show that literal meaning is not processed under some conditions, or indeed, that it might be processed under all conditions, but then abandoned very quickly under most of these conditions. And, I would argue, to continue the distinction between literal and nonliteral, it behooves psycholinguists to identify and understand exactly when the processing of literal meaning might be obligatory, that is, where and when literal and non-literal interpretations might both be active and involved in comprehension. Let me suggest two possible cases.

In the first case, nonliteral language is used in a nondominant (unfamiliar) way. Much figurative language is based on learned convention, such as with idioms, and proverbs. Unfamiliar idioms and proverbs are, in essence, neither idiomatic nor proverbial. So what does a person do when encountering a novel idiom or proverb, such as "A river needs a spring." I would argue that he or she will attempt to understand the item based on the most available information and that would be compositionally based on the usual meaning of the words and the syntax of these words. This, of course, will be most pronounced if the item is presented out of context, as in the example above. And it is highly unlikely that, out of context, such items would make contact with prestored conceptual metaphors, though it is possible that syntactic factors might suggest an item is a proverb.

But what happens when these items are placed in a context that brings out either the figurative or literal sense? Using the example above, one such context, meant to convey a nonliteral meaning, would be as follows: "Even though you are very successful today, you had much help in the past. And you should not forget these people. Remember: A river needs a spring." In contrast, a context talking about lakes, oceans, and other waterways would be used to bring out the literal sense of the phrase. In principle, the context might engage one or more conceptual metaphors, which, in turn, might play a role in comprehension.

We have shown in my laboratory (N. Turner and Katz, 1997) that even with a very elaborated context the "novel" proverb takes longer to comprehend than a literal paraphrase or when placed in a context that makes the proverb literally "true." Cued recall memory tasks indicate that participants are able to recall the proverbial phrase when given either a hint associated with the literal or figurative sense, but only when the unfamiliar proverb is placed in a context structured to bring out the nonliteral meaning. For "literal" contexts the only effective cue is the hint associated with the literal meaning. This suggests that literal meaning is aroused for unfamiliar proverbs even when the context in which it is used supports the nonproverbial literal sense, and the nonliteral sense is generated only when there is sufficient contextual support for that sense.

In the second case, the speaker wishes to contrast the conventional use of language with nonconventional but contextually based use. One could argue that there are instances in which the intent of the speaker is to contrast the figurative and literal senses in order to make some point. For instance, even if the nonliteral use is familiar and placed in a context that clearly points out that the figurative usage, the processing still involves appreciation of the literal sense. Naturally the obverse also obtains: literal usage involving appreciation of a familiar non-literal sense.

Examples can be found in instances of humor, such as those displayed in various films (e.g., *Airplane*) or television programs (e.g., *Get Smart*). For instance, a man with a prosthetic arm might be asked by someone needing help, "Could you give me a hand?"

A second instance can be found with irony. Here the speaker frames what he or she wishes to say in order for the comprehender (at least the audience in the know) to appreciate the difference between the expressed literal and intended nonliteral meanings. In fact, Dews and Winner (1995) argue that the literal meaning is important in "muting" the intended message, what they have labeled the "tinge hypothesis." Thus, an intended sarcastic message conveyed by an expressed positive statement (e.g., "You sure are a good friend") is perceived as more positive than a literal paraphrase of the sarcastic intention. Similarly, an expressed negative compliment is perceived as more negative than the literally expressed compliment.

One can take the examples above as "rare" cases and assume that literal meaning is not generally processed when one encounters a nonliteral statement. In fact, some recent data suggest the tinge hypothesis of Dews and Winner is not generally observed (see Colston, 1997). Leaving aside, for the moment, how the cognitive apparatus would know when literal meaning is obligatory and when it is not, I would like to raise the possibility that perhaps the processing of literal meaning is more widespread than commonly assumed. Much, but clearly not all, the empirical evidence against the tenets of the standard pragmatic model has employed fairly familiar tropes. As noted above, the evidence from these studies (see Gibbs, 1994, for instance) indicates that these tenets are not necessary and that the processing of literal language is not obligatory. Thus, what has been studied most are familiar tropes, and perhaps literal processing is truncated or eliminated in these cases.

Nonetheless, there are indications that, even for familiar tropes, some processing of literal language might occur. Cris Cacciari has found this in the past, in comprehension (Cacciari and Tabossi, 1988), and has suggested it for production as well (Cacciari and Glucksberg, 1991). A recent study (Cutting and Bock, 1997) has confirmed the importance of literal meaning using a novel task. The task was simple: speakers silently read two idioms and were then cued to produce one or the other. The characteristics of the two idioms were manipulated. For example, one contrast would be between a familiar idiom (e.g., "hold your tongue") paired with a literal phrase with the same meaning as the idiom taken to be literally true (e.g., "grab your lip") or paired with a phrase with a different literal meaning (e.g., "sign your name"). Phrases with similar meanings produced more blending errors (e.g., "hold your lip") than did phrases with dissimilar meaning, suggesting that literal meaning was playing a role in idiom production.

In my laboratory we too have found some evidence that literal meaning plays a role in the processing of familiar proverbs. In the N. Turner and Katz (1997) study we found that literal cues were effective even for familiar proverbs placed in a context that supports the conventional nonliteral usage. This indicates to us that literal meaning was extracted, even when the item is conventionally understood as a proverb, and even when the context supports the proverbial (and not the literal) sense of the item.

If these results are not anomalies, we are left with a problem. On the one hand, there is evidence that the arousal of literal meaning is not obligatory, at least for larger verbal units. On the other hand, there is evidence presented here that literal meaning is probably obligatory at the word-by-word level and occurs under some circumstances for idioms, proverbs, and novel tropes, although this occurrence might not be on-line but might occur at later stages of discourse comprehension. I would not like to throw the baby out with the bath water and would like to keep open the possibility that the occurrence might happen on-line. If so, how does the processing system "know" when it is necessary to process literal meaning (as in the examples above) and when such processing is optional? My bet would be that the "knowledge" is somehow conveyed by the ecology in which the statement is embedded and used by a highly interactive processing system. As I tried to show in my review, modular processing approaches are unlikely even for syntactic-level sentence analysis and even more unlikely for analysis of meaning, especially given the findings that I reviewed earlier in my chapter suggesting that social convention (such as status or occupation) might play an early role in comprehension. I would also like to offer the possibility that literal meaning might be aroused (albeit perhaps not in the earliest moments of analysis) even for familiar tropes being used in their familiar nonliteral sense.

CACCIARI: Most often our discussion of the activation of literal meaning in figurative expression comprehension misses what seems to me a relevant point. We might activate the literal meaning of a single word or even a larger linguistic unit because there are semantic features of the literal meaning that are semantically relevant for constructing the figurative interpretation. What we often miss is the semantic contribution of the meaning (considered as something more than features) of the constituent words.

Take, for instance, what Sam Glucksberg and I (Cacciari and Glucksberg, 1991) called quasi-metaphorical idioms. Examples include "carry coals to Newcastle" and "look for a needle in a haystack." These quasi-metaphorical idioms are ideal exemplars of what they represent: the literal action described is a prototypical case of a general class of situations that one can name using such idioms. That is, you can in fact say "doing X is like carrying coals to Newcastle" to describe an extremely useless action. This is a typical case in which the *literal meaning* of the idiom string has to be computed and then extended metaphorically.

This point relates to an old and unsolved question. What kind of information is represented in a lexical entry? And how is the lexically represented information related to more general semantic information? In this reading "ice" for instance, points (or denotes) not only to physical transformation of water but also to the state of mind toward other individuals.

Although Gibbs concedes that literal meaning might be accessed for individual words, in general he argues against the type of distinctions that Katz or Cacciari has put forward. And he makes an argument that puts the question into a larger perspective in which pragmatics and not literality plays a role in comprehension processes.

GIBBS: I want to raise one final point about literal meaning and figurative language that, in my mind, deserves significant consideration. As noted before and in Katz's article, there is a large body of evidence, as well as theoretical argument (Gibbs, 1994; Recanati, 1995), that people need not analyze the literal meaning of many figurative expressions before deriving their intended nonliteral meanings. This conclusion is inconsistent with the traditional claims of philosophers, like Grice (1975) and Searle (1979), who contend that analysis of literal meaning is an obligatory step in the process of understanding many kinds of indirect and figurative meanings. Many scholars, including me, have argued that the psycholinguistic work, reviewed by Katz, suggests that there may not be a principled distinction between literal and nonliteral meanings, between sentence meaning and speaker meaning, or between what a speaker says and what a speaker implicates. The psycholinguistic data, for instance, clearly point to the idea that people can directly access nonliteral meaning, speaker meanings, or a speaker's implication when, say, using a metaphor, especially when figurative expressions are seen in sufficient social-linguistic context. This general idea assumes, however, that what a speaker means literally is isomorphic to what a speaker says (as opposed to what a speaker means or implicates).

I want to now suggest that the conflation of literal meaning with what a speaker says may be unwarranted. There may be many instances when a listener determines what a speaker says prior to, or as part of, their understanding of what a speaker implicates or intends to communicate. This proposal obviously has significant implications for our discussion of figurative language because it may very well be the case that people analyze what a speaker says before or as part of what a speaker implicates when he or she uses a metaphor, metonymy, ironic remark, indirect speech act, and so on. To elaborate on this point, consider the following well-known exchange (Grice, 1975):

ANN: Smith doesn't seem to have a girlfriend these days.
BOB: He's been paying a lot of visits to New York lately.

Grice argued with this example that what Bob said expresses only part of what he meant by his utterance. Thus, although Bob simply stated a fact about Smith's recent visits to New York, Bob likely intended for Ann to understand that Smith has, or may have, a girlfriend in New York. The inference that Smith may have a girlfriend in New York is derived from certain general principles or maxims of conversation that participants in talk-exchange are mutually expected to observe (Grice, 1975, 1989). Among these are the expectation that speakers are to be informative, truthful, relevant, and clear in what they say. When an utterance appears to violate any of these maxims, as Bob appears to do, listeners are expected to derive an appropriate "conversational implicature" as to what the speaker must have intended to communicate in context, given the assumption that he or she is trying to be cooperative.

Grice referred to highly context-dependent implicatures, such as noted in Ann and Bob's exchange, as "particularized" conversational implicatures. Most instances of figurative language (e.g., metaphor, metonymy, irony, indirect speech acts) are traditionally viewed as particularized conversational implicatures where the speaker implicates something different from what he or she says.

On the other hand, Grice referred to conversational implicatures that are normally conveyed regardless of the context as "generalized" conversational implicatures. Consider the following example where the first sentence presents what the speaker uttered and the second sentence reflects what is standardly conveyed or implicated by a speaker: "It took us some time to get there." "It took us a long time to get there." Grice claimed that our understanding of what is meant in each of these examples is best explained by the calculable process of conversational implicature rather than by postulating a large number of distinct, but unrelated, senses for words such as "some." For instance, understanding that "It took us some time to get there" implies that "It took us a long time to get to some location" requires listeners to go beyond what is said by appealing to the cooperative principle, the context in which this utterance was spoken, and certain bits of background knowledge, all of which must be mutually known to be shared by speaker and listener (Levinson, 1983).

Nearly all theorists, including Grice, recognize that certain contextual information relevant to resolving ambiguity and fixing indexical reference must play some role in determining what speakers say. Nevertheless, the long-standing assumption has been that understanding what speakers say, or what is said, refers only to the truth-conditional content of an utterance (its conventional or literal meaning), which is only a small part of speakers' intended, communicative meanings (Levinson, 1987). Many scholars following Grice have argued from such observations that pragmatics plays only a small part in determining what speakers say, as opposed to what they conversationally imply or implicate.

In recent years, however, several linguists and philosophers have persuasively argued that the Grice view ignores the fact that essentially the same sorts of inferential processes used to determine conversational implicatures also enter into determining what is said (Carston, 1988, 1993; Recanati, 1989, 1993; Sperber & Wilson, 1986; Wilson & Sperber, 1992). Consider typical utterances of sentences such as (a) "You're not going to die" and (b) "I haven't eaten." In each case, at least after the indexical references and the time of the utterances are fixed, the literal meaning of the sentence determines a definite proposition, with a definite truth condition, which can be expressed as "The addressee of the utterance in sentence a is immortal" and "The utterer of sentence b has not eaten prior to the time of the utterance." Each of these statements reflects the minimal proposition expressed by the two sentences (Recanati, 1989). However, a speaker of "I haven't eaten" or "You're not going to die" is likely to be communicating not a minimal proposition, but some pragmatic expansion of it, such as "I haven't eaten dinner today" or "You're not going to die from this wound." It appears that significant pragmatic knowledge plays a role in determining both what is said and what is implicated.

Gibbs and Moise (1997) demonstrated in several experimental studies that pragmatics plays a major role in people's intuitions of what is said. Consider the expression "Jane has three children." According to the Grice view, the interpretation that Jane has exactly three children comes from applying specific pragmatic information to the minimally pragmatic proposition of what is said, a process that results in a generalized conversational implicature. But we showed that people do not equate a minimal meaning (i.e., that Jane has at least three children and may have more than three) with what a speaker says. Instead, people assume that the enriched pragmatic meaning that Jane has exactly three children reflects what a speaker says by "Jane has three children." Even when people are alerted to the Grice position, they still reply that enriched pragmatics is part of their interpretation of what a speaker says and not just what the speaker implicates in context.

Other studies in Gibbs and Moise (1997) demonstrated that people recognized a distinction between what speakers' say, or what is said, and what speakers implicate in particular contexts. For instance, consider the following story: Bill wanted to date his co-worker Jane. Being rather shy and not knowing Jane very well, Bill asked his friend Steve about Jane. Bill did not even know if Jane was married or not. When Bill asked Steve about this, Steve replied, "Jane has three children." Steve implicates by his statement "Jane has three children" in this context that "Jane is already married." To the extent that people can understand what Steve says, but not implicates, by "Jane has three children," they should be able to distinguish between the enriched and implicated paraphrases of the final expressions. In fact, the results of one study showed this to be true. These data lend support to theories of utterance interpretation that pragmatics strongly influences people's understanding of what speakers both say and communicate.

Do these data imply that people must analyze what speakers pragmatically say before determining what they implicate in context? At first glance, the idea that people determine what is said before figuring out what is implicated is similar to the traditional view of Grice, Searle, and others that people must analyze the literal meaning of an expression before understanding what it implies in context. However, the traditional view of literal meaning, which, again, many scholars assume is isomorphic with what is said, is that this can be determined apart from significant pragmatic knowledge.

The Gibbs and Moise findings cast doubt on this view. Nonetheless, in an unpublished study we have found that people still take longer to comprehend ''Jane has three children'' when a speaker implies that ''Jane is married'' than to read the same sentence in a context where the speaker only says ''Jane has exactly three children.'' These data show, then, that it takes longer to understand expressions in which speakers communicate some meaning beyond what they pragmatically say than it does to comprehend utterances in which what speakers say and implicate are identical. Drawing conversational implicatures of the sort that arises when we use a statement such as ''Jane has three children'' to communicate that ''Jane is married'' can under some circumstances require additional mental processing. Moreover, it appears that different aspects of pragmatics are differentially available when people understand what speakers say and implicate.

How do we reconcile this conclusion with the extensive data from psycholinguistics that people can quickly understand many instances of figurative language without having to first analyze the literal meanings of these statements? Does not the fact that people can understand the meanings of metaphors and ironies, for instance, more quickly than when these same statements are used literally argue against the idea that inferring what speakers imply takes longer than understanding what they simply say?

There are three responses to these questions worth considering. The first simply argues that most of the studies on figurative language understanding examine conventional instances of figurative language, one reason why people do not appear to take longer to process many metaphors, idioms, indirect speech acts, and so on (Dascal, 1987). On the other hand, understanding that ''Jane has three children'' communicates ''Jane is married'' requires listeners or readers to draw a novel inference about the relation between a statement on the number of Jane's children and the topic of the conversation, namely, whether Jane might be married. Although it is certainly true that one's familiarity with a well-known figurative expression facilitates processing of these statements (see Katz, chap.

1), several studies also demonstrate that people can process novel instances of metaphor and irony in context as quickly as they do literal uses of the same statements (or when what is said and meant are identical) (Gibbs, 1994).

A second explanation for the possible discrepancy between the results of the Gibbs and Moise reading time study and the previous research on figurative language understanding is that some aspects of figurative meaning are understood as part of what speakers say and others as part of what speakers implicate. For instance, several linguists have argued that the nonliteral meanings of certain indirect speech acts (e.g., ''Can you pass the salt?''), metonymies (e.g., ''The buses are on strike''), and ironies (e.g., ''You're a fine friend'') are understood as part of our interpretation of what a speaker says, called ''explicatures'' (Groefsema, 1992; Papafragou, 1996), and not derived as conversational implicatures. Thus, there is sufficient pragmatic information, perhaps part of people's deep background knowledge, that allows them to quickly infer some figurative meanings without having to apply very local, contextually specific, pragmatic information.

A final explanation of the different empirical findings focuses on the different roles that what is said plays in understanding figurative language as opposed to the indicative utterances studies in the Gibbs and Moise (1997) experiments. Consider again the utterance ''Jane has three children'' when used to communicate that Jane is married. Understanding what is meant or implicated by this utterance is accomplished by virtue of our recognition of the pragmatic said interpretation that Jane has only three children. On the other hand, understanding the intended meanings of many metaphors, idioms, ironic statements, and so on is accomplished in spite of what these expressions specifically say.

In many cases of figurative language understanding, processing what a speaker says is short-circuited in favor of what that utterance is intended to communicate in context. For example, our understanding of the metaphorical expression ''The old rock was brittle with age,'' stated by one student to another in reference to an elderly professor, might not require that we first figure out what the speaker specifically says. Instead, the normal process of referential assignment when reading the phrase ''The old rock'' prompts people to quickly seek an alternative figurative meaning that makes sense in the discourse situation. In some specialized and highly available contexts, the metaphoric interpretation is accessed first. This quick search for nonliteral meanings in context provides one main reason why metaphorical utterances can be understood as fast, if not faster, than literal uses of the same expressions. In other cases, understanding what a speaker says will lead us to draw further figurative inferences as implicatures. Just as a speaker might say ''Jane has three children'' to imply that Jane is married, a speaker might say ''I love drivers who signal before changing lanes'' to ironically implicate that he is mad at the driver who just switched lanes without signaling.

What a speaker says in both of these instances determines what he or she wants to communicate. Understanding what the speaker actually intended requires that we comprehend what he or she pragmatically says and also apply additional pragmatic information to infer what he or she really implicates. Drawing inferences about what speakers figuratively communicate beyond what they pragmatically say may, under some circumstances, take additional processing effort.

Interestingly, there are occasions when understanding what someone says automatically leads one to infer a figurative meaning even if the speaker did not necessarily intend that figurative meaning to be communicated. For instance, when someone literally "gets away with murder," he also figuratively "avoids responsibility for his action," an inference from something a speaker says to a figurative meaning that takes people longer to process than if they simply understand the phrase "gets away with murder" when used intentionally as having figurative, idiomatic meaning (Gibbs, 1986).

There is clearly much further empirical work needed to look more closely at the role of pragmatics in understanding what speakers say and implicate by their use of figurative language. My aim in discussing these new ideas and findings is to suggest that some aspects of figurative language are understood as part of what speakers say while others may be understood as part of what speakers implicate in specific discourse contexts. Researchers still need to determine which aspects of pragmatic meaning are best understood as part of what is said as opposed to what is implicated.

One possibility is that there are two kinds of pragmatic processes, primary and secondary, that operate during normal language understanding (Gibbs & Moise, 1997; Recanati, 1995). Primary pragmatic processes apply deep, default background knowledge to provide an interpretation of what speakers say. Secondary pragmatic processes use information from context to provide an interpretation of what speakers implicate in discourse. Listeners' stereotypical background knowledge dominates the application of secondary pragmatic processes to reveal what is said by a speaker's utterance as distinct from what the speaker implicates.

Understanding something of how different aspects of pragmatics interact with different linguistic information may provide essential clues to characterizing people's on-line comprehension of figurative language. The main point here is that people may sometimes construct representations of what speakers say as part of or even before they understand what speakers implicate when they use figurative language, even if these "said" meanings are not related to traditional views of literal meaning.

Turner, in contrast to the position suggested by Katz, and some of the suggestions of Cacciari or Gibbs, sees no need to suggest that literal and nonliteral language suggest different underlying processes. And he suggests how conceptual integration might produce ironic products.

TURNER: Conceptual integration is a basic, general cognitive operation, on a par with others, and interacting with others. The network model shows that there are many kinds of products of conceptual integration, some "felt" to be figurative, some to be literal, some to lie in between, but in all cases the conceptual integration proceeds according to the same underlying basic cognitive operation, with the same structural features and optimality constraints. Different products differ on parameters having to do with distinctions of entrenchment, number and kinds of spaces and domains involved, kinds of projection, and strategies for meeting the multiple competing optimality constraints.

Because conceptual integration is a basic cognitive operation, it is not surprising that it often plays a role in the construction of products judged to be ironic. There is straightforward conceptual integration in ironic "saying the opposite of what you mean": for example, in one input space the speaker loves your sweater and says so; in another input space the speaker hates your sweater and says so; in the blend, the speaker has the hatred from one space and perhaps the sneer from the same space but the words from the other space, "I just love your sweater." Moreover, if the irony is intended to be perceived by the hearer, there must be projection to the blend of intention to make one's meaning understood by the hearer.

In the input spaces, meaning is expressed through conventional forms for evoking it, but in the blend, there is emergent structure: the meaning is expressed in a phrase conventionally associated with the opposite of the meaning. There may also be emergent conventional prosody specific to ironic blends and useful for prompting for their construction: the prosody of the ironic utterance "I just love your sweater" is not in either input space. There is similar straightforward conceptual integration involved in the kind of irony that Adrian Pilkington calls "echo with a shift." Pilkington (1997) gives the example of conversation between Mr. Knightly and Emma in Jane Austen's *Emma*.

MR. KNIGHTLY: If you were as much guided by nature in your estimate of men and women, and as little under the power of fancy and whim in your dealings with them, as you are where these children are concerned, we might always think alike.

EMMA: To be sure—our discordances must always arise from my being in the wrong.

Emma here states an inference carried by Mr. Knightly's conditional, but with a different judgment of its truth-value. This irony presents "disanalogy between two situations that contain the same proposition," but in the blend of these two situations, Emma's statement does not explicitly assert her judgment of that proposition, as it does in the input space in which she explicitly announces what she thinks of this proposition.

There are also cases of conceptual integration in which the blend seems simultaneously metaphoric and ironic. Here is an example from Fauconnier and Turner (1994) and Turner (1996). When Dante in the Inferno encounters Bertran de Born, Bertran is carrying his severed head by hand, like a lantern. Bertran cites his punishment as the appropriate response to his sin, since in life he estranged the son of the English king from his father. Bertran in hell presents a quite complicated blend.

In the cross-space mapping connecting the physically divided object to the socially divided father and son, Bertran is not the counterpart of the divided object. But Bertran is metonymically related as cause to the socially divided father and son, and that metonymy is exploited to deliver a blend in which Bertran is the divided physical object. It seems "ironic" to readers, and even to Bertran, who calls this effect a "contrapasso," that, in the blend, the source counterpart of the sin is visited upon the target sinner as punishment. There is a kind of reversal that "feels" ironic, and that reversal is constructed and revealed through conceptual blending.

A second example comes from Turner and Fauconnier (1995). Consider act 4, scene 2, lines 108–9, in Shakespeare's *King John*. A messenger enters, looking fearful, and King John, reading the disturbance in his face, says: "So foul a sky clears not without a storm. / Pour down thy weather." There is an "ironic" reading of this passage that involves a blended space in which the messenger, the prime example of something absolutely under the king's command, is also nature, the prime example of something absolutely above the king's command. In this blend of contraries, King John is commanding what he can command, but what he can command also turns out to be simultaneously what he cannot command. This shows the instability of his rule. This tension, and some related tensions I pass over, result in a dramatic irony, made possible because of the blend.

Nonetheless, it is important to see that although conceptual integration plays a role in these examples of irony, the structural elements of conceptual integration do not in themselves supply an explanation of why they are judged to be ironic. Consider, on the one hand, a private ironic statement. Ann says, "Why don't you do that for me?" and Barbara says, "I'd love to!" Barbara intends to do it and intends Ann to take her utterance as indicating that she will do it voluntarily, but in fact Barbara is sick to death of Ann's tasking her and enjoys the private irony of her "I'd love to!" as signifying "You are out of your mind thinking that I have nothing better to do than your errands." Barbara's interpretation involves a blended space that is ironic but private, an instrument of self-management. How does this differ from the scene in which Barbara says the same thing but privately interprets it as a straightforward lie, compelled by Ann's power? In both cases, Ann is to construct the identical interpretation, and Barbara's interpretation in both cases involves a blend of the judgment from one space and the utterance from the disanalogous space. But she "feels" one case to be ironic and the other not. The existence of the structural elements of conceptual integration does not in itself tell us why one is judged to be private irony and the other is judged to be private deception.

ON METAPHOR, IRONY AND OTHER TROPES: A ROSE IS A ROSE IS A ROSE (OR IS IT)?

In most of these chapters, the emphasis was on the comprehension or processing of metaphor, though Turner especially discussed a number of figures. There was relatively less discussion of the implications of differences. For instance, in none of the chapters was Wheelright's (1962) distinction between epiphoric and diaphoric metaphor considered, let alone the processing differences between metaphor and irony, irony and hyperbole, and the like. Various comments addressed this issue. Some suggest that differences are important.

Katz wondered about why we have a sense of literality in the first place and how this would affect our reactions to different types of figures. Gibbs speculates about, and reports new data on, differences in processing irony and metaphor. Others have argued in the past that irony, but not metaphor, involves a well-developed theory of mind and have shown how the developmental differences between comprehending metaphor can be explained in such terms (see Winner, 1988). Gibbs argues analogous differences for adult language users. Finally, Turner considers Cacciari's discussion of synethesia (chap. 4) to speculate about neurological mechanisms of integration and responds to Gibbs's new data.

KATZ: I am intrigued by the notion that our sense of literality, vividness, aptness, and other reactions do not reflect basic processing differences but can be described in terms of parameters involved in conceptual integration. And, presumably, different parameters are involved in cases where both the literal and nonliteral might be simultaneously active (such as the instance of humor and of irony that I mentioned earlier), and cases where, depending on context, a given utterance might be perceived as just literal or as just nonliteral (as occurs for nonfamiliar proverbial items).

But why, I wonder, have we developed a sense of literality/nonliterality in the first place, if this difference is not reflective of processing differences? After all, there is no reason that we have to ever experience anything as literal or as nonliteral, especially if this difference is not primary.

I wonder if this difference is tied to other beliefs that we hold: for instance, a common belief is that the world exists (independent of our processing capabilities) and that our mind exists (independent of the world). Thus, physical events can exist to which we are "blind" (e.g., the sound of a dog whistle), and we can experience thought that cannot be externally verified (e.g., hallucinations). Moreover, the perceptual and memory literature is rich with examples in which we confuse the "real" external world with our internal activity, (e.g., the Perkey effect in perception; reality monitoring or false memories). Presumably at least some of this confusion is due to the overlap of representations or processes in the "imaged' and the "perceived" conditions.

So is our sense of literality an instance of a similar phenomenon? That is, do we experience an utterance as literal because the parameters active in integration are parasitic on integration mechanisms that are also active in perceptual processing? If so, we are left with mapping the parameters involved in different types of integration and then relating these to different mechanisms, such as those parasitic on perception and those that are not. Analogous arguments can be made for differences in our sense of aptness, appropriateness, and other "reactions." That is, what parameters are involved?

GIBBS: Metaphor, metonymy, irony, hyperbole, understatement, and indirect speech acts are all types of nonliteral language that are traditionally viewed as classic tropes. Under traditional views of figurative language, there is no reason to believe that one kind of figurative expression requires fundamentally different cognitive processes to understand than any other. Moreover, many scholars now believe, as noted earlier, that similar cognitive processes drive the comprehension of literal and figurative language. I now wish to question both of these views in a certain respect.

Some recent arguments by linguists and philosophers, and some of my own recent empirical research, have lead me to specifically argue that metaphor and irony processing might be quite different precisely because of the use of metarepresentational reasoning in the production and interpretation of irony—something that is not required for understanding metaphor.

Consider the following two stories, each of which ends with the expression "This one's really sharp."

You are a teacher at an elementary school.
You are discussing a new student with your assistant teacher.
The student did extremely well on her entrance examinations.
You say to your assistant,
"This one's really sharp."

You are a teacher at an elementary school.
You are gathering teaching supplies with your assistant teacher.

Some of the scissors you have are in really bad shape.
You find one pair that won't cut anything.
You say to your assistant,
"This one's really sharp."

The expression "This one's really sharp" has a metaphorical meaning in the first context as the teacher refers to the student's intellectual abilities using a familiar metaphorical comparison whereby the mind is conceived of as a cutting instrument. The sharper ability of the cutting instrument refers to greater intellectual abilities. This same expression in the second context has an ironic meaning. Even though the teacher is literally referring to a cutting instrument (i.e., the scissors), she refers to it ironically as possessing a desired property (e.g., sharpness) that, in reality, it does not possess. Ordinary listeners understand linguistic statements such as "This one's really sharp" as overt expressions of and clues to a speaker's thoughts.

Every utterance is more or less a truthful interpretation of a thought that a speaker wants to communicate. Following Sperber and Wilson's (1986) "relevance theory," we can say an utterance is descriptively used when the thought interpreted is itself entertained as a true description of a state of affairs, but it is interpretively used when the thought interpreted is entertained as an interpretation of some further thought, say, an attributed thought or utterance, or an utterance can be an interpretation of some thought that might be desirable to entertain in some context (Wilson & Sperber, 1992). Under this new view, ironic utterances, such as that shown, must be processed interpretively, rather than descriptively, precisely because they require the recognition of a thought about an attributed thought (second-order meta-representation), in order to understand what speakers imply by these statements. For instance, when the teacher says about the scissors "This one's really sharp," she is commenting on her prior belief that the scissors should be sharp and capable of cutting paper. The teacher is essentially alluding to or echoing her prior belief and thus conveying a thought about an attributed thought, belief, or previously stated utterance.

One interesting hypothesis that follows from this is that irony should be more difficult to comprehend than metaphor because irony requires the ability to recognize, at least, a second-order meta-representation (a thought about an attributed thought). This view of irony as involving complex meta-representational reasoning to be understood differs considerably from the traditional, standard pragmatic model, which assumes that understanding irony should not necessitate any ability that interpreting metaphor does not also demand (Gibbs, in press; Happe, 1993).

I have recently conducted a study that examined the above hypothesis. Consider, again, the stories ending with the expression "That's really sharp." I measured the amount of time it took readers to understand the last line of each story, which could be seen as having either a metaphoric or ironic interpretation. This comparison provides the ideal situation for assessing the above hypothesis because the same sentence is read in slightly different contexts (i.e., where the teacher makes an evaluative statement about some person or thing). In fact, people took significantly longer to read the ironic statements (2,013 msecs) than the metaphoric ones (1,791 msecs). This result supports the hypothesis that irony requires extra processing over metaphor because of the extra meta-representational reasoning needed to understand the pretense behind what speakers say in conveying ironic or sarcastic meaning.

Findings from a further study showed that people viewed the ironic utterances as involving pretense and referring to a speaker's prior, mistaken beliefs more so than when they read metaphoric statements. The data from these two studies provide some initial evidence in favor of the idea that irony and metaphor require different kinds of cognitive operations to be understood.

Another set of empirical findings also bear on the importance of meta-representational reasoning in irony understanding (Gibbs, O'Brien, & Doolittle, 1995). Consider the following two situations:

> John and Bill were taking a statistics class together.
> Before the final exam, they decided to cooperate during the test. So they worked out a system so they could secretly share answers. After the exam John and Bill were really pleased with themselves. They thought they were pretty clever for beating the system.
> Later that night, a friend happened to ask them if they ever tried to cheat.
> John and Bill looked at each other and laughed; then John said, ''I would never be involved in any cheating.''

> John and Bill were taking a statistics class together.
> They studied hard together, but John was clearly better prepared than Bill. During the exam, Bill panicked and started to copy answers from John. John did not see Bill do this and so did not know he was actually helping Bill. John took the school's honour code very seriously.
> Later that night, a friend happened to ask them if they ever tried to cheat.
> John and Bill looked at each other; then John said, ''I would never be involved in any cheating.''

Both of these situations end with the identical statement that in each case is understood as verbal irony. The speaker in the first story specifically intends for his audience to understand what is said as ironic, but the speaker in the second situation does not intend for his utterance to be understood ironically. In the second story, only the addressees and overhearers perceive the irony in what the speaker actually said. It is quite possible for people to understand a speaker's utterance as irony even though the speaker did not intend the utterance to be understood as irony.

Several experimental studies showed that people understand utterances in stories like the second one as having ironic meaning even if the speaker did not intend for the utterance to be understood in this way (Gibbs et al., 1995). In fact, readers see the final statements in the unintentional stories as being more ironic than was the case for intentionally ironic statements. Thus, although irony often reflects speakers' communicative goals to identify aspects of ironic situations, speakers may unintentionally create irony by what they say.

An alternative way of distinguishing between these two types of irony is to suggest that understanding intentional irony requires more complex meta-representational reasoning to understand what the speaker pretended to communicate by what he said. That is, when a speaker says, "I would never be involved in any cheating," he intentionally desires for his addressee to recognize the sarcasm in his statement. Listeners must recognize the attributed belief (perhaps shared by the speaker and listener) that a person should not, and would not, cheat (a second-order belief). Understanding unintentional irony, on the other hand, does not require listeners to draw these same types of complex meta-representational inferences (i.e., about what the speaker said nonseriously). Thus, listeners need not construct a hypothetical scenario to which the speaker's utterance, on one level, refers. The results of a reading-time study in Gibbs et al. (1995) showed that people took much less time to read unintentionally ironic statements than to process intentionally ironic statements.

It appears that people find it easier to comprehend verbal ironies that spontaneously create ironic situations than to make sense of ironies that remind listeners of speakers' prior attitudes or beliefs. The main reason for this difference is that understanding the intentional ironies demands a more complex meta-representational process to recover what the speaker really means in alluding to a second-order belief than is the case for comprehending unintentional ironies where second-order beliefs are not being alluded to. The traditional view of irony cannot account for these empirical findings. However, the data are consistent with the hypothesis that ironic statements incorporating more complex meta-representations (i.e., the intentional ironies) take more time to process than ironic remarks that do not reflect second-order beliefs (i.e., the unintentional ironies).

Many other kinds of figurative language, such as hyperbole and understatement, may also require sophisticated meta-representational reasoning to be understood. My general point is that there may be a variety of factors that distinguish how people understand different types of figurative language, including differences in the role of meta-representational reasoning in understanding what speakers mean when they express their thoughts in figurative terms. One challenge for comprehensive theories of figurative language use and understanding, such as Fauconnier and Turner's network model of conceptual integration, is to account for some of these cognitive differences. Moreover, psycholinguists face the challenge of studying in more detail the cognitive processes involved in understanding different types of figurative language to see how these may, or may not, require different theoretical accounts.

Turner on the Neurological Substrate of On-line Processing

Synesthesia seems to raise questions of neurobiological operation, because it involves connections across sensory modalities. One of the most intriguing and difficult questions we face in discussing on-line conceptual integration is: what neurological mechanisms could be doing the work? Unfortunately, there is very little to go on in facing this question, although there are intriguing speculations, and Cacciari's discussion of synesthesia (chap. 4) brings us to one of them.

There appear to be neurological mechanisms for connecting different kinds of features and activating them simultaneously. Gerald Edelman (1989) presents a speculative model of "reentrant mapping" to account for these integrations. Antonio Damasio (1989) proposes a model in which the connections are not direct but go instead through a "convergence zone," a "dispositional representation" that connects to many different sites. Damasio's model might have something to say about the kind of cross-modal integration we see in synesthesia. His model "rejects a single anatomical site for the integration of memory and motor processes and a single store for the meaning of entities or events. Meaning is reached by time-locked multiregional retroactivation of widespread fragment records. Only the latter records can become contents of consciousness" (Damasio, 1989, p. 25). Because a higher-order convergence zone is cross-modal, it offers a site for activating different neuronal patterns.

When we try to imagine what neurological mechanisms could achieve the kind of dynamic binding we see in conceptual integration, it is natural to think of synesthesia, reentrant mapping, and convergence zones. Could sensory integration have provided a mechanism to be exploited for conceptual integration?

Turner on Gibbs's Speculations About Irony

Since particular conceptual integration networks vary along a number of processual parameters—degree of entrenchment of various kinds, amount and kind of on-line projection, number and kinds of input spaces to be constructed, amount of projection from the blend back to the inputs, conventionality of the blend, degree to which the blend is visible, degree of conflict between optimality constraints given the inputs, and so on—it would not be surprising if two different conceptual integration networks judged to be ironic took different amounts of time to construct. (In the case of analogical networks, subjects often struggle for extended periods to achieve a satisfactory product but finally fail.) So while Gibbs may be right in asserting that people take "much less time to read unintentionally ironic statements than to process intentionally ironic statements," it is not clear that this is evidence for different underlying cognitive operations as opposed to different processual parameters of the same cognitive operations.

ON THE NEED AND NATURE OF METAPHORIC REPRESENTATION

A basic issue of contention is the increasingly popular view that there is a metaphoric level of conceptual representation that is reflected in, and motivates our understanding of, linguistic expressions. Three chapters in this book took this as a theme. Turner accepted the view as given, explored some of its historical roots, and described how this form of information is aroused and blended in various ways. Gibbs responded to critiques that questioned whether one needs metaphoric representation. That is, can the data be explained without recourse to an additional hypothetical mental entity? He described various theoretically testable hypotheses that follow from assuming metaphoric representation. Finally, Cacciari explored the nature of nonlinguistic knowledge and what this knowledge suggests about how we process information. Some of these themes were reexamined in the various commentaries.

TURNER: Cacciari insightfully points to possible experiential motivations of metaphoric connections, especially for metaphoric meanings of color terms, and more widely for all sensory terms. Sweetser (1990) comments often on the important experiential motivations of such metaphors. As the principal exponent of the conceptual metaphor THE MIND IS A BODY MOVING IN SPACE and its corollary KNOWING IS SEEING, Sweetser has emphasized the experience of light and seeing: sensory experience of white is associated with light; the presence of light enables us to see objects in the visual field and so perhaps to feel more secure; light, consisting of photons, warms; sunlight is purifying (hence the term "lustration"); light is associated with being awake, with traveling, with social interaction, and so on. I concur with Cacciari that the experience of the sensory phenomenon itself can motivate the metaphoric connection. But I think that Sweetser agrees with Cacciari on this point. Sweetser is instead arguing, correctly I think, that the metaphor cannot be explained as similarity, where similarity is defined in a truth-conditional manner as the sharing of objective features. The metaphoric connection between white and truth is not explained by truth-conditions. It is difficult to see how they could share any objective features, since one is sensory and the other is mental, much less to see how the metaphor could be explained as consisting exclusively of the sharing of objective features.

Katz comes to the issue from the perspective of an experimental psychologist and examines what we have learned from the related questions in the imagery debate: do we need to posit an imagery level of representation or is our experience of imagery a product that emerges from more basic amodal representations and nonimagery-specific processes?

KATZ: I am continually impressed by the elegant analyses of Turner, Lakoff, Gibbs, and others who have argued for a metaphoric level of representation. And, on the face of it, the evidence is very convincing: many expressions appear to share a basic conceptual format, and many expressions require simultaneous consideration of component parts. But how far can we push this? Do we have conceptual metaphors for any set of expressions for which we can find conceptual similarity? Vervaeke and Kennedy (1996) provide a detailed examination of this problem, noting that "we are not given criteria to decide how to subdivide a corpus of metaphors that might be due to several underlying metaphors rather than one unitary and very abstract metaphor, because the theory presently deals with counterexamples only as examples of a different grouping, not as independent, but similar, groupings or as challenges to the theory per se" (p. 279). As an experimental psychologist, I worry that the theory, so elegant, might not be falsifiable. For instance, what unique implications arise that would disprove the existence of conceptual metaphors, or that the nature of these metaphors is embodiment? For instance, we can agree with Turner that we sometimes hold separate ideas simultaneously, that we might merge them, and that in doing so we might have emergent features that would not have been obvious from each idea considered separately. But does this indicate a "blending" that is different than, let us say, the consideration of the perceptual manipulations described in the memory imagery literature? (Consider two triangles, one with the base on the bottom, the other, beside it, with the base on top. Now, in your mind's eye move one triangle over the other. What do you see?)

In fact, much of the discussion of a metaphoric level of representation reminded me of the discussion of the nature of mental imagery found in the experimental literature since the early 1970s. In that literature some argued that imagery was a separate form of representation, with its own properties not explicable as the products of processes working in static propositions. In that literature the early exponents were very careful to make their models of imagery falsifiable, by tieing the experience of imagery to perceptually based mechanisms. And some of those ideas might be interesting to consider here.

Let us, for argument's sake, adopt the view that our conceptual system is modular and that different functions (e.g., language, vision, music) are served by central mechanisms with differing representational formats (e.g., imaginal, propositional, motoric). This position has been taken often in the past (e.g., Aylwin, 1985; Kosslyn, 1980; Paivio, 1971), but the implications for figurative language are not usually considered (though see Paivio and Walsh, 1993).

Let us first consider some of the assumed properties of an imagery-based system. Paivio (1975) describes images as a medium supporting "synchronic" thought, in which disparate mental elements are brought together, organized, integrated, and made available to conscious evaluation. More recently, Kosslyn (1994) also describes imagery as functioning to organize (and, when necessary, to reorganize) simple mental units into higher-order units. Moreover, based on fMRI and PET data, he argues that these functions can be localized within specific areas of the brain, specifically, a dorsal pathway consisting of areas that extend from the occipital lobe to the posterior parietal lobe. These properties are, on the surface, similar to blending activities described by Turner, though it is clear that Turner's descriptions of blending consist of many cases in which the blend is not perceptually based. One possibility that could follow is that there might be two types of blends, with different properties, and different implications for our sense of literality—one for easy to visualize properties and one for more abstract, conceptual thoughts. If so, can we experimentally support two types of blends? One empirical possibility might be to examine various realms of experience that might not be tied to linguistic expression but are, nonetheless, symbolic and syntactic. The work by John Kennedy on understanding raised drawings and this book's description of synesthesia in several chapters would be examples of such realms.

Various art forms might also meet the criteria for experimental disentanglement. For instance, one can consider musical cognition and test the extent to which our understanding of music is analogous to our understanding of linguistic phrases. (What root metaphors underlie musical expression?) Jackendoff (1992) makes such a case but puts it into a larger perspective. He argues, for instance, that we have a rich vocabulary for what we see, suggesting that the conceptual structures underlying language and vision are highly linked. In contrast, we have great difficulty in talking about the state of our bodies (for instance, imagine trying to tell someone how to ride a bike). We also have, he argues, a limited vocabulary for talking about music, suggesting to him that the conceptual underpinnings of music are distinct from those of language (though perhaps more directly linked to conceptual knowledge of our bodies, as reflected in the rich relations between music and dance).

In my reading of Cacciari, she has made the argument that metaphor can serve as the mediator between different conceptual modules. That is, perhaps we should distinguish between metaphor played out by the faculties of language and of vision (which are subserved by highly interrelated central structures) and those that involve faculties less related to the conceptual structures of language, such as motor faculties, musical faculties, and the haptic faculty. The former might demonstrate an intrinsic relation between language and thought, whereas the latter might indicate a special role for metaphor in mapping difficult-to-communicate experiences.

CACCIARI: The main point of disagreement that the recent debate has pointed out concerns whether the choice to speak figuratively instead of literally reflects a surface form preference or springs directly from the metaphorical nature of thought. Specifically, are we first figurative thinkers and consequentially figurative language users or the other way around? This problem has given rise to a lively debate treated extensively elsewhere (Cacciari & Glucksberg, 1994; Hampton, 1989; Jackendoff & Aaron, 1991; Gibbs, 1994, 1996, this book; Langacker, 1988; Quinn, 1991; Murphy, 1996, 1997; Turner, chap. 2). Many scholars working on metaphor today concur that metaphor does not concern only language but also perceptual and categorization processes. However, a crucial difference exists, to try to sketch it in few words, between those for whom metaphor represents a mode of representation and thought where concepts are understood, as Murphy says, (1996, p. 176) "by [metaphoric] reference to a different domain" [the conceptual metaphor view] and those for whom metaphor can be used to produce similarities, new categories, and ways of organization of concepts that are understood "via their own representation" without positing a preestablished metaphorical architecture of the mind (Gentner, Falkenhainer & Skorstad, 1987; Gentner & Wolff, ms; Glucksberg & Keysar, 1990, 1993; Murphy, 1996).

Less attention has been paid to the role played by metaphorical language as a means for expressing the perceptual world that surrounds us and our experiences of it. The stress that many scholars adhering to the Conceptual Metaphor approach have put on the experiential basis of categorization constitutes only the exception that confirms the rule. I concur with Gibbs that knowledge is not (or not only, to me, cf. also Murphy, 1997) "static, propositional, and sentential" (Gibbs, chap. 3). However, the proposed alternative, that knowledge is "grounded in patterns of bodily experience" (Gibbs, chap. 3), reflects a viewpoint for which the perceptual world is mainly constituted by the mental experience we construct about it, and not by the properties and structures that exist before and even without our effort to impose a linguistic structure on it. I treat this point extensively in my chapter when I discuss the relationship between the expressive properties of objects and polysemy.

Gibbs (chap. 3) claims that one of the major innovations of cognitive semantics is the acknowledgment that "knowledge is grounded and structured by various patterns of perceptual interaction, bodily actions, and manipulations of objects," namely, by "image schemas" that emerge throughout the life of an individual, his or her sensorimotor activity, orientation in time and space, and visual perceptions. These recurring body experiences give rise to a set of abstract schemas such as that, for instance, of CONTAINMENT that are then used as a base to understand linguistic metaphors and idiomatic expressions (e.g., those related to anger).

To my understanding, there are at least two crucial problems with the notion of embodiment. The first is that, despite the experientialist stance, the perceptual experience ends up being, once again, "disembodied," so to speak, in the name of a set of well-structured and predictable (from the source domain) mappings described in much the same static and abstract-based format of traditional semantic accounts.

However, something new is happening in the field of meaning representation studies that goes beyond both the traditional truth-value approach and the experientialist view endorsed by Gibbs. A number of researchers are trying to ask new questions concerning the relationship between sensory experience (visual, haptic, olfactory, and so forth), mental representation, and linguistic expression. The way in which a perceptual system holds the information concerning objects and events in time and space is highly complex and sophisticated. The underlying concepts and their verbal labels keep only a schematic trace of such complexity. Not all perceptual properties are in fact captured by the language that speaks, for example, of vision. This leads to the problem of the extent to which the labels that give name to the perceptual actions preserve or filter the complex set of perceptual principles underlying them (cf. Jackendoff, 1987, 1992). A new approach has therefore emerged that tries to account for the mental representation of meaning as comprising not only linguistic information (syntax, morphology, and so on), but also different levels of perceptual information as part of the conceptual representation (cf. Barsalou, in press; Cacciari, 1997; Cacciari & Levorato, 1997; Jackendoff, 1987, 1992). Accordingly, the mental representation of the intension of, for instance, a verb describing visual activities would include also parameters associated with the perceptual "appropriateness" conditions that are required in order to determine the verb's extension (i.e., the class of events that such a verb can be used to refer to). Such mental representation would include also the intuitive models of the perceptual activities that we associate to them.

In Gibbs's approach, no much place or relevance is given, and I come to the second point, to the perceptual world and the properties that objects possess independently from us as cognizers. To pursue the viewpoint I used in my chapter to analyze Woolf's and Musil's metaphors, my claim is that the referential-literal language is fundamentally inadequate to describe the "qualities" and the nuances of many of our perceptions and body experiences (visual, haptic, kinesthetic, and so on). To capture the perceptual and experiential complexity of the world we live in, language has to be "stretched" and hence used metaphorically to increase its descriptive and communicative force. Metaphor is useful and used insofar as it provides a possible contribution to filling this gap between the complexity of the perceptual world and the limitations of our linguistic repertoire to describe it.

CONCLUDING COMMENTS

The problem of metaphor and other forms of nonliteral language has emerged as a central issue in the psycholinguistic literature. Whereas only a few years ago, one would be hard pressed to find mention of metaphor, irony, and other tropes in the experimental psycholinguistic texts, such topics are given a prominent place today. The emergence of nonliteral language as a respectable topic has led to an exciting convergence of many fields: philosophy, linguistic and literary analyses, computer science, neuroscience, and experimental cognitive psychology, to name a few. Each of these fields has enriched the scientific understanding of the relation between language and thought. And in various ways each of these traditions has been expressed in this book.

The value of a book such as this is not to provide a set of definitive answers. Rather it is to stimulate critical and synergetic discussion between practitioners of the various fields and between alternative conceptions of the cognitive and linguistic worlds wherein metaphor resides and is expressed. For much of the recent past, the study of figurative language, when not ignored by the mainstream, has been dominated by schools of thought, populated by zealots who support their position and attack their "opponents." The articles and critiques presented here illustrate not only points of differences and agreements, but also illustrate well the diversity of the phenomenon of metaphor, both in language and thought. Metaphor is not a single entity but shows itself in many different guises. In this volume, we are perhaps seeing, as Cristina Cacciari put it in a preface to her commentary, "hints that the age of 'faith or fight' is maybe fading and new lines of empirical research and theorizing on figurative language are now mature for many of us."

REFERENCES

Aylwin, S. (1985). *Structure in thought and feeling*. New York: Methuen.

Barsalou, L. (1982). Context-independent and context-dependent information in concepts. *Memory and Cognition, 10,* 82–93.

Barsalou, L. (in press). In T. B. Ward, S. M. Smith, & J. Vaid (Eds.), *Creative thought: An investigation of conceptual structures and processes*. Washington, DC: American Psychological Association.

Brugman, C. (1996). Mental spaces, constructional meaning, and pragmatic ambiguity. In G. Fauconnier & E. Sweetser (Eds.), *Spaces, worlds and grammar* (pp. 29–56). Chicago: University of Chicago Press.

Cacciari, C. (1977). *From perception to cognition: how people represent the structure of perception verbs.* Paper presented at the meeting, Semantic Categories: Concepts and Word Meaning, Paris.

Cacciari, C., & Glucksberg, S. (1991). Understanding idiomatic expressions: The contribution of word meanings. In G. Simpson (Ed.), *Understanding word and sentence* (pp. 217–240). Amsterdam: North-Holland.

Cacciari, C., & Glucksberg, S. (1994). Understanding figurative language. In M. Gernsbacher (Ed.), *Handbook of psycholinguistics* (pp. 447–477). New York: Academic Press.

Cacciari, C., & Levorato, M. C. (1997). *Note per usa semantica psicologica dei verbi dell-esperienza sensoriale.* Submitted for publication.

Cacciari C., & Tabossi, P. (1988). The comprehension of idioms. *Journal of Memory and Language, 27,* 668–683.

Carston, R. (1988). Implicature, explicature, and truth-theoretic semantics. In R. Kempson (Ed.), *Mental representations: The interface between language and reality,* (pp. 155–181). Cambridge: Cambridge University Press.

Carston, R. (1993). Conjunction, explanation, and relevance. *Lingua, 90,* 27–48.

Colston, H. (1997). Salting the wound or sugaring the pill: The pragmatic functions of ironic criticisms. *Discourse Processes, 23,* 25–46.

Cutting, J., & Bock, K. (1997). That's the way the cookie bounces: Syntactic and semantic components of experimentally elicited idiom blends. *Memory and Cognition, 25,* 57–71.

Damasio, A. R. (1989). Time-locked multiregional retroactivation: A systems-level proposal for the neural substrates of recall and recognition, *Cognition, 33,* 25–62.

Dascal, M. (1987). Defending literal meaning. *Cognitive Science, 11,* 259–281.

Dews, S., & Winner, E. (1995). Muting the meaning: A social function of irony. *Metaphor and Symbolic Activity, 10,* 3–19.

Edelman, G. (1989). *The remembered present: A biological theory of consciousness.* New York: Basic Books.

Fauconnier, G., & Turner, M. (1994). *Conceptual projection and middle spaces.* San Diego: UCSD Cognitive Science Technical Report 9401.

Fauconnier, G., & Turner, M. (In press). Conceptual integration networks. *Cognitive Science.*

Fillmore, D., Kay, P., & O'Connor, C. (1988). Regularity and idiomaticity in grammatical constructions: The case of let alone. *Language, 64,* 501–538.

Gentner, D., Falkenhainer, B., & Skorstad, J. (1987). *Metaphor: The good, the bad and the ugly.* In TINLAP-3, Theoretical Issues in Natural Language Processing, positions papers, pp. 176–184.

Gentner, D. & Wolff, P. *Metaphor and knowledge change.* Manuscript.

Gibbs, R. (1984). Literal meaning and psychological theory. *Cognitive Science, 8,* 275–304.

Gibbs, R. (1994). *The poetics of mind: Figurative thought, language, and understanding.* New York: Cambridge University Press.

Gibbs, R. (In press). Metarepresentations in staged communicative acts. In D. Sperber (Ed.), *Metarepresentations,* New York: Oxford University Press.

Gibbs, R., Buchalter, D., Moise, J., & Farrar, W. (1993). Literal meaning and figurative language. *Discourse Processes, 16,* 387–403.

Gibbs, R., & Moise, J. (1997). Pragmatics in understanding what is said. *Cognition, 62,* 51–74.

Gibbs, R., O'Brien, J., & Doolittle, S. (1995). Inferring meanings that are not intended: Speakers' intentions and irony comprehension. *Discourse Processes, 20,* 187–203.

Glucksberg, S., & Keysar, B. (1990). Understanding metaphorical comparisons: Beyond similarity. *Psychological Review, 97,* 1, 3–18.

Glucksberg, S., & Keysar, B. (1993). How metaphor works. In A. Ortony (Ed.), *Metaphor and thought,* 2nd ed. (pp. 401–424). Cambridge: Cambridge University Press.

Goldberg, A. (1995). *Constructions: A construction grammar approach to argument structure.* Chicago: University of Chicago Press.

Grice, H. (1975). Logic and conversation. In P. Cole & J. Morgan (Eds.), *Syntax and semantics 3: Speech acts.* New York: Academic Press.

Grice, H. (1989). *Studies in the way of words.* Cambridge, MA: Harvard University Press.

Groefsema, M. (1992). Can you pass the salt—A short-circuited implicature. *Lingua, 87,* 103–135.

Hampton, J. A. (1989). Review article of *Women, Fire and Dangerous Things* by G. Lakoff. *Mind & Language, 4,* 1–2, 130–137.

Happe, F. (1993). Communicative competence and theory of mind in autism: A test of relevance theory. *Cognition, 48,* 101–119.

Honeck, R., & Hoffman, R. (Eds.). (1980). *Cognition and figurative language.* Hillsdale, NJ: Erlbaum.

Jackendoff, R. (1987). *Consciousness and the computational mind.* Cambridge, MA: MIT Press.

Jackendoff, R. (1992). *Languages of the mind. Essays on mental representation.* Cambridge, MA: MIT Press

Jackendoff, R., & Aaron, D. (1991). Review article of *More Than Cool Reason* by G. Lakoff and G. Turner. *Language, 67,* 320–338.

Katz, A. (1996). Experimental psycholinguistics and figurative language: Circa 1995. *Metaphor and Symbolic Activity,* 11, 17–37.

Kosslyn, S. (1980). *Image and mind.* Cambridge, MA: Harvard University Press.

Kosslyn, S. (1994). *Image and brain.* Cambridge, MA: MIT Press.

Langacker, R. (1988). Review article of *Women, Fire and Dangerous Things* by G. Lakoff. *Language, 64,* 384–395.

Lakoff, G., & Johnson, M. (1980). *Metaphors we live by.* Chicago: Chicago University Press.

Lee, K. (1996). Getting at the meaning of "make." In E. Casad (Ed.), *Cognitive linguistics in the redwoods* (pp. 389–422). New York: Mouton.

Levinson, S. (1983). *Pragmatics.* Cambridge: Cambridge University Press.

Levinson, S. (1987). Minimization and conversational inference. In J. Verschueren & M. Bertuccelli-Papi (Eds.), *The pragmatic perspective* (pp. 61–130). Philadelphia: John Benjamins.

Murphy, G. L. (1996). On metaphoric representation. *Cognition, 60,* 173–204.

Murphy, G. L. (1997). Reasons to doubt the present evidence for metaphoric representation. *Cognition, 62,* 99–108.

Ortony, A. (Ed.). (1979). *Metaphor and thought.* New York: Cambridge University Press.

Ortony, A., Reynolds, R., & Arter, J (1978). Metaphor: Theoretical and empirical research. *Psychological Bulletin, 85,* 919–943.

Paivio, A. (1971). *Imagery and verbal processes.* New York: Holt, Rinehart and Winston.

Paivio, A. (1975). Imagery and synchronic thinking. *Canadian Psychology Review, 16,* 147–163.

Paivio, A., & Walsh, M. (1993). Psychological processes in metaphor comprehension and memory. In A. Ortony (Ed.), *Metaphor and thought,* 2nd ed. (pp. 307–328). Cambridge: Cambridge University Press.

Papafragou, A. (1996). On metonymy. *Lingua, 94,* 169–195.

Pilkington, (1997, 7 February). *Shades of Irony.* Paper presented at the Ninth Annual Conference on Linguistics and Literature, University of North Texas.

Quinn, N. (1991). The cultural basis of metaphor. In J. W. Fernandez (Ed.), *Beyond metaphor. The theory of tropes in anthropology* (pp. 56–93). Stanford, CA: Stanford University Press.

Rawson, C. "The character of Swift's satire." Chapter 1 of *Order from confusion sprung: Studies in eighteenth-century literature from Swift to Cowper.* London: George Allen & Unwin, 1985.

Recanati, F. (1989). The pragmatics of what is said. *Mind & Behavior, 4,* 295–329.

Recanati, F. (1993). *Direct reference: From language to thought.* Cambridge, MA: Blackwell.

Recanati, F. (1995). The alleged priority of literal interpretation. *Cognitive Science, 19,* 207–232.

Searle, J. (1979). Metaphor. In A. Ortony (Ed.), *Metaphor and thought* (pp. 92–123). New York: Cambridge University Press.

Smith, E. (1988). Concepts and thought. In R. Sternberg & E. Smith (Eds.), *The psychology of human thought* (pp. 19–49). Cambridge: Cambridge University Press.

Sperber, D., & Wilson D. (1986). *Relevance: Communication and cognition.* Oxford: Blackwell.

Sweetser, E. (1990). *From etymology to pragmatics: Metaphorical and cultural aspects of semantic structure.* Cambridge: Cambridge University Press.

Tabossi, P., & Zardon, F. (1993). Processing ambiguous words in context. *Journal of Memory and Language, 27,* 597–632.

Turner, M. (1987). *Death is the mother of beauty: Mind, metaphor, criticism.* Chicago: University of Chicago Press.

Turner, M. (1996). *The literary mind.* New York: Oxford University Press.

Turner M., & Fauconnier, G. (1995). Conceptual integration and formal expression. *Metaphor and Symbolic Activity, 10,* 183–204.

Turner, N., & Katz, A. (1997). Evidence for the availability of conventional and of literal meaning during the comprehension of proverbs. *Pragmatics and Cognition, 5,* 203–237.

Vervaeke, J., & Kennedy, J. (1996). Metaphors in language and thought: Falsification and multiple meanings. *Metaphor and Symbolic Activity, 11,* 273–284.

Wheelright, P. (1962). *Metaphor and reality.* Bloomington, IN: Indiana University Press.

Williams, J. (1992). Processing polysemous words in context: Evidence for interrelated meanings. *Journal of Psycholinguistic Research, 21,* 193–218.

Wilson, D. & Sperber, D. (1992). On verbal irony. *Lingua, 87,* 53–76.

Winner, E. (1988). *The point of words: Children's understanding of metaphor and irony.* Cambridge, MA: Harvard University Press.

Index